To Aglo

August 8, 2014

Grudge Jim

I See Something GRAND

by Mitzi Chandler

Illustrated by Barbara Epstein-Eagle

GRAND CANYON ASSOCIATION

This book is dedicated to my grandchildren and to the memory of Karen L. Taylor
Thank you to Miss Kelsey Ann Fekkes for giving me the idea for this book.
— Mitzi Chandler

I dedicate the drawings in this book to the memory of my Grandma, Ester Israel Berstein,
who taught me about love, acceptance, beauty, and chicken soup.
—Barbara Epstein-Eagle

Grand Canyon Association

The Grand Canyon Association is the National Park Service's official nonprofit partner raising private funds to benefit Grand Canyon National Park, operating retail stores and visitor centers within the park, and providing premier educational opportunities about the natural and cultural history of Grand Canyon. Proceeds from the sale of this Grand Canyon Association publication will be used to support research and education at Grand Canyon National Park.

"Are we almost there, Grandpa?" Kelsey asked.

"Yes, Kelsey," her grandfather answered.
"The Grand Canyon is just beyond those trees."

"Look, Kelsey!" he exclaimed.
"There's the Grand Canyon!"

"Wow!" Kelsey cried. "We're really high!
It makes butterflies in my tummy.

Hold my hand, Grandpa."

Her grandfather smiled and took her hand.
"Yes, the bottom is very far down.
The Canyon is about one mile deep," he explained.

"What does GRAND mean?" Kelsey asked.

"It means something is SPECIAL," her grandfather said.
"The Grand Canyon is very big and very old.
There is no other place like it on earth.
Look, Kelsey, the Canyon stretches as far as we can see."

"Is the Canyon *this* long?" Kelsey asked her grandfather,
stretching as far as she could stretch.

He chuckled. "It's longer than that, Kelsey.
It's hundreds of miles long."

"Then it's really, REALLY long!" she shouted.

Then Kelsey asked quietly,
"Grandpa, is the Canyon as old as you?"

"Oh, it's much older than me," he answered.
"It's as old as *all* the Grandpas that ever lived."

"Wow!" she exclaimed.
"That's really, really, REALLY old."

Kelsey was curious.
"How did it get here?" she asked.
"Did people dig the Grand Canyon?"

"No, Kelsey," her grandfather told her.
"A long time ago the Colorado River carved
out the Grand Canyon. And each time it
rains, water runs down the canyon walls
and washes tiny pieces of rock and sand
with it.

It's called 'erosion'."

"E-ro-sion," Kelsey repeated. "That's a big word, Grandpa."

"Yes it is," her Grandpa continued. "Erosion also happens when the river at the bottom wooshes between the canyon walls and washes sand and rock into the river."

"Is erosion happening now?" Kelsey asked.

"Yes," her grandfather said.
"The Grand Canyon is getting wider
and deeper all the time."

"Look, Grandpa," Kelsey laughed.
"The Grand Canyon is growing DOWN
and I am growing UP."

"What animals live at the Grand Canyon?" she asked.

"Well," her grandfather said, "this morning
we saw some deer eating leaves."

"They have long ears, Grandpa," she remembered.

"That's right, Kelsey," he said proudly.

"We watched an Abert squirrel
climb a tree," her Grandfather told her.

"We watched ravens soar over the Canyon," he continued. "We saw a chipmunk scamper over rocks."

"He ran fast to his hiding place, Grandpa," Kelsey whispered.

"Yes, he did," her grandfather agreed.

"And remember, Grandpa," Kelsey laughed, "we sat on a bench and watched a rock squirrel eating a pine nut."

"Yes," her grandfather chuckled. "Other animals live at the Canyon too, but we probably won't see them today, Kelsey. I'll tell you about some of them."

"Bighorn sheep live on steep cliffs."

"Coyotes call to each other
by howling."

"Bobcats usually sleep
in rocky dens."

"Collared lizards sun themselves on warm rocks."

"Pink rattlesnakes curl up in rocks at the bottom of the Canyon."

"Scorpions have a stinger
at the end of their tail."

"Elk are the biggest animals living at the Grand Canyon."

"Lots and lots of animals live at the Grand Canyon, don't they, Grandpa?" Kelsey asked.

"Yes they do, Kelsey," her grandfather answered.

"And lots and lots of people from all over the world come to visit the Grand Canyon because it is such a SPECIAL place," he continued.

"Grandpa," Kelsey said suddenly.
"*You* have the same first name as the Grand Canyon.
You are my GRAND father and you are SPECIAL!"

"Thank you, Kelsey," he laughed.
"And did you know that *you* have the
same first name as the Grand Canyon?"

"I do?" she said, surprised.

"Yes," he said. "You are my GRAND daughter and you are very SPECIAL."

"I know, Grandpa," she said, giving him a big hug. "I want to come back when I'm bigger and learn more about the Grand Canyon," Kelsey decided.

"We'll come back when you are big enough to hike down to the bottom," her grandfather promised. "Would you like to do that, Kelsey?"

"Oh, yes!" she said, taking his hand in hers. "That would be just GRAND, Grandpa."

Juvenile Delinquency

The LAW AND PUBLIC POLICY: PSYCHOLOGY AND THE SOCIAL SCIENCES series includes books in three domains:

Legal Studies—writings by legal scholars about issues of relevance to psychology and the other social sciences, or that employ social science information to advance the legal analysis;

Social Science Studies—writings by scientists from psychology and the other social sciences about issues of relevance to law and public policy; and

Forensic Studies—writings by psychologists and other mental health scientists and professionals about issues relevant to forensic mental health science and practice.

The series is guided by its editor, Bruce D. Sales, PhD, JD, ScD(*hc*), University of Arizona; and coeditors, Bruce J. Winick, JD, University of Miami; Norman J. Finkel, PhD, Georgetown University; and Valerie P. Hans, PhD, University of Delaware.

• • •

The Right to Refuse Mental Health Treatment
    Bruce J. Winick
Violent Offenders: Appraising and Managing Risk
    Vernon L. Quinsey, Grant T. Harris, Marnie E. Rice, and Catherine A.
    Cormier
Recollection, Testimony, and Lying in Early Childhood
    Clara Stern and William Stern; James T. Lamiell (translator)
Genetics and Criminality: The Potential Misuse of Scientific Information in Court
    Edited by Jeffrey R. Botkin, William M. McMahon, and
    Leslie Pickering Francis
The Hidden Prejudice: Mental Disability on Trial
    Michael L. Perlin
Adolescents, Sex, and the Law: Preparing Adolescents for Responsible Citizenship
    Roger J. R. Levesque
Legal Blame: How Jurors Think and Talk About Accidents
    Neal Feigenson
Justice and the Prosecution of Old Crimes: Balancing Legal, Psychological, and Moral Concerns
    Daniel W. Shuman and Alexander McCall Smith
Unequal Rights: Discrimination Against People With Mental Disabilities and the Americans With Disabilities Act
    Susan Stefan

Treating Adult and Juvenile Offenders With Special Needs
        Edited by José B. Ashford, Bruce D. Sales, and William H. Reid
Culture and Family Violence: Fostering Change Through Human Rights Law
        Roger J. R. Levesque
The Legal Construction of Identity: The Judicial and Social Legacy of American Colonialism in Puerto Rico
        Efrén Rivera Ramos
Family Mediation: Facts, Myths, and Future Prospects
        Connie J. A. Beck and Bruce D. Sales
Not Fair! The Typology of Commonsense Unfairness
        Norman J. Finkel
Competence, Condemnation, and Commitment: An Integrated Theory of Mental Health Law
        Robert F. Schopp
The Evolution of Mental Health Law
        Edited by Lynda E. Frost and Richard J. Bonnie
Hollow Promises: Employment Discrimination Against People With Mental Disabilities
        Susan Stefan
Violence and Gender Reexamined
        Richard B. Felson
Determining Damages: The Psychology of Jury Awards
        Edie Greene and Brian H. Bornstein
Protecting Society From Sexually Dangerous Offenders: Law, Justice, and Therapy
        Edited by Bruce J. Winick and John Q. La Fond
Treating Chronic Juvenile Offenders: Advances Made Through the Oregon Multidimensional Treatment Foster Care Model
        Patricia Chamberlain
Juvenile Delinquency: Understanding the Origins of Individual Differences
        Vernon L. Quinsey, Tracey A. Skilling, Martin L. Lalumière, and Wendy M. Craig

Juvenile Delinquency

UNDERSTANDING THE ORIGINS OF INDIVIDUAL DIFFERENCES

VERNON L. QUINSEY
TRACEY A. SKILLING
MARTIN L. LALUMIÈRE
WENDY M. CRAIG

AMERICAN PSYCHOLOGICAL ASSOCIATION
WASHINGTON, DC

Published by
American Psychological Association
750 First Street, NE
Washington, DC 20002
www.apa.org

To order
APA Order Department
P.O. Box 92984
Washington, DC 20090-2984
Tel: (800) 374-2721; Direct: (202) 336-5510
Fax: (202) 336-5502; TDD/TTY: (202) 336-6123
Online: www.apa.org/books/
E-mail: order@apa.org

In the U.K., Europe, Africa, and the Middle East, copies may be ordered from
American Psychological Association
3 Henrietta Street
Covent Garden, London
WC2E 8LU England

Typeset in Goudy by Argosy, Waltham, MA

Printer: Sheridan Books, Inc., Ann Arbor, MI
Cover Designer: Berg Design, Albany, NY
Technical/Production Editor: Argosy, Waltham, MA

The opinions and statements published are the responsibility of the authors, and such opinions and statements do not necessarily represent the policies of the American Psychological Association.

Library of Congress Cataloging-in-Publication Data
Juvenile delinquency : understanding the origins of individual differences / by Vernon L.
    Quinsey . . . [et al.] .—1st ed.
        p. cm.
    Includes bibliographical references and index.
    ISBN 1-59147-048-X (alk. paper)
        1. Juvenile delinquency—Psychology. 2. Conduct disorders in children. 3. Conduct disorders in adolescence. 4. Antisocial personality disorders. I. Quinsey, Vernon L.

    HV9069.J795 2004
    364.2—dc21

                                                                                2003048028

British Library Cataloguing-in-Publication Data
A CIP record is available from the British Library.

Printed in the United States of America
First Edition

We dedicate this book to Linda Mealey. Linda devoted her scientific career to the integration of disparate scientific and intellectual disciplines.

CONTENTS

PREFACE

The goal of this book is to explain the origins of individual differences among children, adolescents, and young adults in their propensity to engage in aggressive, antisocial, and delinquent behavior. The theoretical and analytical framework that we employ is provided by evolutionary psychology, behavioral genetics, and developmental psychology. These three fields of scientific inquiry offer different yet complementary levels of explanation for human behavior in general, and delinquent behavior in particular.

Although in this book we focus on individual differences in the propensities to engage in antisocial behavior, we are not so naive to believe that only individual differences are important. One need only read such books as *The Fall of Berlin 1945* (Beevor, 2002), *Hitler's Willing Executioners: Ordinary Germans and the Holocaust* (Goldhagen, 1997), or *The Rape of Nanking* (Chang, 1997); consider the more recent Mylai massacre, wars in Afghanistan, Cambodia, Bosnia, and Africa; or study the more temporally remote wars of the ancient Hebrews, Aztecs, Babylonians, Vikings, or Huns to understand that large-scale, horrific, often genocidal antisocial behaviors do not result simply from the characteristics of particular individuals or even particular cultures. Evolutionary psychology has placed particular emphasis on the commonalities of human nature, leading to the expectation that environmental contingencies act on people in similar ways.

O'Shea's (2000) book *The Perfect Heresy: The Revolutionary Life and Death of the Medieval Cathars* compellingly captures genocidal policies and the brutality of warfare. For example, when the walls of the southern French town of Béziers had been breached in the siege of 1209, soldiers asked Arnold Amaury, the monk who led the first Albigensian crusade, how to distinguish Cathar heretics from Catholics. Amaury is said to have replied, "Kill them all. God will know his own." The slaughter of 20,000 or so of the hapless inhabitants followed. The Albigensian crusade was particularly thorough and barbaric: There is the tale of a long line of men wending their way toward a Cathar fortification, each man with his hand on the shoulder of the man in front. All had been blinded by the crusaders save the first, who was spared one eye. Over the next 200 years, the methods of the inquisition were developed and used to extinguish the Cathar heresy along with the political independence of Languedoc in Southern France. In this book, we make no attempt to deal with such large-scale warfare or intergroup hostilities. Our goal is limited to an attempt to explain individual differences in antisocial behavior within contemporary postindustrial societies.

We were motivated to write this book by our observation that advanced undergraduate students, graduate students, and practitioners whose primary interests are in criminal behavior typically have received little training in evolutionary biology and genetics, and so are often unable to understand or to critique biological explanations of antisocial behaviors. Most psychologists and students concern themselves with either the immediate environmental causes of behavior or the development of behavior within a single organism's life span. The exclusive focus on proximal causation applies even to many students with strong backgrounds in neuroscience. The consideration of more remote causes of behavior requires a Darwinian selectionist habit of thought that does not come naturally to those trained to think solely in terms of proximal causation. We hope to stimulate a selectionist habit of thought.

In part, this neglect of selectionist thinking can be traced to the politically motivated academic controversy associated with E. O. Wilson's (1975) *Sociobiology: The New Synthesis*, of which an excellent history can be found in Segerstråle (2000). In brief, the critics of sociobiology accused it of genetic determinism (the belief that all behavior is determined by genes), facile or panglossian adaptationism (asserting that a characteristic of a species is a result of natural selection on the basis of little or no good evidence), commission of the naturalistic fallacy (believing that what is natural is good), sexism, and racism. Alcock (2001) has documented that the Darwinian approach to understanding behavior not only survived the controversy but also increasingly prospered, leading to his argument that the scientific aspects of the controversy are dead, leaving only its political echoes alive. We do not rehash ideological controversies; this book assumes that its readers concur with us that scientific theories of human behavior should be evaluated solely on their empirical and heuristic merits.

We also wrote this book because we saw an opportunity for integrating what we learned from recent empirical and conceptual advances in evolutionary psychology, behavioral genetics, and developmental psychology. These three fields of inquiry have experienced great successes in explaining human behavior in general, and antisocial behavior in particular, and a conceptual integration of these perspectives offers even greater promise for a more thorough understanding of antisocial behavior and juvenile delinquency. A more thorough understanding of the origins of antisocial and delinquent behavior may in the long-term lead to practical interventions designed to reduce antisocial conduct.

The introduction provides an overview of what an integrated theoretical perspective on antisocial behavior seeks to accomplish. The first three chapters of the book provide the necessary background information. These chapters describe important concepts and findings in the fields of evolutionary psychology, behavioral genetics, and delinquency, and the proximal developmental mechanisms of antisocial behavior. Because it is new, not very well known, and often misunderstood, evolutionary psychology is described at greater length; it also provides the theoretical background for many of the arguments presented in this book. Behavioral genetics, despite very consistent findings, is still not very well-known among social scientists; following a general outline of the concepts and methods in behavioral genetics, we describe several behavioral genetics studies addressing juvenile delinquency and related phenomena. Recent developmental approaches to delinquency have greatly improved our empirical foundations, and we summarize the most important findings in this field. In the fourth chapter of the book, we present an integrated theoretical perspective on delinquency leading to a taxonomy of delinquents. In the final two chapters of the book, we discuss applications of this integrated theoretical perspective. We discuss how an integrated theory can explain differences between male and female delinquency as well as the prediction and prevention of delinquency.

This book is the outcome of our individual efforts to understand juvenile delinquency. The first chapter is adapted from part of the lecture notes of a fourth-year undergraduate course on evolutionary psychology. The second chapter presents material from both this evolutionary psychology course and a graduate course on juvenile delinquency. The remaining chapters are adapted from the graduate course in juvenile delinquency or have been written specifically for this volume. We estimate the difficulty level of the book to be at an advanced undergraduate or graduate level. However, readers do require some knowledge of biology and statistics, particularly for chapters 1 and 2. In order to satisfy more advanced students and not annoy less specialized readers, we have placed additional and more technical information in exhibits or footnotes.

Our aim in writing this book is conceptual. We do not teach readers assessment or treatment methods to be used with delinquents. Rather, we hope that readers will acquire an understanding of what is known about the origins of individual differences in antisocial propensities. This conceptual background is necessary not only to understand current biological theories of antisocial behavior and the fast-moving scientific advances in this and related fields but also to inform considerations of the likely outcomes of proposed interventions designed to reduce delinquency.

ACKNOWLEDGMENTS

Preparation of this book was facilitated by a contract between Vernon L. Quinsey and the Forensic Service of the Kingston Psychiatric Hospital, a sabbatical leave granted by Queen's University, and a senior research fellowship from the Ontario Mental Health Foundation. Tracey A. Skilling was supported by a research fellowship from the Correctional Service of Canada and a postdoctoral fellowship from the Mental Health Centre, Penetanguishene, Ontario, Canada. Martin L. Lalumière was supported by a fellowship from the Social Sciences and Humanities Research Council and by a research fellowship from the Correctional Service of Canada during the early stages of the preparation of this book, and later by grants from the Social Sciences and Humanities Research Council. Wendy M. Craig was supported by grants from the National Health and Research and Development Program, the Ontario Mental Health Foundation, and the Social Sciences and Humanities Research Council. We offer our sincere thanks to Jill Atkinson, Grant Harris, Marnie Rice, and Michael Seto for their comments on earlier versions of this book; to Bruce Sales, the series editor; and to Anne Woodworth, of the American Psychological Association, for her patience and editorial assistance.

Juvenile Delinquency

INTRODUCTION

Throughout this book we use the terms *aggression, antisocial behavior, delinquency,* and *crime.* What is it that we aim to explain in this book? These terms have different meanings but are to some degree conceptually and empirically related. The term *problem behavior* is often used to describe any behavior that breaks social norms. *Antisocial behavior* is usually defined more narrowly and includes breaches of social contracts. *Criminal behavior* is an even narrower term that includes behaviors deemed illegal. *Delinquency* usually refers to illegal behavior committed by juveniles. In the broadest sense, *crime* and *delinquency* refer to all acts or omissions prohibited by law and liable to punishment. This category obviously refers to behaviors that differ greatly in seriousness and frequency. In addition, this category of behaviors varies considerably by country, region, over time, and with the age of the perpetrator.

Based on these definitions, precocious sexual intercourse, truancy, lying, theft, and physical assault would be considered problem behavior, but only lying, theft, and assault would be considered antisocial, and only theft and assault would be considered delinquent and criminal in most places. In this book we attempt to explain why there are variations in young people's tendencies to engage in antisocial behavior, with a particular focus on delinquent behavior. For the rest of this book, however, we will use the terms *delinquency* and *antisocial behavior* interchangeably, and will refer to *antisocial tendencies*—or *antisociality*—as those individual characteristics that increase the likelihood of antisocial behavior. We focus on antisocial behavior engaged in by young individuals, but our theoretical approach necessitates the discussion of issues relevant to children and adults as well.

Our theoretical approach to explaining antisocial behavior in young people will draw from three different fields of research: evolutionary psychology, behavioral genetics, and developmental psychology. These fields

3

offer different yet complementary levels of explanation for human behavior in general, and antisocial behavior in particular. At the most general level of explanation, behavior has two interrelated types of causes: the structure and chemistry of the organism, and the environment. The structure and chemistry of the organism and the manner in which it interacts with the environment are for the most part products of the selective pressures of ancestral environments. The environment affects individual development, often differentially according to genotype (the individual's genetic makeup), and the current environment elicits particular behaviors contemporaneously.

Evolutionary psychology is concerned with the design of all human behavioral characteristics that are the product of natural selection in ancestral environments. These characteristics are called adaptations and make up what is known as human nature. Behavioral genetics is concerned with the partition of individual differences into genetic and environmental variance components. Developmental psychology is concerned with the environmental variance component, that is, the prenatal and postnatal environmental influences affecting individuals during their lifetimes.

Evolutionary psychology, behavioral genetics, and developmental psychology, despite having separate intellectual histories, are intimately linked, and together provide an opportunity for the development of a conceptually broad-based theory of antisocial behavior. Recent developments in evolutionary psychology and behavioral genetics offer new perspectives from which to view juvenile delinquency and provide great hope for the rapid advancement of our scientific understanding of this phenomenon. Theories, however, require findings to explain and it is only in the past quarter century that enough longitudinal research on delinquency has accumulated to make theoretical explanation feasible and productive.

Before beginning, therefore, it may be helpful to consider in broad outline what a theory of delinquency and antisocial behavior must explain. At the aggregate or group level, the most obvious differences in the frequency and severity of antisocial and criminal behaviors are associated with sex and age (e.g., L. Ellis, 1988; L. Ellis & Walsh, 2000; Moffitt, Caspi, Rutter, & Silva, 2001; Rutter, 1996). Males are much more likely to commit crimes than females. The frequency of crimes increases with age through to late adolescence and then begins a graceful decline continuing throughout adulthood. The shape of the age-related changes are roughly the same for males and females.

Continuing at the aggregate level, many correlates of crime appear to reflect competitive disadvantage. In addition to youthfulness and maleness, L. Ellis (1988) identified five cross-cultural correlates of crime in a literature review: large number of siblings, low socioeconomic status, urban location, racial group, and single-parent family of origin. In his literature analysis, Ellis found four studies that examined the relationship between having a large number of siblings and the commission of serious crimes (those involving identifiable victims); all four of those studies showed a significant association. Ellis also identified 28 studies that compared having a large number of siblings and the commission of less serious (victimless) crimes; a significant association was found in 27 of the 28 studies. Low socioeconomic status (variously defined over the studies) was significantly related to serious crime in all of the 46 studies found that compared those variables. A significant relationship between less serious crime and low socioeconomic status was found in 98 of 143 studies identified (35 of those studies reported no significant relationship). With respect to urban or rural status, all 34 studies identified as relevant to this issue found a significant positive relationship between urban status and serious crime, while 20 of 22 studies reported significant correlations of urban status with less serious crime. The relationship of racial group (usually operationalized in these studies in terms of skin color as Black, White, or Asian) to serious crime was examined in 60 identified studies. Significant associations were found in all 60 studies, with Blacks having the highest rates of serious crime and Asians the lowest. Racial group did not show a clear pattern with respect to less serious crimes. Regarding single-parent family of origin, all six studies of its relation to serious crime found a significant positive correlation; of 110 studies of less serious crime, 91 found a significant positive association. Ellis notes that single parent status caused by the death of a spouse does not show as significant a correlation as does single parent status caused by desertion, separation, not marrying, or divorce.

Lastly, there are well-documented differences in crime rates over time and place, most convincingly measured by homicides (Gurr, 1989). For example, the 1980s saw a large increase and the 1990s a large decrease in crimes committed by juveniles and other groups (Blumstein & Wallman, 2000).

At the level of individual differences, however, variables that appear important at the aggregate level may or may not be important (e.g., Gold, 1987; Zajonc & Mullally, 1997). Socioeconomic status of origin, for example, is a statistically significant but relatively unimportant predictor of adult criminality (because most children raised in socioeconomically disadvantaged circumstances do not have adult criminal careers). In contrast, measures of antisocial childhood traits, such as conduct disorder, are very good predictors of adult criminality (e.g., Andrews & Bonta, 1994). Although most people who are arrested for criminal offenses begin their criminal behavior in their teenage years and desist in their 20s, a small group of mostly male offenders exhibit prepubertal antisocial behavior and commit a disproportionate number of serious and often violent offenses as adults. Among adult offenders, this latter group is the most persistent (e.g., Moffitt, 1993b; Quinsey, Harris, Rice, & Cormier, 1998). Also at the individual level, the characteristics of crime careers require explanation—for example, why do few offenders show a high degree of specialization in a particular type of crime? (For an extensive review, see Gottfredson & Hirschi, 1990.)

At the most basic level, therefore, a theory of the development of anti-social behavior must account for sex and age differences in the propensity to commit crimes, the major correlates of criminal behavior at the aggregate and individual levels, the frequent lack of specialization in a particular crime type within individual offenders, and the temporal and geographical variations in the frequency of criminal behavior. Our approach will be to focus on individual differences in the propensity to antisocial behavior; that is, we deal with data primarily at the individual as opposed to the aggregate level.

Readers may well be skeptical about whether an integrated theory of antisocial behavior that involves evolution, genes, and development has real concrete consequences, as opposed to being some vague abstract notion that we must have a biopsychosocial theory so that all theoreticians may have prizes. To illustrate that there are real intellectual consequences of an integrated theory, let us consider a specific finding.

Suppose it were found that antisocial youth were differentially likely to have been abused and neglected by their parents (see chapter 3). Many psychologists and criminologists would be tempted to conclude that the abuse and neglect were the etiological agents that produced the pathological antisocial outcome. However, an integrated theory suggests that this conclusion may be premature. Antisocial parents may be more likely to abuse and neglect their children, so the abuse and neglect may simply indicate what is, at bottom, a genetic influence. Another possibility, not incompatible with the first, is that early antisocial behavior leads to neglect and abuse as a symptom of difficulty in managing an obstreperous child rather than as a cause of later antisocial behavior. Still another possibility is that abuse and neglect are etiological agents but only in the presence of a particular genetic constitution.

An integrated theory also suggests that we examine the notion of pathology very carefully. Could it be that an antisocial behavior is pathological only in the trivial sense that it is undesirable from a societal viewpoint? What if neglect and abuse were environmental signals providing information to the child—not necessarily consciously processed—about the likely outcomes of different courses of action? What if antisocial behavior was often associated, in certain developmental contexts, with the attainment of important developmental goals, such as material resources and sexual relationships? Thus, if we do not consider possible evolutionary or genetic influences, we risk confusing causes with correlates of antisocial behavior; we also risk missing or misinterpreting the functions of particular behaviors and, in consequence, mistakenly target our interventions. This manner of thinking is captured in the following passage:

> Human brains evolved to be molded by experience, and early difficulties were routine during our ancestral development. Is it plausible that

the developing brain never evolved to cope with exposure to maltreatment and so is damaged in a non-adaptive manner? This seems most unlikely. The logical alternative is that exposure to early stress generates molecular and neurobiological effects that alter neural development in an adaptive way that prepares the adult brain to survive and reproduce in a dangerous world. . . . Stress sculpts the brain to exhibit various antisocial, though adaptive, behaviors. Whether it comes in the form of physical, emotional or sexual trauma or through exposure to warfare, famine or pestilence, stress can set off a ripple of hormonal changes that permanently wire a child's brain to cope with a malevolent world. (Teicher, 2002, p. 75)

An integrated theory also leads us to ask the question of whether antisocial behavior is a unitary phenomenon. It is possible that antisocial behavior is a universal human response to certain environmental contingencies; it is also possible that individuals vary in their responsiveness to these contingencies. This, too, is an empirical question that can be addressed by assessing the homogeneity of individuals with antisocial histories. Developmental psychologists have long suspected that there might be different pathways to the development of delinquency. In this book we discuss the notion of developmental pathways, pathology, and adaptive strategies. We argue that there are three major pathways to juvenile delinquency, and we use our integrated perspective to elucidate their proximate and ultimate origins.

All of these questions we have raised are empirically answerable—by, for example, using cross-fostering adoption designs to assess the relative contribution of genes and early environment or longitudinal studies to determine the degree to which antisocial behavior pays off in different circumstances—but in order to find such answers we must formulate the questions more precisely. How should we define pathology? Is it simply poor adjustment and, if so, what exactly does that mean? If we are to think that certain traits or behaviors pay off, what is the payoff and is it the same for everybody? Can these payoffs be manipulated to produce developmental outcomes that are beneficial from the viewpoint of both the individual and society? If people vary in antisocial traits, do they vary quantitatively or in kind?

In order to accomplish the precision required to address these questions and definitional issues, some background material must be covered and some new habits of thoughts formed. We begin chapter 1 with a discussion of the forces that have shaped human nature.

1

EVOLUTIONARY PSYCHOLOGY

In this chapter we review important notions in the field of evolutionary psychology, such as adaptation, parental investment, sexual selection, altruism, genetic conflict, and mating. Our overview shows that the study of antisocial behavior can be informed by theoretical notions that are based on—or at least consistent with—principles of evolution by natural selection, leading to the possibility that some forms of aggressive, risky, and delinquent behaviors can be explained as outcomes of specific reproductive problems encountered in ancestral environments.

This introduction is not a substitute for a careful reading of the recent advances in evolutionary theory. Evolutionary theory is simple in its principles but extremely complex in its ramifications. Descriptions of modern evolutionary thinking that require little in the way of previous background can be found in Dawkins (1986, 1995), Dennett (1995), Mayr (1988, 1991), and Ridley (1993). More advanced treatments are presented in G. Bell (1997), Bock and Cardew (1997), and Crawford and Krebs (1998). Overviews of evolutionary approaches to complex human behaviors can be found in several recent sources: D. M. Buss (1994, 1995, 1999); Hahn, Hewitt, Henderson, and Benno (1990); Lieberman (1984); Loy and Peters (1991); Mealey (2000); Richards (1987); Symons (1979); and R. Wright (1994). The Human Behavior and Evolution Society Web site (www.hbes.com) provides regular updates on new introductory and advanced texts.

EVOLUTION BY NATURAL SELECTION

Evolution by natural selection consists of descent with modification through the differential survival of offspring. In this process the genes that code for morphological, physiological, neuronal, and behavioral characteristics associated with relative reproductive success increase in frequency over generations, along with the characteristics that they code. Thus, changes produced by evolution are inherited.

Evolution by natural selection produces adaptations, which are aspects of organisms that have particular reproductive and survival functions. Thus, the ultimate causes of adaptations are the features of the ancestral environment in which natural selection occurred. Different branches of the life sciences, including psychology, are now involved in what is called the adaptationist program (Mayr, 1983; Nesse & Williams, 1994; Williams, 1966, 1992), which is aimed at discovering the possible adaptive functions of particular morphological, physiological, and psychological characteristics. Not all characteristics reflect adaptive design: A characteristic that is not an adaptation is either a by-product of other adaptations (e.g., nipples in males); the result of nonselective forces, such as genetic drift; or the result of pathology (e.g., lesions caused by infection). In this book, we discuss the possible adaptive functions of characteristics associated with juvenile delinquency, such as risk taking, aggressiveness, and promiscuity.

Thinking about how characteristics are selected over evolutionary time is not that different from thinking about how behavior is selected over an organism's lifetime. In fact, evolutionary theory is related to traditional psychological theory in the great similarity between evolutionary selectionist thinking and operant or instrumental conditioning.[1] Both deal with the effects of the environment on behavior. In evolution, aspects of the ancestral environment have determined gene frequencies over generations, thus becoming the ultimate causes of a variety of behaviors. In learning, environmental contingencies select certain behaviors through reinforcement and punishment, and these behaviors become more or less frequent. Current environmental contingencies are thus proximal causes of behavior. The conceptual loop is closed by the observation that proximal causes of behavior (i.e., the way the environment affects certain behaviors) often have their ultimate origins in ancestral environments.

---

[1] Skinner, for example, recognized early on the relation and the similarity between phylogenetic and ontogenetic selection (Alessi, 1992; Skinner, 1966).

COMMON MISUNDERSTANDINGS

There are several common misunderstandings about evolution (Alcock, 2001; P. Gray, 1991). Despite the marked tendency of people to think the contrary, modern evolutionists have concluded that evolution has no fore-sight and that people are not more highly evolved than other animals.

Characteristics that have been produced by evolution are not morally good or bad; to think otherwise is to commit the naturalistic fallacy. For example, we might find evidence that evolution has designed men to be more aggressive than women or to desire a greater number of sexual part-ners, but that makes neither aggression nor promiscuity any more, or less, morally desirable than if evolution had nothing to do with it. Understand-ing what people tend to find morally good or objectionable, however, could be informed by selectionist thinking by considering what advantages those moral judgments have had for those who hold them (e.g., the advantages afforded by people's tendency to condemn those who cheat and lie).

Characteristics that have been produced by evolution can have bad, good, or neutral effects on our physical and mental health in our current environment. For example, we are likely to have been designed to find sugar and animal fat rewarding because they were rare but important sources of calories in our environment of evolutionary adaptation. Presently, sugar and animal fat are superabundant and our evolved taste for these foods can make us overweight (for other examples see Nesse & Williams, 1994). Adaptations are clearly related to reproductive and survival success only in those environments that closely resemble the environments in which the adaptations were selected. Similarly, a characteristic or tendency that has been produced by evolution does not necessarily make people happy in their current environment; indeed, it may not have done so in the historical environment in which the characteristic was developed. Evolution works on relative reproductive success, not relative happiness.

All characteristics that have been produced by evolution need an environment in which to express themselves and are often very influenced by environmental context. To think otherwise is to commit the genetic deterministic fallacy (this is not a criticism of determinism per se). Psycho-logical adaptations, for example, are seen as information-processing devices, or mental algorithms (Cosmides & Tooby, 1987), that selectively process and respond to environmental inputs. In that sense, the study of behavior from an evolutionary perspective is an environmentalist science (Crawford & Anderson, 1989). D. M. Buss (1995) described evolutionary psychology as a perspective that "jettisons the outmoded dualistic thinking inherent in much current discourse by getting rid of the false dichotomy between bio-logical and social" (p. 167). Furthermore, behaviors and characteristics that have strong genetic loadings and that are minimally affected by naturally occurring environmental variations can still be modified by environmental change engineered by humans. For example, the severe mental retardation caused by the genetic disorder phenylketonuria can be avoided with a restricted phenylalanine diet. Thus, a finding that individual differences in antisociality can be attributed to genetic influence is not a reason to conclude that environmental interventions must be useless.

IDENTIFYING AN ADAPTATION

Williams (1966, 1992; see also Mayr, 1983) has provided the groundwork for the adaptationist program. An adaptationist view of the phenotype (the observed characteristic of an organism) asks, "What is the function of a particular feature?" For the purpose of this book it is sufficient to mention the following criteria for the identification of a human adaptation (P. Gray, 1991): (a) It is obviously designed in a manner to accomplish some biological purpose; (b) it operates in a similar manner over cultures and time; (c) it is plausibly related to reproductive and survival success in ancestral environments; and (d) it is not more parsimoniously explained on other grounds (e.g., as a by-product of another characteristic or adaptation, or as pathology). Adaptations have historically contributed to the reproductive success (fitness) of individuals or to the reproductive success of individuals and their relatives (inclusive fitness).

Sexual aggression, for example, has been studied in the context of the adaptationist program (e.g., Lalumière, Chalmers, Quinsey, & Seto, 1996; Thornhill & Thornhill, 1992; Thornhill & Palmer, 2000). The question is whether the use of sexual aggression by men is a direct result of a psychological mechanism designed for that purpose, a result (by-product) of some other evolved mechanisms designed for other purposes (such as a desire for obtaining multiple mateships), or a result of pathology (such as a paraphilic sexual preference). In this book, we pay considerable attention to differentiating the effects of pathology from those of natural selection.

Daly and Wilson (1988) have argued that "our perceptions of self-interest have evolved as proximal tokens of expected gains and losses of fitness" (p. 10). In this view, evolution has designed people so that they desire things and experience emotions that increased the inclusive fitness of people in ancestral environments. It is important to understand that the theory does not assert that people consciously or even unconsciously attempt to maximize their reproductive success or increase the proportion of their genes in subsequent generations. People are not fitness maximizers. Rather, our psychological mechanisms are adaptations designed to solve reproductive and survival problems that existed in ancestral environments; people are adaptation executors (D. M. Buss, 1995; Tooby & Cosmides, 1990).

A clear example of an adaptation involved in sexual reproduction is a male sexual preference for partners that have reproductively relevant characteristics. At the most basic level, we would expect male sexual preferences to focus on conspecifics. A computer search of the Kinsey Institute's extensive files of thousands of people interviewed between 1938 and 1963 revealed 96 cases involving intensive sexual activity with animals, but in not a single case was the animal contact or the fantasy of contact with animals the preferred source of achieving sexual excitement (Spitzer, Gibbon, Skodol, Williams, & First, 1994). Apart from some very rare exceptions (see Earls & Lalumière, 2002), sexual activity with animals is a nonpreferred choice.

Male sexual preferences are, of course, more than species specific. Researchers using a variety of methods have consistently found that heterosexual men sexually prefer young, average-weight females with prototypically female waist-to-hip ratios (G. T. Harris, Rice, Quinsey, & Chaplin, 1996; Kenrick & Keefe, 1992; Quinsey & Chaplin, 1988; Quinsey, Rice, Harris, & Reid, 1993; Quinsey, Steinman, Bergersen, & Holmes, 1975; Singh, 1993; Singh & Luis, 1995). There is also strong interrater and cross-cultural agreement on female attractiveness (reviewed in Quinsey et al., 1993, and Silverthorne & Quinsey, 2000). Infants 3 to 6 months old spend more time looking at faces judged by adults as attractive than at those judged unattractive. Average and symmetrical faces are preferred, probably because they have signaled the absence of genetic or developmental anomalies (Langlois & Roggman, 1990). V. S. Johnson (1999) has found, using a computer program that allows subjects to design an optimally attractive face, that preferred female facial features reflect not only symmetry but also attributes that are associated with the presence of hormones during development that facilitate female fertility.

This exquisite tuning of male sexual interest to signs of reproductive capability—such as sex, youthfulness, body shape, absence of genetic anomalies, and developmental precision—strongly indicates that sexual interest is an adaptation (for more detailed accounts see Quinsey, in press; Quinsey & Lalumière, 1995). This adaptation makes sense in light of parental investment theory described in the next section. The male sexual preference system is obviously designed to do something (maximize attraction to and motivate behavior toward reproductively viable partners), is similar over cultures and time, is plausibly related to reproductive and survival success in ancestral environments in that men who had this sexual preference system were likely to out-reproduce those men who did not, and is not more parsimoniously explained on other grounds, such as a general preference for particularly shaped objects. Female sexual preferences are, of course, different in some respects from male sexual preferences. Parental investment theory explains these sex differences in mating preferences and behavior.

PARENTAL INVESTMENT THEORY

Parental investment theory is one of the great achievements of late-20th-century biological science. It is the cornerstone theory for the study of human mating and for many of the theoretical formulations presented in this book. Parental investment consists of the energy, time, resources, and opportunity cost associated with producing offspring and is contrasted with mating effort, which consists only of securing and preserving mating opportunities (Trivers, 1972).

Sex differences in the costs associated with parental investment create different life histories for the sexes through two simple rules: First, members of the sex that incur the largest minimal parental investment have a lower potential reproductive rate (the maximum number of offspring that can be produced in a breeding season or in a given unit of time) than members of the other sex (Clutton-Brock & Vincent, 1991). Second, the reproductive success of members of the sex with the largest minimal parental investment is not limited by access to members of the other sex but by access to resources, support, or other kinds of help. Conversely, the reproductive success of members of the sex that incurs the smallest minimal parental investment is limited by access to sexually receptive members of the opposite sex. In other words, the sex that is the least sexually available is a limited resource for the other sex while the reverse is very seldom true.

The sex that has the highest potential reproductive rate is under greater selection pressure to compete, directly or indirectly, for access to members of the other sex. That sex often develops sex-specific morphological structures, such as antlers, and behavioral tendencies, such as seeking sexual opportunities, while experiencing larger intrasex variations in reproductive success (Trivers, 1985). Interestingly, these life histories are not dependent on which sex incurs the largest minimal parental investment. When females incur the largest investment, as in all primates, they are choosier concerning sexual partners, are less competitive among themselves than males, and experience smaller variations in reproductive success. When females incur the smallest investment, as in some species of seahorses, they fight for access to males, are less discriminating than males, and experience larger variations in reproductive success (Daly & Wilson, 1983; Gwynne, 1991; Williams, 1966).

Parental investment theory is well exemplified by the mating strategy of elephant seals. Males are physically much larger than females and contribute no parental investment after copulation. Males fight with each other for access to females, and only a few males inseminate most females. Female elephant seals show less resistence to the mating efforts of dominant males than to those of other males (Cox & Le Boeuf, 1977).

In mammals, females invest more in offspring than males because of lactation and internal gestation. Thus, mammals tend to exhibit polygyny to varying degrees. Polygyny means that some males have multiple female reproductive partners and some have very few or none at all. Somewhat paradoxically, having a higher ceiling on reproductive success also means, for many males, complete reproductive failure. Polygyny is often associated with greater male size, as illustrated by the marked dimorphism of elephant seals. The different size of human males and females and other evidence reviewed by D. M. Buss (1995) implies moderate polygyny in the human ancestral environment.[2]

Parental investment theory may have something to say about antisocial and delinquent behavior. Because of the greater reproductive variance (or stakes) in male mammals, males would be expected to take more risks than females (M. Wilson & Daly, 1985). Among humans, risky behavior and its sometimes unfortunate consequences are most often related to competition for status, resources, and mates, and are most common among young men of poor economic prospects.

Some of the proximal causes of sex differences in mating strategies, risk acceptance, and aggression are hormonal. Recently, investigators have been able to link ecological selection pressures, hormones, and behavior. Sex hormones are steroids produced from cholesterol. Steroids within cells that contain appropriate receptors act on particular genes. Steroid receptors are highly specific and therefore are interesting psychologically because of their highly specific motivational effects. They act both as organizers of fetal neural tissue and as context-sensitive activators of biologically significant behaviors throughout life, including many behaviors and characteristics associated with delinquency. A description of some of the major hormones is given in Exhibit 1.1.

SEXUAL SELECTION

The observation that female elephant seals prefer large, dominant males raises the question of whether female preferences can cause males to evolve particular characteristics. Andersson (1982) provided an elegant

---

[2] Given that one man can have children with many women, why are there the same numbers of males as females? A satisfactory explanation of why the sex ratio is equal was first proposed by Fisher (1930). The modern version of this theory asserts that the ratio of parental investment in the two sexes should be equal. Because each offspring is the product of a male and a female, members of the rare sex will produce more offspring than members of the common sex. Members of the rarer sex, therefore, will be more reproductively successful than members of the more common sex, resulting in an equal sex ratio at equilibrium. Note that if one sex is less likely to survive to reproduce (is more fragile), more offspring of this sex would be produced at birth.

demonstration of this phenomenon, called epigamy, which is one of two forms of sexual selection. (For a review of female mate choice in general, see Andersson, 1994.)

The male African long-tailed widow bird is the size of a sparrow and has orange shoulder flashes. In the breeding season, the main tail feathers of the male are 18 inches long. Although the males are grounded in wet weather because of the length of their tails, they exhibit spectacular display loops over grassland in the breeding season. In this species, the females do the choosing and breeding males have a harem of six or so females (thus, most males do not breed). Andersson (1982) designed an experiment to determine whether male tail length was caused by female preference. Four groups of subjects were employed: (a) a half-tail group, in which the tails were cut in half; (b) a double-tail group, in which half a tail was glued onto the normal tail; (c) an untouched group; and (d) a sham operation group, in which the tail was cut and glued back on.

The double-tail group had four times the females and eggs as the half-tail group. The other two groups had intermediate numbers. It appears that female preference for long tails has caused males to develop them. Different models exist to explain this phenomenon, but Williams (1992) convincingly argued that exaggerated or dominant male characteristics could evolve simply as a result of the great care females take in choosing a mate. Females that make poor mating choices suffer greater consequences than males and are thus more careful. Males who do not display sexually selected characteristics, such as a long tail, are either too young, have bad genes, or have a set of genes that is not resistant to current pathogens.[3] This kind of female choice is also evident in humans: Females are more likely to have sex with males who have symmetrical physical features, a reliable indicator of developmental precision (Thornhill, Gangestad, & Comer, 1995).

The second form of sexual selection involves competition between individuals of the same sex—intrasexual selection. Like epigamy (or intersexual selection), intrasexual selection produces characteristics that provide reproductive advantages, sometimes even to the detriment of survival advantages (up to a point). Because of sex differences in parental investment, males are often (or to a greater degree) subjected to sexual selection pressures of both types.

One interesting and important outcome of sexual selection is the evolution of male alternative and conditional strategies. Alternative strategies refer to different strategies adopted by genetically different males. For example, male bluegill sunfish either grow big and adopt a parental strategy or grow small and adopt a sneaky mating strategy (Gross, 1991). The small-sneaky strategy works quite well, reproductively speaking, as long as there are not too many sneakers around (something called frequency-dependent selection). Alternative strategies are quite rare among animals.

In conditional strategies, individuals are genetically the same but may adopt different sets of behavioral tactics, depending on conditions encountered during their lifetime. They may even change their morphology conditionally. Unlike alternative strategies, conditional strategies are quite common in the animal world. Belovsky, Slade, and Chase (1996) have provided an interesting example of a conditional strategy involving aggressive behavior. Males of one species of grasshopper either display to court females or stalk them and attempt forced copulation. Females prefer to mate with the males with the best foraging success (even though they get no direct investment from the males). Males therefore use display or stalking tactics dependent on their foraging success. If they are successful, they display; otherwise they stalk. Thus, stalking/forced copulation in the grasshopper appears to be an alternative mating tactic used by males that are less successful and less preferred by females. Biologists use the phrase "making the best of a bad job" to describe those tactics that are not as successful as others but that are used as a last resort to achieve at least some success. The notions of alternative and conditional strategies are very important for

---

[3] One theory asserts that there is variability in tail length and female preference for tail length over individuals (Andersson, 1994). In this situation, genes for female preference for long tails are carried in male bodies but are not expressed. Genes for male tail length are carried in female bodies but not expressed. Because of prior female choices, the two sets of genes are correlated or exhibit "linkage disequilibrium." Because of this coupling, the genes that make females choose long male tails are choosing copies of themselves. The genes can then choose a copy of themselves by using tail length as an identifier. Any small perturbation in preference for longer tails starts a runaway process that reaches equilibrium only when utilitarian effects balance sexual selection effects.

understanding individual differences and will be central to our discussion of pathways to delinquency (see Lalumière, Quinsey, Harris, & Rice, in press, for an in-depth discussion of alternative and conditional strategies in relation to forced copulation among animals).

ALTRUISM, COOPERATION, AND DEFECTION

So far our discussion has focused on various forms of competition engendered by natural (including sexual) selection. But sometimes the best way to compete is to be cooperative or even altruistic. Altruistic behavior, when defined as not merely being helpful but as sacrificing one's fitness in the course of being helpful, may appear at first glance paradoxical in the context of a selectionist view of behavior.

Kin-Directed Altruism

One would expect that altruistic individuals would be taken advantage of by others, leave fewer descendants, and thus be bred out of any population. The answer to the paradox of altruism involves focusing on the proper unit of selection. What is actually selected for in evolution? Most commonly, people think it is the individual organism—that is, fitter organisms out-reproduce the less fit. However, as we illustrate later in the discussion of maternal–fetal competition, that idea is somewhat inaccurate. Hamilton's (1964) alternative proposal, that the gene is the unit of selection, has had profound effects in biology and evolutionary psychology. In this way of thinking, an organism is simply the gene's way of getting by (Dawkins, 1978).

Hamilton recognized that, although altruistic individuals may be less likely to leave progeny than nonaltruistic individuals, altruistic genes can be selected for and increase in frequency. This is a result of the mathematics of inheritance. Organisms share varying numbers of their segregating or polymorphic genes[4] with their relatives by common descent. Fifty percent are shared for first-degree relatives (parents, offspring, and siblings); 25% for second-degree relatives (nieces, nephews, uncles, aunts, half-siblings, and grandchildren); and 12.5% for third-degree relatives (cousins and great-grandchildren). One would expect, therefore, that self-sacrificing behavior would be positively associated with degree of kinship and, from a gene-centered viewpoint, that there would be many circumstances under which an organism would do well to sacrifice itself for its relatives. These circumstances involve gene frequencies: Ego is worth at least two children, four nieces, or eight cousins. If an organism sacrifices itself for three rather than

---

[4] Different genes, called alleles, that can occupy the same locus on a chromosome.

two first-degree relatives, for example, the gene associated with that sacrifice would increase in frequency. This is even truer if the reproductive potential of the relatives is higher than that of the altruist (e.g., if they are of better reproductive age). Thus, in a gene-centered nomenclature, one can speak of an organism's inclusive fitness, defined as the sum of an individual's Darwinian fitness (personal reproductive success) and his or her influence on the Darwinian fitness of relatives, weighted according to their coefficients of relatedness to the focal individual.

In accord with this gene-centered selectionist theory, altruistic behavior in animals has often been found to be nepotistic. Animals act to increase not only their own fitness but also that of their relatives. R. D. Alexander (1979), Daly and Wilson (1983), and Trivers (1985) describe many human and nonhuman examples of nepotistic behavior.

Because crimes are often courses of action in which the interests of victim and perpetrator are in conflict, we expect nepotistic variation in crimes. Committing crimes against relatives is, in a sense, the opposite of nepotism. In accord with this view, homicide victims are relatively unlikely to be biologically related to their perpetrators (Daly & Wilson, 1982, 1988). We might also expect notions of kinship to be important in one's judgments of the actions of others as well. Other group-living primates, such as vervets, are aware of which individuals are related to each other and use this information in interacting with nonkin (Cheney & Seyfarth, 1990). One might think of kinship as an implicit premise of social contracts (Cosmides & Tooby, 1992) in which people have behavioral expectations of any persons who are connected by these contracts. People should thus be sensitive to differences in the genetic relatedness of others and expect kinship-based variations in nepotistic behavior among them. Exhibit 1.2 describes three studies that examined people's ratings of the severity of crimes

---

EXHIBIT 1.2
Genetic Relatedness and Judgments of Crime Severity

There is a surprising degree of consensus among people from different social classes and different societies on the relative severity of different crimes (Akman & Normandeau, 1967; Wolfgang, Figlio, Tracy, & Singer, 1985). Wolfgang et al. (1985) developed a magnitude estimation scaling technique to measure perceived crime severity based on Fechner's law of psychophysics, which asserts that the logarithm of rated stimulus intensity is a linear function of actual stimulus intensity. Perceived severity is one of a number of elements determining societal responses to a particular crime; other determinants include the offender's previous criminal history and the degree to which the offender lacks criminal intent.

A prediction concerning the perceived severity of crimes can be derived from the notion of inclusive fitness: Crimes should be viewed as more severe to the degree that the victim is genetically related to the perpetrator. To test this prediction, Quinsey, Lalumière, Querée, and McNaughton (1999) had 230 university students estimate the magnitude of the severity of brief crime descriptions in three separate studies. In the first of these, 40 male and 40 female first-year university undergraduates rated the severity of various acts using a magnitude estimation procedure. In this procedure, a modulus or standard comparison stimulus was included (stealing a bicycle) and assigned a severity score of 10. Participants rated the severity of the other items by considering how many times more (or less) serious each of the other crimes or sexual interactions were than the modulus. The perpetrator or protagonist was always described as an adult male when the event involved two persons.

There were 36 items, of one line of text each. Four of these items were taken from Wolfgang et al.'s (1985) National Crime Survey (a murder, a theft, an obscene phone call, and an underage intoxication). The remaining 32 items presented the rater with sexual offenses and legal sexual interactions that differed across genetic relatedness; victim age; the nature of the sexual act; and, within the no-genetic-relatedness condition, whether the nature of the social relationship proscribed sexual intimacy or not.

There were four levels of biological kinship. In the no-genetic-relatedness condition there was either an authoritative or a proscribed relationship with the victim (teacher, stepfather, minister, priest, professor, or stepbrother) or not (involving protagonists who lived in the same apartment, lived in the same neighborhood, played on the same softball team, lived on the same street, were in the same park, or were in the same university class). The genetic-relatedness conditions involved third-degree relatives (cousin–cousin), second-degree relatives (uncle–niece or half-brother–half-sister), and first-degree relatives (father–daughter or brother–sister). Within each degree of genetic relatedness, items included victims or partners who were either 11, 16, or 21 years of age. The sexual activity described alternated between sexual intercourse and fondling of the female's genitals. The results for sexual intercourse for adult victims and partners are shown in Figure 1.1.

The prediction that the log mean severity ratings of sexual acts would be linearly related to degree of genetic relatedness was strongly supported for age 21 with respect to intercourse and at ages 21 and 16 with respect to fondling. In interpreting this effect it is important to remember that the no-genetic-relatedness condition involved authoritative relationships that are ordinarily thought to proscribe sexual relationships. Even when the no-genetic-relatedness condition was omitted, a

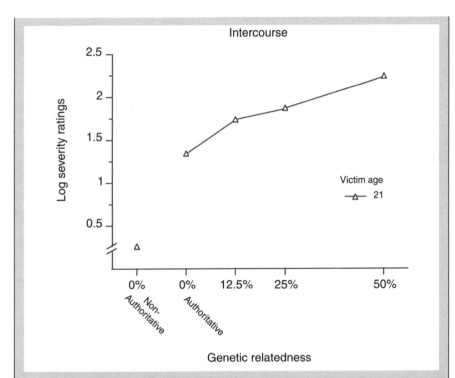

Figure 1.1. Severity ratings of sexual intercourse as a function of social and genetic relatedness. From "Perceived crime severity and biological kinship," by V. L. Quinsey, M. L. Lalumière, M. Querée, and J. K. McNaughton, 1999, *Human Nature, 10,* 399–414. Adapted with permission of the authors.

significant linear trend was found for each variation of age and sexual act across genetic relatedness.

In the second study, the effect of genetic relatedness of victim and perpetrator on ratings of the severity of nonsexual crimes was varied, and in the third, the hypothetical genetic relatedness of the participant and the fictitious victims was varied. These two studies, like the first, found a linear relationship between genetic relatedness and perceived crime severity, as predicted by kin-directed altruism theory. For example, physically assaulting one's sister was seen as more severe than physically assaulting one's cousin. Perceptions of the severity of particular crimes thus appear to be related not only to the nature of the crime but also to the genetic relationship of the victim and perpetrator.

involving either perpetrators and victims who varied in their genetic relatedness to each other or victims who varied in their genetic relatedness to the rater.

Reciprocal Altruism and Defection

Altruism is not always nepotistic. Humans, like other organisms, develop alliances based on what Trivers (1971) called reciprocal altruism. Reciprocal altruism involves the cooperation of two or more nonrelatives and is characterized by a payoff matrix in which the gain obtained from cooperation is greater than the sum of the gain obtained by each party without cooperation. But with cooperation comes the possibility of defection. Game theory describes a social exchange matrix in which the payoffs and the costs of cooperation are pitted against the benefits and costs of defection (noncooperation) in an ongoing social exchange. Usually game theorists determine the costs and payoffs such that defection produces the highest payoff in the short run and cooperation produces the highest payoff in the long run (Axelrod, 1984). Many forms of antisocial behavior can be seen as defection in social contracts in which one individual obtains a benefit without paying the attached cost.

R. H. Frank (1988) has developed an interesting evolutionary model that predicts that the proportion of altruistic and nonaltruistic individuals in a population will stabilize at a value determined by the costs and accuracy of identifying defectors. Because exploitative characteristics are likely to be increasingly costly for an individual over time in stable social situations, defectors (or cheaters) are likely to maximize their outcomes through geographic and social mobility (Harpending & Sobus, 1987). Cooperators are likely to do better in interacting with the same people over time. As discussed in Exhibit 1.3, the benefits to altruistic individuals are sometimes reputational and subtle.

EXHIBIT 1.3
Altruism as Display

Researchers have long noticed that the benefits of altruistic acts to the altruists are sometimes not obvious. In many circumstances, the actions of altruists do not have benefits for their relatives and do not seem to be reciprocated. This happens, for example, when the best hunters in subsistence societies share the meat they bring back from the hunt but, being the best, do not as often receive meat from others.

A recent twist on altruism has arisen from Zahavi's notion of honest signaling (Zahavi & Zahavi, 1997). Honest signals provide information to recipients that cannot be faked by the signaler. For example, the peacock signals his good health and good genes with his exaggerated and expensive tail. Similarly, the gazelle jumps very high in front of the lion as if saying, "Look at me—I'm in great shape and you would waste your time running after me. Pick on someone else!" Signals that are easily

---

faked do not provide reliable information to the recipients, and are selected to be ignored.

Smith and Bliege Bird (2000) recently examined turtle hunting among the Meriam of Torres Strait in Australia. Turtle hunting is a very costly behavior in terms of time, energy, and money involved, and is considered a form of public generosity (altruism). The researchers collected data suggesting that this behavior meets many of the conditions of honest signaling. It is costly, not reciprocated, reaches an audience, and provides a true test of ability and strength. Altruism, then, may serve as a display of the altruist's qualities.

R. H. Frank also postulated an evolutionary role for emotions, especially secondary emotions such as guilt and shame. In his view, emotions evolved in part as a buffer against short-term material motivation. As he put it, "people who love, who feel guilty when they cheat, vengeful when they are wronged, or envious when they get less than their full share will often behave in ways that reduce their material payoffs. But precisely because of this, they will also enjoy opportunities that would not be available to a purely opportunistic person" (R. H. Frank, 1988, p. 237). In chapter 4 we describe a group of opportunistic individuals who seem designed to pursue a life history of social defection.

GENETIC CONFLICT

As mentioned before, evolutionists view the unit of selection as the gene (loosely defined as parts of DNA that cause particular phenotypic effects and are inherited together), not the vehicle that carries the gene (the actual organism). As noted previously, this way of thinking about the unit of selection has many consequences for understanding conflict and cooperation and has led to several interesting discoveries. In this section we discuss one of these discoveries—genetic conflict between the mother and the fetus—and in the exhibits we present other examples of genetic conflicts and their outcomes.

In humans, the mother–fetus coefficient of relatedness is .5. As noted earlier, this means that mothers and their offspring share 50% of their polymorphic genes by common descent. This lack of genetic identity has a number of implications. The first is that the immune system of the mother must be prevented from attacking the foreign element in the fetus (the paternal genome). This is accomplished in part by the placenta, which does not display the human leukocyte antigen (HLA) markers and thus screens the fetus (containing the foreign paternal genome) from the maternal immune system (Bodmer & McKie, 1994). The fetus also seems to defend itself actively against the maternal immune response (Munn et al., 1998).

Haig (1992, 1993, 1995, 1997, 1999) has extended Trivers's (1972) model of parental investment to intrauterine events. Because the mother and fetus do not have identical genetic interests, there is opportunity for competition between them. It may be in the fetus's interest to obtain more maternal resources than it is in the mother's interest to give them. The hormones that maintain pregnancy (luteinizing hormone and progesterone) are initially produced by the mother but by day 50 are produced by the fetus in large quantities. The mother responds by becoming less sensitive to the hormones.

The fetus attempts to maximize its share of each maternal meal. One of the ways in which this is accomplished is through raising the mother's blood pressure, a common problem of pregnancy. Placental cells also kill the muscles in the arteries leading to the womb so that the mother cannot contract these muscles; the mother responds by spiraling these arteries (hence "spiral arteries") to increase their resistance to blood flow.

In addition to fetal–maternal genetic conflict, maternal–paternal gene conflicts can also occur under certain conditions (Haig, 1992, 1993, 1995). Information on these conflicts is presented in Exhibit 1.4, and information

---

EXHIBIT 1.4
Maternal–Paternal Genetic Conflicts

Some genes change their expression depending on whether they are paternally or maternally derived; this phenomenon is termed *genomic imprinting* (Haig, 1992). Genomic imprinting results in interesting phenomena when females bear the offspring of more than one male and display more parental investment than males. In this situation, paternal genes that exploit the mother are selected through intermale competition.

Insulin-like Growth Factor II (IGF-II) is a growth enhancer. Type 1 receptors are required for IGF-II to function. In mice, where females mate with more than one male, there are also Type 2 receptors. Type 2 receptors soak up and degrade IGF-II. Type 2 receptors are preferentially expressed by the maternal chromosome. Thus, within the cell, the paternal allele produces the growth factor and the maternal allele destroys it. Type 2 receptors do not have this function in birds, where the offspring have no influence over the amount of yolk their eggs receive.

Genetic material can be obtained from mice after fertilization but before fusion of the maternal and paternal DNA. Male–male, female–female, or male–female DNA can then be placed in an (empty) egg.

Contrary to expectations derived from classical genetic theory, neither of the same sex combinations results in viable offspring (revealing genomic imprinting). The placenta resulting from two females implants very weakly, but the placenta resulting from two males exhibits explosive growth.

Several imprinted genes that are expressed in the brain have now been identified in humans. These genes control the actions of other genes or regulate their products. Sexual dimorphism in the human brain then may reflect the actions of imprinted X-linked genes in addition to the effects of intrauterine sex hormones (Skuse, 1999). Skuse et al. (1997) studied females with Turner's syndrome, caused by deletion of all or part of one X chromosome. Females whose X chromosome was maternally derived displayed poorer social cognition than those who had a paternally derived X chromosome. If the genes involved in social cognition are expressed only from the paternally derived X chromosome, the existence of this locus could explain why 46,XY males (whose single X chromosome is maternal) are more vulnerable to developmental disorders of language and social cognition, such as autism, than are 46,XX females.

Skuse (1999) has speculated about how a paternally imprinted gene on the X chromosome that facilitated social cognition could arise in evolution. If there were a gene on the X chromosome that was related to social competence, it would be likely to have greater expression in females than males (because there was likely no homologue on the Y chromosome). If the locus were silenced in maternal gametes, the dose of imprinted gene expression in daughters would be halved, and in sons reduced to zero. A reduction in aspects of social cognition, such as empathy, might provide an advantage to sons in intermale status competition. Thus, mothers could confer a dominance advantage to their sons and fathers could confer a social skill advantage to their daughters. Goos and Silverman (2001) have written an accessible review of the role of genomic imprinting on human brain development and behavior.

on other genetic conflicts is presented in Exhibit 1.5. For our purposes, the important point is that genetic conflicts between mothers and their offspring can affect the developing fetus in important ways, as discussed in chapter 3. This same theme of the partially divergent genetic interest of parents and children will reappear at a different level when we consider family influences on delinquent behavior. To anticipate, one might expect that the behavior of children and adolescents would be sensitive to the amount and quality of parental investment received.

EXHIBIT 1.5
Other Examples of Genetic Conflicts and Their Outcomes

Sexually Antagonistic Genes

Early work on the guppy suggested that sexually antagonistic genes, those that confer a benefit to one sex to the detriment of the other, can spread in the population when they are tightly linked to the gender-determining gene(s). The evidence was that the genes associated with gaudy color in males were near the chromosomal region determining gender; such color would benefit males by increasing their success in courtship but only harm females by increasing their risk of predation.

The physical proximity of sexually antagonistic genes to the sex-determining genes ensures that they segregate with the sex-determining genes most of the time. If sexually antagonistic genes were not linked to the sex-determining genes, they would be found in both sexes and not provide a net benefit (averaged over both sexes) that would facilitate their spread.

There are two strategies for dealing with leakage of sexually antagonistic genes from the Y to the X chromosome: Sex-limited expression of the trait(s) and suppressed recombination of the area on which the sexually antagonistic allele rests. The second mechanism is faster and thus may be more likely to evolve. Such suppressed recombination may spread along the X chromosome in a chain reaction.

Location of Sexually Antagonistic Genes

Experimental support for the evolution of sexually antagonistic genes in "hot spots" close to the gender-determining area comes from W. R. Rice (1992; 1996a) working with drosophila. In *Drosophila melanogaster*, females are XXY and males are XY. There are four chromosomes. Among males, the genes from the two parents do not recombine.

An autosomal dominant gene for red eye color was made to act as a new sex-determining (female) gene. Each generation, only subjects heterozygous for the eye color gene were female (heterozygous males were discarded) and only homozygous subjects were male (homozygous females were discarded). In the control populations, hetero- and homozygous individuals were alternated over generations of red-eyed flies.

After 29 generations, the two female-determining areas from the experimental lines were put into males. The fitness of these males was decreased by 50%, mostly due to their poor mating performance. Therefore, the chromosomal region proximate to a new sex-determining gene is a hot spot for the accumulation of genes detrimental to the homogametic sex.

Arms Race Between the Sexes

The existence of sexually antagonistic genes implies that relations between the sexes parallel those between predators and prey and between parasites and hosts, with the constraint that alleles that are too strongly antagonistic cannot evolve unless sex-limited in expression.

Drosophila males ejaculate about 5,000 sperm, but females can only store about 500. Male flies produce one peptide that encourages egg laying and dampens sexual interest among females and another that kills rival sperm and in the process poisons the female. Females produce chemicals that fend off the male proteins, reduce the number of sperm, and switch off the sex appetite suppressant.

In an ingenious experiment, W. R. Rice (1996b) prevented females from evolving in response to changing male reproductive strategies. By using artificial selection and chromosomal marking, Rice enabled the paternal set of genes (the male haplotype) to be transmitted exclusively from father to son. The female-derived genes (the female haplotype) passed to sons but had no effect on the population because all female haplotypes were culled. The nonresponding stock donated target females unidirectionally to the experimental adapting male line each generation. Each generation of males was mated with females from a large stock population. Mutations beneficial to male reproductive success were thus passed from father to son. After 40 generations, experimental males fathered more offspring, prevented competitors from siring progeny, and caused females to die young. Clearly, males and females are in an evolutionary arms race.

EMOTIONS

If natural selection has designed our psychologies, then our emotions are likely to be adaptations to different reproductive and survival problems encountered by our ancestors (Nesse, 1990). Ekman (1992, 1993) has presented evidence that there are six basic human emotions: surprise, happiness, anger, fear, disgust, and sadness. Ekman produced a book comprising facial photos of actors asked to pose these emotions and found that isolated tribal New Guineans could reliably identify them. Similarly, American college students could reliably identify facial photos of New Guineans portraying the emotions. Blind children exhibit the six basic emotions as well. Recent data from a carefully designed cross-cultural investigation strongly support the universality of human perception of emotions (Hejmadi, Davidson, & Rozin, 2000).

Although there has been controversy about the universality of facial displays and their relationship to basic emotions (for a complete discussion see Russell & Fernández-Dols, 1997), there does seem to be some consensus among researchers, summarized by Ginsburg (1997) as follows:

> As a species, we are very attentive to faces and their expressions . . . and appear to have some neurological sensitivity to both facial identity and facial displays. . . . It is not clear whether we are particularly attentive to facial displays in contrast to postural and vocal displays, but all such displays carry information about what acts the displayer is embarked upon or is prepared to undertake. The neural and muscular anatomy of the human face, especially those parts innervated by the seventh (facial) nerve, affords exceptionally fine variation of feature movement and therefore extremely high resolution of configurations. Nuances of both quality and intensity are readily produced, readily controlled, and readily perceived. . . . The function of facial actions is interpersonal and implicative—they imply what is about to occur or could occur. (pp. 376–377)

THE CASE OF JEALOUSY

The action implications of emotional expression may be a sufficient explanation for the evolution of facial-expression production and recognition. An evolutionary viewpoint suggests that there will be particular emotions associated with particular problems of survival and reproduction that occurred in ancestral environments. A very good candidate for an evolved emotion is jealousy. Jealousy is expected to express itself differently and to have different functions in men and women if our male and female ancestors faced different reproductive problems (D. M. Buss, 1995; D. M. Buss, Larsen, Westen, Semmelroth, 1992; Daly, Wilson, & Weghorst, 1982).

As noted in the section on parental investment theory, an ancestral woman was limited in the number of offspring she could produce because of pregnancy, lactation, and menopause. The number of offspring of an ancestral man, on the other hand, was limited mainly by the number of fertile women with whom he could mate. The number of surviving offspring of either the man or woman would be further limited by the resources available to raise them. Because the principal limitation on a man's reproductive success was the number of his fertile women partners, men competed among each other for mating opportunities. Because the principal limitation on a woman's reproductive success was the resources available to raise offspring successfully, women competed among themselves for access to men with resources and willingness to commit those resources to them.

One important way that men could compete among themselves, therefore, was in the acquisition of status and wealth. Powerful, wealthy men, having more resources to commit, would be more attractive to women. The women that they would be more attracted to would be the most fertile: healthy and young (for a review of empirical support for this proposition, see D. M. Buss, 1994). But men had another problem that women did not have; they could not be sure that "their" offspring were theirs. This is the problem of paternity uncertainty.

A man who invested his resources in raising another man's children had fewer surviving offspring of his own than one who did not. A woman who mated with men who did not invest their resources in her children had fewer surviving offspring than other women. Given the different reproductive problems that our male and female ancestors faced, men and women would be expected to have somewhat different psychologies. They should desire different things in romantic and sexual relationships. This is the simple result of the competition within each sex that designed male and female psychologies through differential reproductive success.

An ancestral man who desired many sexual partners (i.e., was very interested in partner novelty), sexually desired women to the extent they appeared fertile, was sexually jealous regarding a woman to the extent that he had committed resources to her, and was socially and materially ambitious was more likely to have had more surviving offspring than men who did not have these characteristics. Contemporaneous men, therefore, are expected to express these characteristics more than women. In contrast, an ancestral woman who was concerned with her potential partner's emotional commitment to her, his health, status, and resources, and his generosity would likely have more surviving offspring than other women. A contemporary woman, therefore, would be expected to be less concerned about her partner's sexual fidelity than her partner would be about hers but more concerned about his emotional and material commitment to her and her children than he would be about her commitment to him and his children.

In accord with this view, D. M. Buss and his collaborators (D. M. Buss, Larsen, Westen, & Semmelroth, 1992; Buunk, Angleitner, Oubaid, & Buss, 1996) have shown using physiological measures that a woman's jealousy focuses more on her partner's emotional commitment to her, whereas a man's jealousy focuses more on his partner's sexual fidelity. Of interest, men are more likely to state concern about sexual fidelity if they have actually experienced a committed relationship. This finding implies that male sexual jealousy is context specific; that is, it is activated by having experienced a committed relationship (see also L. Paul, Foss, & Baenninger, 1998). Geary, Rumsey, Bow-Thomas, and Hoard (1995) obtained the same results in China.

Daly and Wilson (1988) reviewed cross-cultural and cross-national data and found that homicide rates vary in a manner expected from these considerations of the different reproductive problems faced by ancestral men and women. Marital violence appears to arise out of men's desire to control the reproductive capacities of women. Male sexual proprietariness is a common source of conflict, and sexual jealousy is the most common motive for men assaulting—and sometimes even killing—their wives.

MATING

Several studies that compared the mating motivations and interests of young men and women support the view that men and women faced different reproductive problems in human ancestral environments (D. M. Buss, 1987, 1989). Sex differences in preferred partner characteristics have been extensively documented. Heterosexual men have been found to prefer females that are increasingly younger than themselves as they get older and to place more importance than females on characteristics associated with peak and potential fertility, such as physical attractiveness. Heterosexual women have been found to prefer men who are slightly older than themselves, regardless of their own age, and to place more importance than males on characteristics associated with resource acquisition, such as industriousness and social dominance, and behavioral cues of willingness to commit resources (see reviews in Batten, 1992; D. M. Buss, 1994).

There are also sex differences in preferred relationship characteristics: Men, compared to women, are more interested in partner variety, are more willing to engage in impersonal sex, and have a greater propensity to seek extrapair romances (e.g., D. M. Buss & Schmitt, 1993; B. J. Ellis & Symons, 1990; Landolt, Lalumière, & Quinsey, 1995). For example, in two studies (Clark, 1990; Clark & Hatfield, 1989) male and female confederates approached opposite-sex individuals on a university campus and asked them one of three questions: "Would you go out with me tonight?" "Would you come to my apartment tonight?" or "Would you go to bed with me tonight?" Male and female respondents were about equally interested in a date, but very few women accepted a visit to the apartment (less than 15%) and no women accepted the sexual invitation. In contrast, more than half the men agreed to a visit or to having sex.

Some of these sex differences in partner and relationship characteristics have been observed across sociodemographic groups, cultures, and time periods (D. M. Buss, 1987, 1989; Kenrick & Keefe, 1992; Sprecher, Sullivan, Hatfield, 1994). These findings are among the most stable and replicable in the social sciences and are of direct relevance to individual differences in delinquency.

Juvenile delinquency is related to mating effort in both sexes, as assessed by age at first intercourse or number of lifetime sexual partners (Bogaert, 1993; Bogaert & Rushton, 1989; Rowe, Rodgers, Meseck-Bushey, & St-John, 1989). Rowe, Vazsonyi, and Figueredo (1997) found that questionnaire items whose manifest content reflected delinquency, such as, "Other guys respect me because they know I have a lot of friends who would support me," loaded with items such as, "I would rather date several girls at once than just one girl," on a scale designed to measure mating effort. Mating effort is also associated with the use of sexually coercive tactics among young adult males (Lalumière & Quinsey, 1996; Malamuth, Heavy, & Linz, 1993).

Aggressive and antisocial tendencies in both boys and girls are associated with early sexual intercourse and its occasional consequence, reproduction (Bingham & Crockett, 1996; Jessor, Costa, Jessor, & Donovan, 1983). Middle adolescent risk taking is among the best predictors of adolescent pregnancy involvement for both males and females (Scaramella, Conger, Simons, & Whitbeck, 1998). Serbin et al. (1998) found that mothers' aggression measured in childhood predicted teen motherhood and close spacing of births in a large longitudinal study of the intergenerational transfer of psychosocial risk between mothers and children.

Stouthamer-Loeber and Wei (1998) found in a longitudinal study of inner-city public schools in Pittsburgh that 12% of 506 males fathered a child before age 19. These fathers were over 200% more likely than other men in the sample to have committed serious crimes. Delinquency did not decrease after fatherhood. In the Oregon Youth Study sample, Fagot, Pears, Capaldi, Crosby, and Leve (1998) followed 206 boys ages 9 and 10. As early as sixth grade, the 35 boys who became fathers by age 20 were different from those who did not. The adolescent fathers were characterized by low socioeconomic status of origin, parental antisocial behavior, poor parental discipline, deviant peer group membership, academic failure, and antisocial behavior. They had more substance abuse problems and arrests than boys who had not become fathers. Antisocial behavior was a better predictor of age at first intercourse than it was a predictor of early pregnancy. Forty percent of the adolescent fathers had no contact with their offspring by the time the children were 2 years old. The at-risk fathers showed more negative reactions when their children worked on a puzzle task than control fathers.

The link between delinquency and mating seems so obvious to researchers that there are not many studies specifically designed to address this issue. Instead, precocious and promiscuous sex is often part of the very definition of delinquency. Rowe and Rogers's (1989) concept of d (or deviance) is in fact meant to explain the strong association between delinquency and precocious and varied sexual behavior.[5] In an interesting study of siblings, Rowe, Rogers, Meseck-Bushey, and St-John (1989) observed

---

[5] Other authors have demonstrated, through factor analyses, that one factor underlies propensity for "problem behavior," including violence, and precocious and varied sexual activities. Jessor and his colleagues have labeled this factor *unconventionality* (e.g., Donovan, Jessor, & Costa, 1988).

that knowledge of one sibling's delinquency predicted the other siblings' sexual behavior, and vice versa, for both sexes.[6]

Because aggregate data show that poverty and having a teenage mother predict subsequent antisocial activity in offspring, and because poor young women were differentially more likely to obtain an abortion than wealthier and older women after abortion was legalized in the United States as a result of the 1973 *Roe v. Wade* decision, it might be expected that crime rates would fall some years later. Donahue and Levitt (2001) have reviewed the data showing reductions in crime; for example, since 1991, the U.S. has had the largest drop in murder rates since the end of prohibition. Crime began to fall 18 years after *Roe v. Wade*. The five states that legalized abortion earlier showed earlier reductions in crime. In states with high abortion rates, only arrests of those born after the legalization of abortion fell relative to states with low abortion rates; there was no change in crime rate for older cohorts. Donahue and Levitt (2001) found that the effect remained after controlling for incarceration rate, number of police, and level of poverty at the state level. They concluded from their quantitative modeling that legalized abortion accounted for about half of the reduction in crime.

COMMENTS

Evolutionary psychology is concerned with human psychological features that are shared by all members of the species. It is also concerned with variation in human behavior. People can develop different psychologies and adopt different courses of action based on their sex, their age, their developmental conditions, and the conditions of their current social and biotic environments. In that view, variations in age, sex, kinship, access to resources, future prospects, and so on are tied to variations in individuals' desires, motivations, and behaviors—including antisocial tendencies and behaviors—in a manner that is consistent with selectionist principles. We now turn to a very different but not necessarily incompatible conceptual approach to the study of individual differences.

---

[6] L. Ellis (1988; L. Ellis & Walsh, 2000) has identified a large number of studies documenting the link between early onset of sexual activities or number of sexual partners and criminality, drug use, and sensation-seeking.

2

BEHAVIORAL GENETICS AND DELINQUENCY

The notion of individual differences is central to behavioral genetics. In this chapter we describe the basic methods and statistics behavioral geneticists use to partition sources of individual differences, explain that behavioral genetics is as concerned with environmental effects as it is with genetic effects, and then review and discuss findings related to juvenile delinquency. In the spirit of conceptual integration we also spend some time linking behavioral genetics to development and experience (ontogenesis), and to evolution (phylogenesis).

HERITABILITY AND INHERITANCE

The subject matter of behavioral genetics is the genetic and environmental influences on behavioral differences among individual members of the same species. Genetic influence is measured by a statistic called *heritability* (h^2). Heritability describes the proportion of the observed variance in a behavior that can be attributed to genetic differences among individuals. Thus, a trait that shows high heritability (e.g., intelligence, as opposed to binocular vision) necessarily varies within a population, and this phenotypic variation can be attributed to genetic differences. A trait that is *inherited* is passed on through genes. An inherited trait can therefore have low or high heritability, but a trait that is not inherited always has, in principle, zero heritability. Heritability estimates are a function of the environmental heterogeneity of the population studied. A population with a relatively homogeneous environment, such as in Scandinavian countries, would be expected to produce higher heritability estimates than a population in a relatively heterogeneous environment, such as the United States. For this and other reasons, heritability estimates for a given population or group may not generalize to other populations or groups.[1]

Before turning to the methods of behavioral genetics and to delinquency research, we briefly discuss the relationship between development, genetics, and evolution.

GENETIC AND EXPERIENTIAL DETERMINANTS OF BEHAVIOR

Cairns and his colleagues (Cairns, 1996; Cairns & Gariepy, 1990; Cairns, Gariepy, & Hood, 1990) have argued that there are parallels between developmental and evolutionary processes. They make three empirical generalizations. First, social behaviors can be changed very rapidly through genetic selection: For example, highly aggressive and nonaggressive lines of mice can be differentiated in one to four generations. Such differentiation can be reversed even more quickly, such that organisms are said to exhibit genetic homeostasis (see also Weiner, 1994).

Second, the effects of genetic selection tend to be susceptible to experiential modification, such that the magnitude of strain and breed differences in mammalian social behaviors depends heavily on social rearing experiences. For example, genotype–experience interactions are found in aggression among strains of mice. Even when rearing conditions are held constant, repeated experiences affect the magnitude of genetically based differences in aggressive behavior between strains. These effects are related to the Brelands' "drift toward instinctive behavior" (Breland & Breland, 1961) that sometimes undermines instrumental performance in a variety of species. Another example involves the ease with which a variety of very young animals will form cross-species attachments; these attachments are typically reversed as the animals become juveniles, and these reversals are biased toward species-typical (i.e., intraspecific) preferences. Thus, there is a buffering mechanism in ontogeny that biases the organism toward species-typical trajectories. Individual adaptations tend to be context specific, time

---

[1] One common mistake is to believe that heritability estimates, which characterize a group of people, can be interpreted at the level of individuals (for example, that 40% of a person's aggression is due to genetics). Behavioral genetics is solely about individual differences.

constrained, and age dependent. This phenomenon is termed *developmental homeostasis*.

Third, the age at which a behavior first appears and its rate of development are keys to understanding differences between individuals and among species. For example, differences in aggressive behavior among mice are nonexistent in infancy, largest around puberty, and smaller in adulthood. As we shall see, age and rate of development are also crucial notions in the area of juvenile delinquency and aggression.

Cairns and his colleagues (Cairns, 1996; Cairns & Gariepy, 1990) concluded that both evolutionary homeostasis and developmental homeostasis operate to stabilize adaptations in social behaviors, although organizational features of certain behaviors offer windows of opportunity for rapid change. Behavior that is most modifiable by experience is most likely to be sensitive to genetic modification, albeit by different mechanisms. Certain features of behavioral organization (e.g., latency to attack in mice) are open or modifiable, whereas others (e.g., topography of attacking behavior in mice) are more closed. Changes in the evolutionary and ontogenetic time frames typically support each other, and dual genesis of behavior is the rule.[2]

BEHAVIORAL GENETICS AND THE FUNDAMENTAL THEOREM OF NATURAL SELECTION

There is a relationship between evolutionary change and behavioral genetics. Fisher's fundamental theorem (Andersson, 1994; Plomin, DeFries, McClearn, & McGuffin, 2000) states that changes in evolutionary fitness require additive genetic variance. Additive genetic variance is due to gene dosage, as opposed to interactions among different genes (called nonadditive variance), and is responsible for the resemblance of parents and offspring. If additive genetic variance for fitness-related characteristics is present in a species, then there is opportunity for further selection. When maximal fitness in the population is reached, the additive genetic variance is zero. The genes are said to have gone to fixation. The heritability of major components of fitness, such as fertility, should be low. This does not necessarily mean, however, that phenotypic characteristics with low heritability are important components of fitness. The fundamental theorem does suggest that most of the genetic variance of characteristics related to fitness should be nonadditive. The theorem thus leads us to expect inbreeding depression (the expression of harmful traits due to homozygosity at certain

---

[2] The notions of developmental and genetic homeostasis raise the more general question of the relationships of genetic constraint to evolutionary plasticity, a question that has received a great deal of attention at the intracellular and embryonic levels. Gerhart and Kirschner (1997) have presented a detailed overview of the developmental understanding of phenotypic variation and evolutionary adaptability.

loci), hybrid vigor (the superior qualities arising from the mating of genetically different individuals), and low heritabilities for fitness characteristics in stable populations.

A number of forces, however, can maintain or create additive genetic variance in a population (Hughes & Burleson, 2000).[3] Hughes and Burleson review evidence showing that life history (fitness-related) traits are moderately heritable. Genetic variance in humans (and drosophila) is about 10%, and heritabilities are approximately .20. About 12% of phenotypic variance in humans appears to be maintained by selective forces; the remaining variation is nongenetic or accounted for by mutations. Recent studies have confirmed the heritability of fitness-related traits in humans and have suggested that the availability of contraception may have changed the nature of the heritable precursors of variations in fertility (Rodgers et al., 2001). Snieder, MacGregor, and Spector (1998) have provided an excellent example of heritable differences in a fitness-related trait, age at menopause, in a study of identical and fraternal twins. A further example comes from a large twin study of the heritability of variations in the propensity to engage in casual sexual activity (measured by the Sociosexuality Inventory). Bailey, Kirk, Zhu, Dunne, and Martin (2000) found that familial resemblance in sociosexuality was attributable to additive genetic factors and not shared environment.

Behavioral genetics and evolutionary psychology are related. Behavioral genetics deals with the differences among members of a species. It seeks to characterize the sources of behavioral variation or individual differences. Evolutionary psychology is typically more interested in inherited characteristics of all members of a species (Daly, 1996). Thus, the characteristics of interest to an evolutionary psychologist may be inherited but show no heritability in behavioral genetics analyses because there is no variance in the population (Crawford & Anderson, 1989). However, central to the viewpoint developed in this book is Gangestad's (1997) explication of the role of genetic variation in behavioral characteristics from an evolutionary perspective. Gangestad argues persuasively that some phenotypic variance is fitness related and, as noted previously, this argument has empirical support. From our perspective, evolutionary considerations may play an important role in understanding individual differences.

---

[3] These forces include mutations, heterozygote advantage, frequency-dependent selection, environmental heterogeneity, sexually antagonistic genes, antagonistic pleiotropy, and gene flow between populations.

PARTITIONING THE VARIANCE

Heritability statistics can be computed using contrasts between identical (monozygotic, or MZ) and fraternal (dizygotic, or DZ) twins or between genetically related individuals reared together (T) and apart (A). Because MZA twins share identical genetic material but no common environment, the correlations of MZA twins directly reflect heritability. Another estimate is provided by twice the difference between MZT and DZT correlations,[4] because fraternal twins share on average half of their polymorphic genes. For example, a correlation of .60 for intelligence among identical twins reared together and .40 among fraternal twins reared together leads to a heritability estimate of .40. The environmental influence, then, is .60 (assuming no measurement error).

The environmental influence can be partitioned into *shared environment* (the aspects of the environment that are shared by all family members, such as household socioeconomic status) and *nonshared environment* (the aspects of the environment that are not shared by all members, such as differential parental treatment of siblings). The difference in correlation between MZA and MZT twins directly estimates the effects of shared environment (also called between-family variance). Shared environment can also be estimated using adoption and cross-fostering designs.

The effects of nonshared environment (or within-family variance) can also be estimated using the twin design (Plomin & Daniels, 1987). For example, the total nongenetic variance in the preceding example is .60. Identical twins share all their genes, but their correlation is only .60. Thus, assuming perfect reliability of the measure, the total nongenetic variance (.60) can be divided into .20 for shared influences (twice the correlation for DZT minus the correlation for MZT) and .40 for nonshared influences (1 minus the heritability coefficient minus the nonshared component). Thus, in this example, two thirds of the nongenetic variance makes identical twins different from one another (the nonshared environment effect) and one third makes them similar (the shared environment effect). Genetic modeling offers another way to estimate genetic, shared environment, and nonshared environment effects (Loehlin, 1989).

---

[4] Assuming equality of the environment and the absence of assortative mating, genetic dominance, and nonadditive effects for the trait under consideration.

The vocabulary and basic behavioral genetics equations are shown in Exhibits 2.1 and 2.2. The discussion that follows assumes an understanding of the terms defined in Exhibit 2.1 and the general idea behind the equations given in Exhibit 2.2.[5]

EXHIBIT 2.1
The Polygenic Model

Phenotype: The manifest characteristics of an organism. A phenotypic character may be influenced by genes from many different parts of the chromosomes (loci). Phenotypic deviations from the mean for some character in a population are a function of environmental and genetic deviations and their interaction.

Genotype: The genetic constitution of an organism.

Heritability: The proportion of phenotypic variance that is attributable to genetic variance. Heritability (h^2) is the proportion of variance among individuals in a trait that is due to genetic differences.

Dominance: The nonadditive interaction of alleles at a single locus.

Epistasis: Interlocus interaction. The interaction of two or more genes at different chromosomal loci to produce a distinct phenotypic effect. If many genes are involved, the term used is emergenesis (the interaction of polygenic systems). Emergenesis is indicated by a very high correlation between MZA and a very low correlation between DZT.

Genetic variance is due to additive genetic variance, dominance variance, and variance resulting from epistatic interactions. Broad heritability is all of the genetic influences that make monozygotic twins reared apart (MZA) alike. For IQ, broad heritability is about .75.

Additive (or narrow-sense) genetic variance is that due to gene dosage. Narrow heritability is the proportion of phenotypic variance that is attributable to additive genetic variance. It is that genetic influence that is responsible for the resemblance of parents and offspring. For IQ, narrow heritability is about .5.

Genotypic value due to all loci = sum of additive genetic values across all loci + sum of dominance deviations across all loci + deviation due to epistatic interactions.

The proportion of variance among individuals in a trait that is due to common environment (the environment shared by family members) is symbolized by c^2.

---

[5] Plomin, DeFries, McClearn, and McGuffin (2000) have written an accessible book on behavioral genetics methods.

The total phenotypic variance is equal to the genetic variance plus the environmental variance plus twice the covariance of the genetic and environmental variances. The covariance of genetic and environmental influence is given by the correlation between them multiplied by the square root of the genetic variance times the square root of the environmental variance.

Note: See Andersson (1994, pp. 64–66); Jensen (1997); and Plomin, DeFries, and McClearn (1990, pp. 221–285).

Heritability estimates from twin data can be compromised by differences between twins in their intrauterine environments. For example, identical twins who share a common placenta are more similar to each other than those who, like fraternal twins, do not (Phelps, Davis, & Schartz, 1998). This placentation difference can result in artifactually high heritability coefficients (cf. Devlin, Daniels, & Roeder, 1997). In twin studies, data on placentation can be obtained in order to improve the precision of the heritability estimate; in cross-fostering studies, paternal half siblings can be studied to eliminate the confounding of intrauterine environment and genes (e.g., Kety, 1988; Kety, Rosenthal, Wender, Schulsinger, & Jacobsen, 1978). Other limitations of the behavioral genetics basic twin and adoptive design have been discussed at length in references cited herein.

EXHIBIT 2.2
The Heritability Equations

The components of variance in twin and adoption studies can be estimated using the formulas given below (Jensen, 1997). Phenotypic variance (V_{phen}) is standardized so that each variance component is a proportion.

$V_{TOTAL} = V_{BF} + V_{WF}$ (where BF is between-family and WF is within-family)

$r_i = V_{BF} / V_{TOTAL}$ (the intraclass correlation)

$V_{phen} = V_g + V_e + 2cov (SQRT\ V_g) (SQRT\ V_e)$

$V_{TS} = r_{xx}$ (where TS means true score and r_{xx} means reliability)

$r_{MZA} = V_g = h^2$

$r_{MZT} = V_g + V_e + V_{ge} + V_{BF} = h^2 + c^2$

$r_{UT} = V_{BF}$ (where UT means unrelated raised together)

$1 - (r_{MZT}/r_{xx}) = V_{WF}$

INTELLIGENCE, PERSONALITY, AND DELINQUENCY

It has long been known that crime runs in families, but it has been more difficult to determine the extent of genetic similarity. Family similarity could occur through either the shared family environment or the influence of genes on intelligence, personality, the predisposition to develop substance abuse problems, or other characteristics associated with deliquency, such as high mating effort.

Longitudinal and cross-sectional studies have consistently found an association between personality variables and delinquency (Andrews & Wormith, 1989). The personality measures most commonly investigated include the Socialization scale of the California Psychological Inventory, the Psychopathic Deviate scale of the Minnesota Multiphasic Personality Inventory, the Porteus Maze Test Q score, and the junior version of the Eysenck Inventory. A good example of the longitudinal relationship between personality and later criminal behavior is provided by Sigvardsson, Bohman, and Cloninger (1987), who studied the criminal histories of 431 Swedes who had been assessed at ages 11, 15, and 27. Three dimensions of personality were rated without knowledge of the outcome. The three dimesions were Novelty Seeking, Harm Avoidance (responsiveness to aversive cues), and Reward Dependence (comprising traits such as sensitivity to social cues, sentimentality, and industriousness). As we discuss later in this chapter, these traits are highly heritable. Aggressive behavior at age 15 and violent criminal behavior in adulthood were predicted by high Novelty Seeking, low Harm Avoidance, and low Reward Dependence—all characteristics associated with antisocial personality.

Many cross-sectional and longitudinal studies have found that intelligence is inversely related to criminality (Hirschi & Hindelang, 1977; Kandel et al., 1988; Moffitt, 1990; Moffitt & Silva, 1988; Quay, 1987; J. Q. Wilson & Hernstein, 1985). In longitudinal studies, researchers have identified low IQ as a predictor and correlate of childhood aggression and adult violence (e.g., Farrington, 1991; Huesmann, Eron, & Yarmel, 1987). Significant negative correlations between IQ and delinquency have been found after controlling for socioeconomic status (Wolfgang, Figlio, & Sellin, 1972); race (Lynam, Moffitt, & Stouthamer-Loeber, 1993); academic achievement (Denno, 1990); and the child's motivation during the IQ test (Lynam et al., 1993). The relationship between IQ and delinquency is significant even when IQ is assessed long before the development of the antisocial behavior (Denno, 1990; Raine, Yaralian, Reynolds, Venables, & Mednick, 2002).

High intelligence appears to protect against the risk of delinquency. Kandel et al. (1988) assessed four groups of men in a Danish birth cohort: high-risk men (with severely delinquent biological fathers) who had engaged in criminal behavior, high-risk men who had not engaged in criminal behavior, low-risk men (with nondelinquent biological fathers) who had engaged in criminal behavior, and low-risk men who had not engaged in criminal behavior. High-risk men were 5.6 times more likely to be offenders than low-risk men. As predicted, the noncriminal high-risk men were significantly more intelligent than the men in the other three groups. The mean Wechsler Adult Intelligence Scale IQs were 113 for high-risk noncriminals, 100 for high-risk criminals, 105 for low-risk criminals, and 105 for low-risk noncriminals. The interaction of risk and intelligence remained significant when socioeconomic status (uncorrelated with intelligence) and education ($r = .36$ with intelligence) were partialed out. The role of intelligence as a protective factor for delinquency has been replicated in a prospective longitudinal study of self-reported and officially recorded delinquency in a New Zealand birth cohort (White, Moffitt, & Silva, 1989).

The IQ–crime relationship could be interpreted as meaning that the crimes of less intelligent delinquents are more likely to be detected. Using a sample of 654 thirteen-year-olds from an ongoing longitudinal study of a New Zealand birth cohort, Moffitt and Silva (1988) directly tested the differential detection hypothesis by comparing the Wechsler Intelligence Scale for Children–Revised IQ scores of delinquents matched on frequency and severity of self-reported delinquency who had or had not been officially detected. Contrary to the differential detection hypothesis, the IQs of delinquents known to the police did not differ from those of unidentified delinquents, but both groups scored six points less than nondelinquents.

Questions remain about the contribution of IQ to the prediction of antisocial behavior independently of other predictors. Huesmann and Eron (1984) found that IQ was no longer a significant predictor of aggression at age 30 once the effects of aggression at age 8 had been extracted. Huesmann and Eron suggested that low IQ may contribute to the early development of aggressive behavior patterns but not to their maintenance. This perspective is consistent with current findings about the relation between early disruptive behavior, poor school achievement, and delinquent behavior. While it is often suggested that aggressive behavior is a result of academic failure, a stronger case may be made that aggressive behavior contributes to failure at school, which in turn contributes to delinquent tendencies in later childhood and adolescence (Huesmann et al., 1987; Patterson, DeBaryshe, & Ramsey, 1989).

In the following section, we review behavioral genetics research on intelligence and personality. Findings from this research are now so well established that researchers have moved on to other research areas, such as the molecular genetics of cognitive abilities, personality, and psychopathologies.

HERITABILITY OF INTELLIGENCE AND PERSONALITY

Data from a large number of studies indicate that genetic differences are responsible for at least 50% of differences in IQ and educational achievement, and that genetic effects increase with age (Plomin, 1989). The heritability estimates for intelligence are particularly convincing because of converging evidence from studies of identical and fraternal twins reared together and apart, siblings reared apart, and adoption studies (for a complete discussion, see Sternberg & Grigorenko, 1997). Shared environment accounts for very little of the phenotypic variance; the correlation of adult intelligence test scores among unrelated persons reared together is zero (Bouchard, 1997). There is some assortative mating for intelligence (the correlation between spouses is about .3) and strong assortative mating for social and political attitudes but little assortative mating for personality traits (Bouchard, 1997). The effect of assortative mating is to reduce within-family variance and increase between-family variance.

There is a growing consensus that personality is best described by a minimum of three and a maximum of nine central traits (Bouchard, 1997; Zuckerman, Kuhlman, Joireman, Teta, & Kraft, 1993). These traits have emerged in factor analyses of people's self-ratings and others' ratings where the descriptors are supplied by dictionaries, clinicians' suggestions, or the participants themselves. A five-factor structure has been found in studies of English, German, Dutch, and Filipino participants. Some of the Big Five traits are consistent with studies of infant temperament (John, 1990).

The Big Five traits measured by the NEO Personality Inventory–Revised, as described by Costa and McCrae (1985), are (a) Extroversion: talkative, fun-loving, sociable, affectionate; (b) Neuroticism: anxious, insecure, guilt-prone, self-conscious; (c) Agreeableness: sympathetic, warm, trusting, cooperative; (d) Conscientiousness: ethical, dependable, productive, purposeful; and (e) Openness to experience: daring, nonconforming, broad interests, imaginative. A useful mnemonic for the Big Five is OCEAN (or CANOE, for Canadians). All researchers on the structure of personality concur on Extroversion and Neuroticism (or Negative Emotionality). Zuckerman's group (1993) adds Impulsive-Unsocialized Sensation Seeking, Aggression-Hostility, and Activity to these two.

Recent studies have been conducted using behavioral genetic methods to determine the influence of genetics on personality differences, but most have used three- or four-trait systems on the basis that these traits can be observed in infancy. The most commonly studied traits are Emotionality, Activity, Sociability, and Impulsiveness (EASI; A. H. Buss, & Plomin, 1975). Although it is clear that genes influence differences in these traits, heritability estimates vary with the methods employed. For example, observational studies of the Emotionality, Activity, and Sociability traits show less pervasive influence of genetics than questionnaire and parent rating studies (A. H. Buss & Plomin, 1975).

Among the best-known behavioral genetic investigations is the Bouchard, Lykken, McGue, Segal, and Tellegen (1990) study from the University of Minnesota. It involved 217 pairs of identical twins and 114 pairs of fraternal twins reared together, and 44 pairs of identical twins and 27 pairs of fraternal twins reared apart. Twinship status was established using blood and fingerprint analyses. For those reared apart, the median age of separation was 2.5 months and the median length of separation was 34 years.

Bouchard et al. (1990) used Tellegen's Multidimensional Personality Questionnaire. This is a 300-item self-report inventory measuring three factors: Positive Emotionality (extroverted, achievement-oriented, having a sense of well-being); Negative Emotionality (anxious, angry, alienated); and Constraint (inhibited, cautious, deferential, conventional). Variance in test scores was apportioned among the effects of heredity (genetic differences), shared family experience (shared environment), and unique experience (nonshared environment). The basic finding was that identical twins were much more similar to each other than same-sex fraternal twins whether they were reared together or not. As in other studies, heritability coefficients increased with age.

Seventy percent of the variance in intelligence was accounted for by genetic influence (i.e., r for MZA = .70; note that no portion of this correlation is due to a common environment and that the total observed variance is set to 1.00). This is a higher estimate than reported in the literature, perhaps due to the relatively older age of the sample. Heritability coefficients were 40% for Positive Emotionality, 55% for Negative Emotionality, and 58% for Constraint. Family influence was small and notable only for Positive Emotionality. The investigators concluded that personality differences are more influenced by genetic differences than by environmental diversity. The effect of a common rearing environment was very small.

Similar findings were reported for religious interests (Waller, Kojetin, Bouchard, Lykken, & Tellegen, 1990). Two scales were employed: the Religious Leisure Time scale (interest in attending church, taking religious studies courses, etc.) and the Religious Occupational Interests scale (being a minister, a rabbi, a missionary, etc.). The intraclass correlations for the Religious Leisure Time scale were .39 (MZA), .01 (DZA), .60 (MZT), and .30 (DZT). Genetic modeling showed that 50% of the variance in these two measures was due to genetic differences.

From meta-analytic results and a review of several large-scale investigations, Bouchard (1997) concluded that the broad heritability of four of the Big Five personality factors is about .45, and is somewhat lower for Agreeableness. In addition, there is nonadditive genetic variance (recall that nonadditive effects involve unique effects of genes that contribute to the similarity of identical twins but not first-degree relatives). The effect of common family environment is small for all of the five traits.

A large literature confirms the small effect of shared environmental effects within families. Children from the same family are not very similar to each other (Plomin & Daniels, 1987). Correlations among siblings are about .40 for cognitive variables and about .20 for personality variables. Nearly all of this resemblance is due to shared genes as opposed to shared environment.

Unique (nonshared) environmental influences may include differential treatment of children in the family, birth order, outside friends, schooling experiences, illnesses, and so on. These contribute more than shared environmental influences on personality and intelligence (Rowe, 1994). Environmental differences operate to make children within a family different from one another, such that twins reared together are less similar in some variables than twins reared apart even at very early ages. In certain studies of personality, however, some of this dissimilarity may be an artifact resulting from a contrast effect caused by parents rating their children in comparison to each other.

Bouchard et al. (1990) believe that genes primarily affect psychological characteristics indirectly through gene–environment covariation. Genes cause people to seek congenial environments, that is, to seek a niche where certain learning effects take place. In this view, the proximal cause of personality differences is learning, and learning augments the effects of genotypic differences. Simply put, the genotype determines the organism's responsiveness to environmental opportunities (Scarr & McCartney, 1983). The interplay between genotype and environment in causing developmental outcomes has been referred to as the "art of genes" (Coen, 1999), in which the art itself is a product of natural selection.

EVOLUTION AND NONSHARED ENVIRONMENT

Evolutionary explanations may account for variations in personality characteristics and criminality within families. Elsewhere we proposed a theory to explain why common or shared environment accounts for so little variance in development (Lalumière, Quinsey, & Craig, 1996). This theory attempts to explain both the process by which siblings become different from each other and the evolutionary origin of this process.

According to a Darwinian view, all organisms, including humans, compete for limited resources associated with growth, survival, and reproduction. The manner in which the competition takes place and the resources that are sought are determined by the particular evolutionary history of a given species. Individuals compete with members of other species, with conspecifics, and with kin.

Within multichild families, siblings compete for the same resource: parental investment. Trivers (1972) defined *parental investment* as "any investment by the parent in an individual offspring that increases the off-spring's chance of surviving (and hence reproductive success) at the cost of the parent's ability to invest in other offspring" (p. 139). Parental investment is by definition limited, and siblings attempt to maximize their share (Trivers, 1974). Parents do not indiscriminately invest in their children (as commented in the same context by D. M. Buss, 1987; see also Daly & Wilson, 1980), and, to the extent that investment is discriminate, sibling competition is expected.

Differential parental solicitude is likely associated with initial differences among siblings on characteristics related to survival and reproduction. These initial differences can be accounted for by genetic differences, age, birth order, or sex of offspring. Initial differences among two siblings on a given characteristic, such as verbal or athletic ability, may put one child at advantage over the other, and to receive an equivalent share of parental attention the less skilled child may have to display (instead of or in addition to the given characteristic) another type of ability or propensity. In this process siblings are steered toward different developmental trajectories.

As would be expected from this family dynamic, studies report that differences in sibling characteristics are related to variation in parental behavior and that siblings do not perceive their familial environment in the same way (also, parents tend to perceive differences among siblings even when others do not; Saudino, 1997). More important, measures of psychological adjustment correlate with measures of parental treatment within the family (Daniels, Dunn, Furstenberg, & Plomin, 1985; Daniels & Plomin, 1985; Dunn, Stocker, & Plomin, 1990; Lytton, 1990; Plomin et al., 1988). Although more study is needed, research supports the view that sibling differentiation may occur within the family as an outcome of initial differences among siblings and discriminative parental solicitude (Hertwig, Davis, & Sulloway, 2002).

Sibling differentiation may have had Darwinian consequences in ancestral environments in steering siblings toward different developmental trajectories (Sulloway, 1996); and, to the extent that these different trajectories produced average fitness gains superior to the average gain of multiple copies of a single trajectory in ancestral environments, the process underlying differentiation may have been selected for and refined. Thus, sibling differentiation, begun as a by-product of ontogenetic competition for parental investment, may have been maintained and furthered by its long-term fitness effects.

Processes producing developmental specialization contingent on one's characteristics and the characteristics of one's siblings may have been selected for in ancestral environments for two reasons. First, specialization would have reduced competition among siblings for the same resources outside the family. Second, developmental specialization would have been advantageous in the context of stable environments that contained a number of niches or in the context of rapidly changing environments. It is thus possible to imagine a gene or a set of genes coding for a within-family process that would support the development of meaningful variations among offspring on personality and other characteristics associated with different, specialized developmental trajectories. One example of variation in developmental trajectories is the allocation of male energy to status competition or to early mating attempts (e.g., Belsky, Steinberg, & Draper, 1991).

This model of sibling differentiation leads to a very specific and counterintuitive prediction: Siblings should grow more dissimilar the more time they spend together in the same family. Contemporary socialization theories would predict exactly the opposite (see Maccoby & Martin, 1983). Naturally occurring experiments where twins are separated during the first few years of life offer a test of this prediction. R. C. Johnson (1963); Pedersen, McClearn, Plomin, and Friberg (1985); and Vandenberg and Johnson (1968) reported that the lengths of time twins were reared in the same family was negatively related to similarity in cognitive abilities (but see Bouchard, 1983, who found no relation). Pedersen, McClearn, Plomin, and Nesselroade (1992) found for some personality measures, such as extroversion, agreeableness, and openness to experience, that "twins separated earlier, with the greatest separation or for the longest time were more similar than those pairs separated later, with the least separation or separated for the shortest time" (pp. 261–262).

Another prediction is that the characteristics most likely to be susceptible to influence by an evolved within-family differentiation process should be those more closely associated with particular developmental trajectories than those more generally associated with reproductive and survival success. For example, within a given sample, personality characteristics such as impulsivity and extroversion may show more within-family variability than a general factor of intelligence or characteristics such as height and weight. (For support of this hypothesis, see Lynn, Hampson, & Agahi, 1989; McCartney, Harris, & Bernieri, 1990; and Pedersen, Friberg, Floderus-Myrhed, McClearn, & Plomin, 1984.)

Finally, the differentiation process should affect boys more strongly than girls because males in general compete with each other more than females for access to mates (Clutton-Brock & Vincent, 1991), often through competition for within-group status. Within-sex competition often leads to the selection of alternative strategies (Trivers, 1985), and sons should thus be more strongly subject to the differentiation process. Schachter (1982) reported greater same-sex than opposite-sex "deidentification" but did not distinguish by sex; Rowe, Rodgers, and Meseck-Bushey

(1992) reported larger effects of nonshared environment (in this case birth order) on delinquency for brothers than for either sisters or opposite-sex siblings. Braungart-Rieker, Rende, Plomin, DeFries, and Fulker (1995) reported greater shared environment effects on behavior problems for girls than for boys. If characteristics associated with juvenile delinquency are part of one or more specialized developmental trajectories, one would expect characteristics associated with delinquency to be promoted in some families.

HERITABILITY OF DELINQUENCY AND ANTISOCIAL BEHAVIOR

The evidence for a genetic influence on antisocial conduct has become overwhelming. Reviews of selected studies only are provided in the following subsections because the literature is now too large to be reviewed in detail in a single chapter.[6]

Twin Studies

Rutter (1996) provides a simple summary of genetic influence on antisocial conduct: Resemblance in antisocial conduct declines in order from MZT siblings (within-pair correlation of .81) to DZT siblings, full siblings, half siblings, and unrelated siblings reared together (within-pair correlation of .27, an estimate of shared environment). Carey and Goldman (1997) have provided a useful review of behavioral genetic studies concerning antisocial behavior. Of 17 twin studies, 16 found evidence for a genetic effect. Antisocial behavior was defined in various ways over these investigations, including officially recorded offenses, self-reported offenses, antisocial personality symptoms, and conduct disorder symptoms. Examples of individual twin studies are given below.

Rowe (1986) conducted a mail survey of 107 female and 99 male MZ twins, and 59 female and 38 male DZ twins. Participants averaged 17.5 years of age. Included in the survey were an antisocial behavior inventory; the anger, fear, impulsivity, and sociability scales of the EASI-III temperament survey (A. H. Buss & Plomin, 1975); and three measures derived from social control theory: Perceived Parental Behavior, Value Placed on Academic Achievement, and Deceitfulness (defined as self-serving dishonesty with people with whom a person ordinarily has affectional bonds).

---

[6] Whitney (1990) has reviewed the history of this area of research. The most concentrated summary of the earlier work on genetics and antisocial behavior can be found in Van Dusen and Mednick (1983). A recent summary of the research can be found in Rowe (2002). Research in this area has a long and controversial history; for a somewhat jaundiced review, see Walters and White (1989).

Most of the antisocial behavior reported was quite minor; less than 10% of the males reported a serious offense. The heritability estimate for antisocial behavior was 43% for males and 47% for females, similar to the estimates obtained in behavior genetic studies of a variety of nonintellectual traits. As in behavioral genetic studies of personality, there was no effect of common family environment on antisocial behavior; that is, variables such as social class, child-rearing styles, and parental attitudes that would affect both twins of a pair equally did not have much of an effect. The genetic determinants of delinquency appeared to operate through temperamental traits such as anger, impulsivity, and low empathy. In males, the hereditary factor accounted for more than 25% of the variation in anger, impulsivity, and antisocial behavior. In females it accounted for more than 13% of the variability in impulsivity, perceived parental rejection, and antisocial behavior. The hereditary factor accounted for almost 50% of the variance in deceitfulness among both males and females.

A very small but more detailed study was conducted by Ghodsian-Carpey and Baker (1987), who measured the aggressive behaviors of 21 MZ and 17 DZ primarily middle-class twins between 4 and 7 years old. Zygosity was determined by a parental questionnaire that is known to be about 90% accurate. A behavioral checklist for mothers was developed based on Patterson's (1976) work identifying nine behaviors that best discriminated between aggressive and nonaggressive children: rejection, destructiveness, negativism, noncomplying, teasing, attacking, insulting, verbal threatening, and yelling. Previous studies have shown a correlation of .69 for mean frequency of behaviors reported by parents and those obtained by trained observers. Mothers also completed the Achenbach Childhood Behavior Checklist (CBCL; Achenbach, 1991). Each twin was observed separately on two nonconsecutive days for 2 hours, during which behaviors were recorded every 15 minutes, and the twins were observed together for one further day. The largest heritability estimate (.94) was obtained for the Aggressive subscale of the CBCL, and the estimate for the total checklist was 68%. Although these heritability values are likely overestimates (for methodological reasons), they point to substantial heritability of antisocial behavior in childhood.

Eley (1998) has reported findings from several large sets of data on twins. Of particular interest in the context of juvenile delinquency are data from the CBCL. The Aggression and Delinquency subscales of this instrument correlated at .55. Sixty-five percent of the variance in aggression was attributable to genetic influence, 5% to shared environment, and 30% to nonshared environmental influence. In contrast, 40% of delinquency was due to genetic influence, 30% to shared environment, and 30% to nonshared environmental factors. The influence of genes was greater in females, and the influence of shared environment greater in males. An extremes analysis indicated that the same genetic factors were involved at the extremes of the Aggression subscale as in the normal range.

Eley (1998) also examined the extent of genetic influence on the correlation between delinquency and aggression. Fifty percent of the shared variance in these traits was due to genetic factors, 40% to shared environment, and 10% to nonshared environment. Very surprisingly, aggression was also correlated with depression, and genetic influence accounted for two thirds of this relationship. The finding that genes account for relationships within persons across the internalizing–externalizing dimension of the CBCL suggests that there are at least some general genes for behavioral deviance and psychopathology, in agreement with the molecular genetic literature (see the next section of this chapter).

In a study of 389 male twins ages 11 to 16 years, Silberg et al. (1996) performed a latent class analysis on interview and questionnaire data obtained from parents, teachers, and children. They identified four classes of boys. The first and largest class (with an estimated population prevalence of 72%) contained nonsymptomatic boys. Membership in the first class appeared due to additive genetic and shared environmental effects. The second class of boys (14%) presented symptoms of hyperactivity and conduct disorder attributable to nonadditive genetic effects or parental contrast effects and additive genetic effects. Boys in the third class (8%) exhibited only conduct disorder symptoms largely attributable to the effects of shared environment. These boys had a later onset of antisocial behaviors and appeared to be adolescent-limited offenders (Moffitt, 1993b). Multisymptomatic boys were identified as a fourth class. Membership in this class was attributable to additive genetic effects; only small effects of unique environment were observed.

Although there is an important genetic influence on antisocial conduct, there are variations in the size of the heritability coefficients across studies. Using measures of conduct disorder in an Australian twin sample, Slutske et al. (1997) have produced one of the largest heritability estimates in this area. Although they could not exclude a small effect of shared environmental effects, an estimated 71% of the variance was genetic. Even with 2,682 twin pairs, however, the confidence interval for the heritability estimate was very large (32 to 79%). In Exhibit 2.3, we provide a summary of twin studies that examine antisocial behavior among miliary service members.

Cross-Fostering Studies

Carey and Goldman (1997) identified 29 modern adoption studies of antisocial behavior. Almost all of these studies identified a genetic effect; some individual studies are reviewed in the following paragraphs.

In a seminal investigation, Schulsinger (1977) studied 854 biological
and adoptive relatives of 57 carefully diagnosed psychopaths (defined here
as impulsive and manipulative men without psychotic symptoms) and 57
closely matched control participants. The frequency of psychopathic spectrum disorders was higher among the biological relatives of the psychopathic probands than among their adoptive relatives or the biological or
adoptive relatives of the control participants.

Mednick, Gabrielli, and Hutchings (1983) used the Danish Adoption
Cohort Registry on all extrafamilial adoptions between 1924 and 1947 for
whom the biological parents were known. Males whose biological fathers
and adoptive parents had criminal backgrounds were the most frequently
convicted of criminal behavior, followed by males whose biological fathers

had criminal backgrounds but who were adopted by noncriminal parents; the females showed the same relationship at a much lower rate.

Biological parents' criminality was more closely associated with the adoptees' convictions than was adoptive parents' criminality. For boys whose adoptive parents were noncriminals, there was a linear positive relationship between the number of (biological) parental convictions and the number of adoptive offspring's convictions. Almost all of these convictions were for property crimes. There was no relationship between parental criminality and violent crimes. As in many other studies, a small group of men (4%) had most convictions (69%).

Moffitt (1987) used the same Danish registry to examine the effects of biological parent psychiatric hospitalization. The pool selected contained 6,700 male adoptees for whom the biological parents were known. Although neither adoptive parent criminality nor psychiatric disorder has been found to influence adoptive sons' criminality, those adoptees with deviant adoptive parents were excluded, leaving 5,659 individuals.

Psychiatric hospitalization of at least one biological parent was associated with the likelihood of adoptee conviction to a slightly lesser degree than biological parent criminality. If neither biological parent had been hospitalized, the conviction rate was 14.4%; if one had been hospitalized, the rate was 19.2%. Biological parent hospitalization had no effect on the adoptee's likelihood of being a chronic offender, but the effect of the combination of parental multiple conviction and hospitalization was significant (though small). The types of parental psychiatric problems related to criminal behavior were alcohol abuse and personality disorder as opposed to psychosis. Neither biological parental hospitalization nor multiple convictions alone were related to the probability an adoptive son would be convicted for a violent offense (the base rate was low, at about 4%). The combination of these variables doubled the rate, but the difference was not significant. Of course, prenatal and perinatal factors may have played a role in the later development of criminal behavior, along with genetic transmission of vulnerability.[7]

Bohman (1996) has reviewed the Stockholm study of 913 female and 862 male adoptees. Two kinds of criminal career were identified, one involving male alcoholics who exhibited repeated crimes of violence and a second involving male petty property crime. Petty criminals were likely to have parents who were also involved in petty crime. The risk of criminality in the male alcohol abusers increased with the severity of alcohol abuse. Unstable preadoptive placement increased the risk of both petty criminality and male limited alcoholism. In this study, low socioeconomic status did not lead to petty criminality unless combined with genetic influence.

---

[7] Brennan, Mednick, and Jacobsen (1996) have reported more recent data from the Danish adoption cohort, showing that a heritable characteristic increases the risk of violence in the biological father and the risk of schizophrenia in the adopted-away offspring. The explanation for this finding is yet unclear.

Because of the success in measuring the heritability of various characteristics, the focus of investigation has been shifting in recent years toward identifying the specific genes underlying these characteristics, particularly those associated with psychiatric disorders. Until recently, investigation of the genetics of behavioral disorders has been guided by the one gene, one disorder (OGOD) hypothesis. This approach has led to such successes as the discovery of the gene for Huntington's chorea. Unfortunately, this strategy has not been successful in the area of major mental disorders, leading to replication failures and withdrawn claims. The principal reason for this lack of success appears to be that the etiology of major mental disorders does not involve single genes of large effect. Therefore, the staple of investigations of psychiatric disorders, pedigree studies of affected kindreds, has not been very informative.

The search for many genes of small effect has led to the increasing use of allelic association designs, in which affected and unaffected individuals are compared regardless of their kinship status. The Human Genome Project has identified a large number of markers on many chromosomes. The identification of these markers means that genes of modest effect size can be identified in association studies. This improvement allows pedigree studies to be bypassed and, because association studies are easier to conduct, will contribute to progress in the study of polygenic and oligogenic disorders and other conditions.

Association designs also have been applied to personality characteristics, such as Cloninger's (1995) Novelty Seeking (Sigvardsson et al., 1987). Novelty Seeking corresponds negatively to the Big Five or NEO-PIR Conscientiousness factor and Tellegen's Constraint, and positively to Zuckerman's Impulsive Sensation Seeking and Eysenck's Psychoticism (Bouchard, 1997). It is a personality characteristic involved in antisocial behavior (e.g., Sigvardsson et al., 1987). The broad-sense heritability of Novelty Seeking obtained from twin studies is 41%. A gene for a particular dopamine receptor (D4DR) has been linked to Novelty Seeking (Ebstein et al., 1996). The D4DR polymorphism accounts for about 10% of the genetic variance in Novelty Seeking.[8]

Because of its importance, there have been attempts to replicate the link between Novelty Seeking and the D4DR polymorphism, with mixed results. There have been at least six successful replications: Benjamin et al. (1996), Ebstein et al. (1998), Hamer (1997), Mel and

---

[8] The D4DR polymorphism has been related to patterns of human dispersal in the manner that novelty-seeking individuals are more apt to migrate. Chen, Burton, Greenberger, and Dmitrieva (1999) found a strong relationship between prehistoric migration and the frequency of the long D4DR allele in 39 populations and a moderate difference between peoples who were more recently sedentary or nomadic.

Horowitz (1998), and Ono et al. (1997). Noble et al. (1998) found that D2DR and D4DR polymorphisms among boys were individually associated with Novelty Seeking but that the combined D2DR and D4DR polymorphisms contributed more markedly to this trait than either alone did. On the negative side, Jonsson et al. (1998) found a nonsignificant but positive relationship between D4DR polymorphisms and Novelty Seeking, and there have been six other failures to replicate (Benjamin, Osher, Belmaker, & Ebstein, 1998; Castellanos et al., 1998; Kuhn et al., 1999; Pogue, Ferrell, Deka, Debski, & Manuck, 1998; Sander et al., 1997; Sullivan et al., 1998). Despite these failures, it is highly likely that a meta-analysis will confirm a small but significant relationship between D4DR polymorphisms and Novelty Seeking. This belief is strengthened by studies showing relationships between dopamine-related genes and conditions related to Novelty Seeking, such as attention-deficit/hyperactivity disorder (Faraone et al., 1999; Rowe et al., 1998; Swanson et al., 1998; Waldman et al., 1998).

Other personality characteristics associated with juvenile delinquency have been linked to specific genes. Lesch et al. (1996) found that variations in a DNA regulatory sequence of a serotonin transporter gene (5-HTT) accounted for approximately 8% of the inherited variance of the NEO-PIR Neuroticism facets of Anxiety, Depression, Angry Hostility, and Impulsiveness. Similar results were reported for Cloninger's Harm Avoidance dimension (which is highly correlated with Neuroticism). As expected, the polymorphism associated with these traits is linked to decreased serotonin expression. The polymorphism was also negatively associated with the Agreeableness facet of Compliance and positively to the Aggressiveness facet of Neuroticism (Hamer, 1997). Because of the longitudinal stability of impulsiveness and aggressiveness, the "good intra-individual stability over development for concentrations of the principal 5-HT metabolite 5-HIAA in cerebrospinal fluid" (Stoff & Vitiello, 1996, p. 101) is a critical observation supporting the role of serotonin. Virkkunen et al. (1989) found that one of the strongest predictors of recidivism among a small sample of male violent offenders and impulsive arsonists was their cerebrospinal fluid 5-HIAA concentration. (For a general review of serotonin and psychiatric disorders, see Scalzitti & Hensler, 1997.)

The molecular genetic literature has identified what appear to be "general" genes for psychopathology. Comings (1997) has argued from association studies that "polygenes" (mutant genes involved in polygenic inheritance) are involved in a spectrum of disorders that occur when individuals inherit a greater than threshold number. These polygenes are thought to cause an imbalance between dopamine and serotonin (and norepinephrine), resulting in a variety of impulsive, compulsive, addictive, anxious, and affective behaviors. Blum et al. (1997) have reviewed a large number of investigations suggesting a link between the dopamine D2 receptor gene locus and severe alcoholism and polydrug abuse. A higher frequency of the A1 allele of this gene is associated with not only severe alcoholism but also a wide variety of other behavioral problems, including polydrug dependence, smoking, conduct disorder, pathological gambling, obesity, Tourette's syndrome, and posttraumatic stress disorder. In a recent study of parents' reports of externalizing problems, S. E. Young et al. (2002) identified the 9-repeat variant of the DAT1, a dopamine transporter polymorphism, as a significant risk allele at ages 4 and 7 years.

Molecular genetic research is progressing at a staggering rate, and is producing remarkable findings concerning the origins of variations in behavior. Exhibit 2.4 provides an intriguing example of these findings regarding the role of specific genes in mating effort, parental investment, and monogamy in rodents.

EXHIBIT 2.4
Evolution of Monogamy in Rodents

Naturally occurring variations in mating behavior in two vole species has allowed the relationship of receptor genes, hormones, hormone receptor distribution in the brain, and social behavior to be elucidated. Vasopressin is a peptide hormone that facilitates affiliation, pair bonding, and paternal care in the prairie vole (*Microtus ochrogaster*) but does not facilitate social behavior in the closely related but polygamous montane vole (*Microtus montanus*).

These different vasopressin effects in prairie and montane voles are associated with a different pattern of vasopressin receptors in the brains of these monogamous and polygamous species (L. J. Young, Wang, & Insel, 1998). These differences are in turn related to differences in the DNA sequence of vasopressin receptor genes. A long DNA sequence is inserted in the promoter region of the vasopressin receptor gene of the monogamous and gregarious prairie voles. This region of the gene appears to determine when and where the gene is turned on. The receptor gene does not have this insert in the promiscuous and less gregarious montane voles.

In one experiment, the prairie vole vasopressin receptor gene, with its long promoter sequence, was inserted into the genome of mice. Mice are normally much less social than prairie voles. In these transgenic mice, the vasopressin receptor was expressed in a pattern that resembled that found in the prairie vole brain. Moreover, the transgenic mice responded to vasopressin injections with increased social behavior, exactly as prairie voles did but different from normal mice or montane voles. While these transgenic mice were not monogamous, when given vasopressin they showed an increase in social contact with a female, a response that was not seen in normal mice (L. J. Young, Nilsen, Waymire, MacGregor, & Insel, 1999). Thus, a change in the promoter sequence of a single gene led to a new pattern of receptor expression in the brain, resulting in a profound difference in complex social behavior. Although many genes may be involved in the evolution of monogamy, these studies are beginning to identify the links between DNA sequences, brain chemistry, and social behavior.

COMMENTS

Most variable human characteristics show nonzero heritability. This is particularly true of psychology's triumvirate—cognitive abilities, personality, and psychopathology—and of delinquency. Behavioral genetics has also confirmed that the environment matters, but not in the way most psychologists and sociologists have thought: Most of the environmental influences that have a lasting influence on development are not shared by family members. Many of the traditional suspects of psychological and sociological studies (e.g., household socioeconomic status of origin, neighborhood conditions, family adversity, divorce, parental intellectual stimulation) account for little variance. In contrast, features of the environment that are not shared by siblings (possibly prenatal events, differential parental treatment, peers) account for much more variance.

Notwithstanding the convergence of twin and adoption studies in identifying heritable individual differences in delinquency and criminality, the genetic issues remain complex. Phenotypic characteristics are caused by various nongenetic proximal mechanisms in addition to and in combination with genes. Phenotypic complexity can be introduced by the interaction of genes and environment; for example, a genetic–environment interaction has been found in the etiology of aggression and conduct disorder in which an adverse adoptive home environment was associated with aggression and conduct disorder only among adoptees whose biological parents exhibited antisocial personality disorder (Cadoret, Yates, Troughton, Woodworth, & Stewart, 1995). This kind of genetic–environment interaction has recently received dramatic confirmation in a large longitudinal study of New Zealand boys (Caspi et al., 2002). Abuse and neglect were highly associated with later aggression, but only among boys with a particular polymorphism in the gene encoding the neurotransmitter-metabolizing enzyme, monoamine oxidase A.

Genes may influence delinquency through personality and intelligence, and through alcohol tolerance or its reinforcing properties. It is also possible, as we see in chapter 4, that genes influence criminal and aggressive conduct more directly through their effect on the adoption of an alternate life history strategy.

We now turn to more direct investigations of environmental (proximal) factors associated with the development of delinquency.

3

PROXIMAL MECHANISMS AND THE DEVELOPMENT OF JUVENILE DELINQUENCY

A developmental theoretical perspective can help one understand the proximal mechanisms that contribute to juvenile delinquency, as this perspective emphasizes the importance of person–environment interactions at key life transition points. The development of delinquent as well as prosocial behavior is shaped by risk and protective factors residing within both individuals and their environments. Risk factors are those that lead directly to problem behavior, whereas protective factors operate to buffer risk.

There is a cumulative effect of risk across time. At a given point in time, children are at greater risk for juvenile delinquency if they experience multiple risk factors than if they experience single or no risk factors (Rutter, 1983). Over time, there is a progressive accumulation of the consequences of individual factors (cumulative continuity) and the responses they elicit during social interactions (interactional continuity). Within this developmental framework, life phases and transitions are particularly important in understanding behavior because they present either crises or challenges, engendering stress that can undermine development or revealing resources and opportunities (Garmezy, 1985). A developmental perspective considers both stability and transformations in behavior in their developmental

57

context. The challenge for any theory of delinquency is to explain the emergence and the change in form and frequency of antisocial behaviors over the course of development.

The great amount of research in the past 20 years on the development of juvenile delinquency has spawned a variety of theoretical positions regarding its etiology and developmental course (e.g., Moffitt, Caspi, Rutter, & Silva, 2001; Patterson & Yoerger, 1997). Despite the fact that the risk factors for juvenile delinquency are relatively well known (Robins, 1991), there is a lack of theoretical convergence on the etiology of delinquency. There is fairly strong agreement, however, that no single factor can explain delinquency. Rather, it is a combination of risk factors (e.g., perinatal problems, difficult temperament, hyperactivity, family disadvantage, and peer rejection) interacting with a number of protective factors (e.g., positive parenting skills and high parental monitoring) that best predicts delinquency (L. Ellis & Walsh, 2000; Kolvin, Miller, Fleeting, & Kolvin, 1988; Loeber & Farrington, 1998).

In this chapter we review a large number of proximal variables associated with juvenile delinquency, starting with biodemographic and socioeconomic indicators. We briefly review major sociological theories of delinquency—which typically use these indicators—and present examples of empirical tests of these theories. We then spend the majority of the chapter discussing in detail several individual proximal factors associated with delinquency in the context of childhood and adolescent development. These factors cover early neurodevelopment, family characteristics and dynamics, and peer influences.

EPIDEMIOLOGY OF DELINQUENCY AND SOCIOECONOMIC INDICATORS

Farrington (1987) has discussed the epidemiology of delinquent acts committed by juveniles, focusing on general delinquency (primarily theft and burglary) because of its high frequency and on the finding that delinquents tend to show a low degree of specialization in the types of crime they commit. *Prevalence* refers to the number of persons committing delinquent acts (in contrast to *lifetime prevalence*, the number of persons who have ever committed a delinquent act); *incidence* refers to the number of delinquent acts per offender. This distinction can be important; for example, peak age of offending appears to reflect peak prevalence rather than peak incidence (i.e., more offenders are involved in crime at this age, but the rate at which they commit crimes is the same). Self-report data agree with officially recorded data more on prevalence than on incidence. The two methods agree on the effects of ethnicity, age, and sex. Black American males, however, appear to underreport their crimes (Hindelang, Hirschi, & Weis,

1981). Official and self-report data indicate that the prevalence of general delinquency peaks between ages 15 and 17 for both males and females. Both the prevalence and the incidence of delinquency are higher for males than for females, independent of age and race. The sex ratio varies from 1.5 to 7 over studies but appears to have declined somewhat in recent years.

Elliott, Huizinga, and Morse (1986) have examined juvenile violent offense patterns longitudinally as measured by self-report in their nationally representative sample of U.S. youth, the National Youth Survey. They found that self-reported offense rates were much higher than arrest rates. There were no effects of age, social class, sex, or race in individual offending rates for serious (index) offenses. The period of involvement in violent offending tended to be short. Individual offending rates increased over time, and there was increasing diversification of offense types with the duration of the youths' involvement in crime. Serious violent offenders did not specialize in seriously violent offenses. In agreement with arrest data, the self-report data indicated that serious violent offenders were more likely to be Black urban males from lower social classes. Elliott et al. (1986) concluded that demographic differences in aggregate violent offense data are more likely to result from differences in prevalence than from different rates of offending.

Some of the central questions in criminology have involved variations in crime rates among youth from urban areas that differ in socioeconomic indicators. Among the most influential early empirical efforts in criminology was Shaw and McKay's (1969) ecological research in Chicago (Gold, 1987). This research was planned and begun in the 1920s, a time when there was a strong movement in America to stop immigration on eugenic grounds. Using aggregate data, Shaw and McKay studied the distribution of juvenile crime over different areas in Chicago. They concluded that juvenile crime was strongly related to socioeconomic segregation that led to concentrations of economically disadvantaged people, leading in turn to social disorganization and then to strong regional differences in criminal traditions.

Historically, Sutherland and Cressey's (1974) theory of differential association has been the dominant criminological theory. This theory posits that criminal behavior is learned like any other, primarily in intimate association with others. Using Sutherland and Cressey's theory of differential association, Shaw and McKay (1969) argued that youth living in high-crime areas had a greater chance of being exposed to procriminal attitudes than those living in low-crime areas and that their families, being impoverished, were less effective agents of socialization and control. This work has spawned a number of replications and similar research. The basic finding that crime rates vary with the socioeconomic status of geographical areas has reliably been supported. For detailed reviews of modern ecological work on delinquency, see Byrne and Sampson (1986).

Although poorer urban areas have higher delinquency rates, it is the ecological fallacy to suppose that poor urban families necessarily have the most delinquent children (Gold, 1987). First, correlations of aggregated data are larger than correlations of individual data obtained with the same variables. But, more important, it is difficult to draw conclusions at the individual level from area-level data. For example, it was found in Kentucky that the higher the proportion of Blacks in an area, the higher the delinquency rate, but it was the Whites' rate of delinquency that was higher, not the Blacks'. Similarly, in London, England, delinquency was found to be negatively correlated with the divorce rate, although the children of divorced parents were more likely to be delinquent (Gold, 1987). Primarily for this reason, we focus on individual data in this book.

Self-report data have not shown very high correlations with areal socioeconomic indicators. Part of this lack of relationship can be attributed to the trivial nature of many of the delinquent acts reported, particularly in the early self-report studies. With respect to more serious acts, such as violent predatory crime, there is a modest relationship with these indicators (e.g., Elliott, Huizinga, & Menard, 1989). It is also the case that very serious juvenile delinquents are unlikely to participate in such surveys and, even if they do participate, are likely to underreport serious crimes. It is poor children who live in affluent neighborhoods who turn out to be the most delinquent on self-report measures; next most delinquent are middle-class children living in poor areas.

It is likely that an urban area's victimization rate rather than its delinquency rate is responsible for its reputation for crime. An areal reputation for crime leads to increased police surveillance (Gold, 1987). From more recent work, it appears that the large correlations between socioeconomic areal indicators and delinquency reflect dense population, lesser willingness of residents to deal with delinquency informally, and greater police surveillance. The deeper into the justice system the data are collected, the higher the correlations between criminal and socioeconomic indicators (Gold, 1987).

Sociological Theories of Delinquency

J. Q. Wilson (1983), a political scientist, has discussed early sociological theories of juvenile delinquency, concluding that most of these theories shared the assumptions of the theory of differential association. Criminological theories have thus been primarily sociopsychological (Sacco & Kennedy, 1998). Following the Gluecks' research in the 1950s (see Glueck & Glueck, 1950, 1967), many criminologists argued that the roots of crime lay in family problems such as instability, lack of affection, and poor discipline (J. Q. Wilson, 1983). The major figures in criminology rejected poverty as a cause of crime because crime did not increase during periods of economic depression and because many crimes are not economic in nature. Similarly, racism was rejected as a cause of crime because of the differences in crime rates between Japanese and Black Americans. Instead, Wilson believed that criminologists have in one way or another advocated that attitudes inculcated by family and peers are a cause of crime. Because the attitudes conducive to some forms of crime were thought to be related to social class, social class was also seen as a cause of crime.

Traditional sociological theories of delinquency are either cultural, as is Wolfgang and Ferracuti's (1967/1982) subculture of violence thesis, or structural, as are Hirschi's (1969) control theory, which postulates that crime results from a breakdown in structural controls over behavior, and Merton's (1938) strain theory, which argues that crime results from an anomic imbalance between culture and social structure. Cultural and structural theories are not necessarily incompatible with each other and are not incompatible with differential association theory. They each, however, emphasize different causal variables at the expense of others, leading investigators to compare variables derived from the various theories in an effort to develop integrated theories of delinquency.

Rosenfeld (1986) conducted an interesting comparison of the classic sociological theories using aggregate data from the U.S. Federal Bureau of Investigation's Uniform Crime Reports and the U.S. census. Strain theory was evaluated by measuring the effects of relative deprivation, defined as the intensity of deprivation, its scope, and the level of economic aspiration among poor families. Relative deprivation was operationalized as the product of (a) the difference between the mean income of families below the poverty level and the mean income of all families in the Standard Metropolitan Statistical Area, (b) the percentage of families below the poverty level, and (c) the ratio of the median years of schooling completed by heads of families below the poverty level to the median years of schooling completed by all family heads. In a regression analysis, relative deprivation, as predicted by strain theory, was significantly related to a variety of crimes (murder, rape, assault, burglary, larceny, and motor vehicle theft) after statistically controlling for population, unemployment rate, and region. Robbery, unfortunately for this theory, was not significantly related to relative deprivation.

From a control theory perspective, the function of social structure is to link culture with the behavior of individuals. Rosenfeld (1986) investigated the provision of welfare as a control theory variable because both conservative and radical commentators have thought that welfare undermines the control of both the family and the labor market. Murder and motor vehicle theft rates were both related to welfare dependency after controlling for the proportion of people eligible for welfare, region, unemployment, and population. There was no effect on any of the other five offense types. These data provided very weak support for control theory.

The subculture of violence thesis posits a southeastern U.S. subculture with attitudes that support violence. This subculture has moved into U.S. cities with Black migration. (For an interesting historical approach to this issue, see Lane, 1989.) Rosenfeld (1986) found that, after controlling for population size, unemployment rate, and relative deprivation, there were substantial regional effects predicted by the theory on murder, rape, robbery, and assault; as well, no differences in burglary, larceny, or motor vehicle theft were found, as predicted. In a further analysis of the subcultural thesis, the percentage of Blacks in an area was found to be significantly associated with murder, robbery, and assault (but not rape, burglary, larceny, or motor vehicle theft) after controlling for population, unemployment, and relative deprivation.

In summary, Rosenfeld (1986) found substantial support for strain theory in that crime rates were more strongly connected to inequality than to poverty and in that the relation of crime and inequality was higher in the presence of high achievement aspiration. There was weaker support for the effect of welfare on crime derived from control theory. Cultural explanations were supported by finding regional and race effects on crime rates after controlling for a variety of other variables. Rosenfeld's study cannot be considered conclusive for our purposes because it employed aggregate data. It does, however, nicely illustrate how sociologists use aggregate data to test competing theories.

Mak (1990) tested elements of control theory using cross-sectional individual data obtained by questionnaire from 793 Australian high school students. Social control was measured by attachment to parents, attachment to school, commitments to educational and occupational goals, and belief in the moral validity of the law (perceived seriousness of delinquency). Personal control (an expansion of Hirschi's, 1969, conceptualization) was measured by impulsiveness and empathy scales. Background variables (age, sex, home intactness, and father's education) were included. Self-reported delinquency was predicted by background, social control, and individual control variables in a blockwise hierarchical regression analysis. Background variables accounted for 6% of the variance in delinquency; social control, 40%; and personal control, 6%. Interaction effects accounted for a further 2% of the variance. Despite possible problems of shared method variance, these data provide strong correlational support for control theory.

Elliott et al. (1989) conducted a longitudinal predictive test of an integrated theory involving elements of control, strain, and social learning theories. This study used 1,200 individual respondents from the National Youth Survey. Exogenous or background variables included in Elliott et al.'s (1989) path analysis were sex, race, parental socioeconomic status, urban/suburban/rural status, family size, sibline position, and age. Endogenous (theoretically relevant) causal variables were derived from theory. Occupational strain was measured by respondents' ratings of chances to get the job they want after finishing school. School strain was indexed by grade point average, rating of school success, and rating of likelihood of obtaining a college education. From control theory, internal bonding was measured by the extent to which a respondent believed it was necessary or acceptable to engage in lying, cheating, and breaking rules to achieve desired goals in family and school contexts. A second measure of internal bonding, belief, measured the extent to which an individual believes it is morally wrong for someone of the same age to commit a variety of acts (assault, theft, drug use, and cheating on tests). External bonding was measured as the amount of time devoted to family and school (excluding such activities as sports). A further measure of external bonding was delinquent peer group bonding; it was measured by the degree of peer group delinquency (the number of friends who had engaged in delinquent acts) multiplied by the amount of time the individual spent with the group. This measure, although derived from control theory, is more reflective of social learning theory.

Thirty-one percent of the variance in general delinquency offending rate was predicted by deviant peer group bonding and sex, with the former much more important (27%) than the latter (4%). Other theoretical variables had influence only through deviant peer group bonding. Similar but smaller effects (15% of the variance) were found for the rate of index offenses. Peer group bonding was also the best predictor of alcohol, drug, and polydrug use, followed by internal bonds to society. In contrast, mental health problems (loneliness, depression, emotional problems, and utilization of mental health services) were predicted by school strain, family normlessness, and low family involvement.

In conclusion, the integrated sociological theory worked fairly well in the National Youth Survey. Theoretical variables always had larger effects than exogenous variables. Strain theory variables influenced delinquency and substance use only through deviant peer group bonding but had a direct effect on mental health problems. Control theory variables, particularly belief, directly influenced substance use, and family-related control theory variables directly influenced mental health problems. Social learning theory provided the principal explanation for both delinquency and substance abuse problems but, as expected, did not predict mental health problems.

More recent research has shown no difference between murder rates among Blacks in the North and Blacks in the Southeast but has breathed new life into the subculture of violence thesis, by confirming a large regional difference in argument-related homicides among young White men (D. Cohen, 2001). Using aggregate data, D. Cohen (1998) found that argument-related (but not felony-related) homicide was positively associated with indices of social organization, including family cohesion, in accord with the existence of a southern and southwestern American culture of honor; the opposite pattern was found in the North. The finding that intact families and social structures are better able to inculcate culturally approved conduct, including criminal conduct, places strong constraints on the generality of strain and control theories but fits nicely with differential association theories.

Recent sociological theories of crime recognize cross-cultural similarities in the individual correlates of crime while continuing to endorse a differential association viewpoint. For example, Gottfredson and Hirschi (1990) make the following assertion in describing their general theory of crime:

> Individual-level correlates of delinquency that appear everywhere include sexual precocity, limited scholastic aptitude, and drug use (including alcohol and tobacco). The available data are thus consistent with attempts to construct a general—that is, cross cultural—theory of crime and delinquency, a theory that sees crime as short-sighted pursuit of self-interest and sees criminality as the relative absence of the self-control required to produce concern for the long-term consequences of one's acts.

> Self-control is presumably a product of socialization and the current circumstances of life. Individuals in stable families are more likely to be socialized to take into account the long-term consequences of their acts, and they are more likely to suffer from failing to do so. Individuals with limited scholastic aptitude are less likely to have favorable long-term prospects, and their behavior is therefore less likely to be governed by them. . . . With limited time and space horizons, the individual is vulnerable to spur-of-the moment impulses, impulses that are implicated everywhere in the commission of criminal acts. (pp. 178–179)

Comments

Many sociological (and psychosocial) theories of delinquency emphasize the effects of variables that are shared among members of a family, such as social class and family composition. As noted in chapter 2 of this volume, shared environmental effects account for a very small part of the variation among people. Unique (nonshared) environmental influences, however, have a much greater impact on individual differences. This general finding helps explain the very small association between socioeconomic indicators (measured at the level of the individual) and delinquency.

The literature on the heritability of criminality does lead to expectations about the relationship between socioeconomic status and criminality. Within individuals, low intelligence and antisocial traits (e.g., recklessness, dishonesty, imprudence, and aggressiveness) are likely to be associated with decreased socioeconomic status. To the extent that these traits are genetically influenced, the genes themselves would be associated with decreased socioeconomic status. The children of antisocial individuals would necessarily, therefore, be more likely to be of low socioeconomic status of origin, unless they were to be adopted. Moreover, highly antisocial individuals are likely to show little parental investment in their children, to have unstable marriages, and to be more likely than more restrained individuals to have children outside marriage (for a review, see Barr & Quinsey, in press). The children of antisocial individuals are therefore more likely than those of less antisocial people to be raised by single mothers, with the higher risk of poverty that that entails. These observations raise a question: To what extent does the modest individual-level link between socioeconomic status and crime reflect genetic influences?

Caspi, Taylor, Moffitt, and Plomin (2000) have shed some light on this question by examining, in a genetically informative design, the influence of neighborhood characteristics on toddlers' mental health. The sample consisted of 1,081 pairs of monozygotic twins and 1,061 pairs of same-sex dizygotic twins. Data were provided by the parents of the twins when the latter were 2 years old. Both emotional and conduct problems were measured by questionnaire. Neighborhood conditions were measured with a multi-attribute questionnaire resulting in a classification of neighborhoods into six categories, ranging from the most affluent to the poorest (government-subsidized housing, low incomes, high unemployment, and single parents).

The model that best fit the behavioral problem data included additive genetic variance (55%), child-specific environment (24%), and familywide environment (20%). Neighborhood accounted for 5% of the familywide environment effect and 1% of the total variance. The authors put the effect of neighborhood in context as follows:

> Though small, the effect is hardly trivial. It is similar in size to the impact of dramatic environmental events, such as premature loss of a parent through death or separation. . . . The neighborhood effect is likely to accumulate strength as children experience prolonged deprivation . . . and when, as adolescents, they spend more time outside their homes and in the neighborhood. The neighborhood effect is also similar in magnitude to the impact of a single, identifiable genetic allele on a behavioral trait. (p. 341)

As we observed earlier, neighborhood may not be a purely environmental variable because heritable parental traits may be related to selective migration to deprived neighborhoods. Caspi et al. (2000) comment, however, that studies find neighborhood effects even when controlling for highly heritable parental characteristics, such as maternal education, and, more important, that "there is no necessary connection between the origins of a risk factor and its mode of risk mediation. For example, the tendency to smoke may be genetically influenced, but the effects of tar and nicotine on health are environmental" (pp. 341–342).

NEURODEVELOPMENT

Much recent empirical work has focused on the relationship between neurodevelopment and delinquency, especially violent crime. In this section we examine the phenomenon of selective male afflictions generally. We then examine the relation between neurodevelopment, parental psychopathology, and delinquency. Finally, we examine more specifically how aspects of neurobiology and physiology have been linked to delinquency.

Selective Male Afflictions and Neurodevelopmental Problems

There are many disorders for which the male:female sex ratio is larger than 1. These disorders, called *selective male afflictions* (Gualtieri & Hicks, 1985), include (a) childhood psychiatric disorders such as hyperkinetic disorder, conduct disorder, and autism; (b) neurological disorders such as seizure disorders, cerebral palsy, stuttering, and dyslexia; and (c) perinatal disorders such as spontaneous abortion, toxemia, pulmonary infection, and cerebral birth trauma. The neurodevelopmental disorders tend to strike males more frequently and females more severely. The disorders appear to be mediated genetically in females and prenatally and perinatally in males.

One explanation for the relative male disadvantage is that females are diploid for many alleles on the X chromosome, whereas males are haploid. Males thus become the victims of uncompensated dosage effects. X-linked recessive genes are expressed in males but not in females. However, this explanation cannot explain the male disadvantage for most of the disorders listed in the preceding paragraph because none of the disorders are X-linked and few show an inheritance pattern characteristic of chromosomal abnormalities.

Gualtieri and Hicks (1985) argued that successive pregnancies are not independent events because a memory of previous pregnancies exists. Pregnancy difficulties run in families and are correlated with parity, suggesting an immunological phenomenon. The inherited characteristic could be a proclivity to react immunologically to some aspect of the male fetus. The H-Y antigen is a candidate for triggering the immunological effect because it is expressed in every somatic mammalian male cell but is not expressed in the placenta. Recently, it has been shown that fetal cells persist in the mother, providing a possible mechanism for the maternal bodily "memory" of previous pregnancies. Bianchi, Sacerdote, and Panerai (1996) discovered male fetal progenitor cells in the venous blood of nonpregnant women originally produced by fetuses carried up to 27 years earlier. Pregnancy appears to establish a long-term, low-grade maternal chimeric state.

Neurodevelopment and Parental Psychopathology

Brennan, Mednick, and Mednick (1993) described two studies on the association among parental psychopathology, congenital factors, and violent crime. In the first study, 72 male children of psychiatrically disturbed parents were compared with 36 control participants matched on sex, pregnancy number, mothers' and fathers' age at delivery, social class at birth, and mothers' height and weight. Delivery complications were rated by the senior obstetrician, and the ratings were split at the median. Participants were also rated on hyperactivity between ages 11 and 13 by a pediatric neurologist. Among children of psychiatrically disturbed parents, 4% of the nonhyperactive/low-delivery-complications group, 8% of the hyperactive/low-delivery-complications group, 17% of the nonhyperactive/high-delivery-complications group, and 53% of the hyperactive/high-delivery-complications group were arrested for a violent crime by age 22. Children of psychiatrically normal parents had low arrest rates for violent crime (< 5%) and showed no effects of hyperactivity or delivery complications.

The second study was a replication involving 108 males with parents who were psychiatrically disturbed (where either parent was hospitalized or the mother was taking psychoactive medications during the child's adolescence) and 312 males with parents who were not psychiatrically disturbed. Hyperactivity was assessed by a maternal retrospective interview. Again, after controlling for age, socioeconomic status, childhood conduct disorder, childhood school performance, and parents' criminality, the researchers found an interaction between hyperactivity and delivery complications in the violent arrest data only among the children of psychiatrically disturbed parents. Minor physical anomalies, thought to reflect disruption to the central nervous system (CNS) during pregnancy (e.g., low-set ears, a curved fifth finger, attached earlobes), interacted with delivery complications in predicting violent arrest in the same manner as hyperactivity.

Brennan et al. (1993) suggested that "a genetic factor in the children of the mentally ill may act to predispose them to criminal violence. This genetic factor may be triggered by perinatal factors with the result being CNS damage that is characterized by impulsive, fast-moving behavior and a short attention span. The CNS damage triggered by perinatal factors, in turn, results in an increased propensity for criminal violence" (p. 253).

Neurological Functioning

Carlson, Earls, and Todd (1988) suggested that developmental neurobiology may contribute to understanding personality development, sex differences, and behavior problems by elucidating how genetic and environmental experiences and early brain insults interact to affect later development. In the same vein, Post (1992) suggested that both sensitization to stressors and episode sensitization occur and become encoded at the level of gene expression. This prenatal as well as postnatal disruption of the brain may cause compromised neuropsychological functioning, which in turn could contribute to juvenile delinquency. Prenatal disruption of the development of the fetal brain (caused by maternal drug use, poor prenatal nutrition, or prenatal exposure to toxic agents) may combine with child abuse or neglect and genetic influences to result in a chain of parent–child as well as peer interactions that cumulate to produce antisocial and aggressive behavior characteristic of juvenile delinquency.

Toddlers with neurological impairments are delayed in reaching developmental milestones and are more likely than nonimpaired toddlers to be awkward; to be very active; and to display deficits in attention, self-control, language, and learning (Rutter, 1983). All of these characteristics are related to antisocial outcomes (Moffitt, 1990). Minor physical abnormalities, which are observable markers of problems in neural development, are elevated among hyperactive (Firestone, Levy, & Douglas, 1976) and aggressive boys (Waldrop, Bell, McLaughlin, & Halverson, 1978), as well as among juvenile delinquents (Kandel, Brennan, Mednick, & Michelson, 1989). Furthermore, brain insults that occur at birth have been related to later antisocial behavior: 80% of violent offenders scored in the range indicating delivery complications, compared with 47% of the normal population (Kandel & Mednick, 1991). This research is not entirely consistent; for example, both Denno (1990) and Farrington (1997) found no relationship among pregnancy or birth complications and later violent behavior.

Moffitt (1993a) suggested that behavioral problems associated with neurological deficits may evoke a series of negative parent–child interactions. It is known that neurological problems increase the risk of maltreatment and abuse, punitive and harsh disciplinary techniques, and coercive interactions (Parke & Tinsley, 1983; Patterson et al., 1989). Thus, children with neuropsychological deficits may be more difficult to parent and may elicit problematic reactions from parents, especially under conditions of family adversity or stress. Over time, these negative and adverse interactions may generalize to the school setting (Patterson & Yoerger, 1997). Although supportive home environments buffer the risk of developing juvenile delinquency (see Moffitt, 1990), there is a significant correlation between unsupportive environments and neurological deficits (Harris, Rice, & Lalumière, 2001; Moffitt, 1993b). Evidence supporting some of the specific neurological functioning deficits is reviewed in the following subsections.

Executive Functioning

Moffitt (1993a) concluded from a literature review that two cognitive factors play an important role in the etiology of juvenile delinquency:

(a) deficits in verbal skills, such as expression and comprehension, and (b) deficits in executive function, as reflected in poor inhibitory control. Skoff and Libon (1987) found deficiencies in executive functioning in approximately two thirds of the juvenile delinquents in their sample. Moffitt and Henry (1989) found that juvenile delinquency was related to impulsivity as well as to attention modulation problems. Furthermore, results from neuropsychological tests examining frontal lobe functioning among delinquents have been consistent with the executive functioning deficit hypothesis: Delinquents scored low on tests of selective attention (Wolff, Waber, Bauermeister, Cohen, & Ferber, 1982); on tests assessing the ability to inhibit an inappropriate response (Krynicki, 1978); and on tests requiring sequencing of motor behavior (Brickman, Mcmanus, Grapentine, & Alessi, 1984).

Poor inhibitory control is the primary characteristic of attention–deficit/hyperactivity disorder. Hawkins et al. (1998) concluded, from 11 studies on the relationship between these variables and juvenile delinquency, that there was a consistent relationship between hyperactivity, concentration or attention problems, and impulsivity and later violent behavior.

Although there is clearly a relationship between neurological impairment, particularly impairment of the frontal lobe, and antisocial behavior, Hare's (1984) conclusion that "psychopaths are less likely to display gross symptoms of neurological impairment or dysfunction than are individuals who exhibit some of the features of psychopathy but who fall short of fitting the complete clinical syndrome" (p. 139) is of considerable interest. This finding suggests that the most persistent antisocial offenders may belong to a separate category of individuals who are not neurologically impaired. We explore this idea more fully in chapter 4 of this volume.

Sensory and Perceptual Difficulties

Penner (1982) and Lawson and Sanet (1992) concluded from a literature review that juvenile delinquents were much more likely to experience perceptual deficits than nondelinquent adolescents. Furthermore, young offenders were much more likely to have multiple sensory and perceptual processing deficits (e.g., eyesight or hearing deficits) compared to more isolated deficits in the comparison groups (Anderson & Snart, 1999). With respect to visual difficulties, the young offenders almost all had refractive errors (compared to 50%–60% of comparison adolescents) and had a higher incidence of a variety of visual anomalies and visual memory deficits. Furthermore, on visual perception tasks, young offenders were more likely than nonoffender adolescents to demonstrate reversals, rotations, and distortions of visual stimuli. Anderson and Snart concluded that these visual deficits contributed significantly to the findings that young offenders read between one to seven grades below expected grade level. Longitudinal research has found that remediation of visual and perceptual difficulties is associated with improved reading as well as a reduction in recidivism for young offenders (Dzik, 1975; Kaseno, 1985).

Wolff et al. (1982) found that delinquents scored lower than nondelinquent adolescents on tests of reading, naming vocabulary, and receptive language. Similar results have been found with respect to visual processing and auditory-language functioning (Karniski, Levine, Clarke, Palfrey, & Meltzer, 1982); verbal language skills; abstract verbal reasoning; and semantic and sequential memory (Sobotowicz, Evans, Laughlin, 1987). For example, Karniski et al. (1982) found that 22% of delinquents in their sample, compared to 4% of control participants, had visual processing deficits, and that 30% of delinquents as opposed to 2% of control participants had deficits in auditory-language functions. Anderson and Snart (1999) noted that there were very few studies examining auditory perceptual difficulties and none that addressed the issue of intervention or recidivism. The research does suggest that this is an important area for future investigation because of its implications for intervention, at least in addressing the high incidence of school failure among delinquents.

In summary, there is a consensus that sensory and perceptual deficits contribute to learning problems and juvenile delinquency. The combination of learning deficits and disruptive behavior appears to contribute to the increased likelihood of school dropout and the corresponding increase in opportunities to engage in delinquent activities. Thus, these deficits may have a cumulative effect over the life course.

Biochemical and Psychophysiological Functioning

Biochemical and psychophysiological studies of children with conduct-disorders and aggressive tendencies suggest that there are differences in the brain's noradrenenergic and serotonergic systems associated with the activation and inhibition of aggression. For example, Krusesi et al. (1990) found significantly lower levels of serotonin in children and adolescents hospitalized for disruptive behavior than in a matched comparison group.

Daugherty and Quay (1991) found that children with conduct disorder have a specific learning deficit that is characterized by a tendency to persist at a task in the face of failure, suggesting an inability to learn from experience. In this regard, C. E. Lewis (1991) reported serotonergic dysfunction in antisocial individuals, linking the inability to learn from experience to similar findings from animal learning research on low serotonin levels. Low serotonin levels may contribute to academic problems and put affected individuals at risk for juvenile delinquency because they are less likely than unaffected individuals to learn from their mistakes.

In a prospective study of 101 boys, Raine, Venables, and Williams (1990a, 1990b, 1990c) showed that those who later committed criminal offenses by age 24 had lower resting electroencephalogram readings, heart rates, and skin conductance scores at age 15 than did control participants. Moreover, the future criminals also displayed lower skin conductance and heart rate responsiveness to orienting stimuli at age 15. The investigators concluded that underarousal was a possible etiological factor in the development of delinquency.

Hormones

Testosterone has been positively related to antisocial behavior, aggression, dominance, and impulsiveness (for a review, see Archer, 1991; Book, Starzyk, & Quinsey, 2001), although in one study (Schaal, Tremblay, Soussignan, & Susman, 1996) it was related to dominance and low aggression among young adolescent males. Testosterone has a stronger correlation with antisocial behavior among low-socioeconomic-status men than among high-socioeconomic-status men (Dabbs & Morris, 1990). Testosterone has also been positively correlated with number of sexual partners among men (Bogaert & Fisher, 1995; Dabbs, 1992). Another hormone, cortisol, has been positively related to autonomic arousal, anxiety, and behavioral inhibition (for reviews, see Raine, 1993, and Zuckerman, 1995). Low levels of cortisol have been found in habitually violent incarcerated offenders (Virkkunen, 1985). Similarly, children's saliva cortisol level has been found to be negatively associated with their conduct disorder symptom count and with their father's antisocial personality symptom count (Vanyukov et al., 1993). There is some evidence that the relationship between testosterone and aggression may be stronger among people with low cortisol levels than among those with normal cortisol levels (Dabbs, Jurkovic, & Frady, 1991). Finally, there is research linking low levels of platelet monoamine oxidase (MAO), a neurologically active enzyme, to criminality and related behavior problems such as alcohol and drug abuse, and sensation seeking (L. Ellis, 1991).

The striking effect of the hormones testosterone and androstenedione on masculinization, dominance, and aggression is explored in Exhibit 3.1 for a species in which females are dominant over males.

Alcohol and Substance Use

As the seriousness of offending increases in adolescence, so does the seriousness of substance use (Loeber & Farrington, 1998). A greater proportion of juvenile offenders not only use drugs but also use them on a more frequent basis than do nonoffenders (Fergusson, Lynskey, & Horwood, 1996; Saner & Ellickson, 1996; Thornberry, Huizinga, & Loeber, 1995). This result holds true for both male and female offenders. Despite the strength of these relationships, the nature of the developmental progression

EXHIBIT 3.1
Testosterone, Masculinization, and Aggression in Spotted Hyenas

Spotted hyenas, *Crocuta crocuta,* are in the family Hyaenidae, a group that is more closely related to cats than dogs. Spotted hyenas hunt medium-sized ungulates both alone and in groups (Holekamp et al., 1997). Spotted hyena females are highly masculinized and 10% larger than males (Yalcinka et al., 1993). The proximal mechanism is massive prenatal androgen exposure that causes aggressiveness and genital masculinization in females. The female has a "scrotum" that is made from fused labia and contains no testes. Her "penis" is the clitoris. Both sexes get erections in greeting; the erections function as an appeasement display. Males provide no paternal care and are not feminized. Males are usually interested in sex, and females seldom are.

Spotted hyenas are organized into a matrilineal hierarchical dominance structure where a mother and her offspring are dominant over another matriline, which is dominant over another matriline, and so forth. This means that youngsters from higher ranking matrilines outrank adults from lower matrilines and natal males outrank females from subordinate matrilines. Immigrant males occupy the lowest dominance rank (Smale, Frank, & Holekamp, 1993).

During sex, the female retracts her penis into an orifice, into which the male can insert his. The female's full cooperation is required for intromission. The urogenital canal runs the length of the penile clitoris. She mates and gives birth through it. The birth canal makes a sharp turn, and the birth canal is 60 cm, twice the length of the canal in similar sized mammals. The umbilical cord is only 12–18 cm, so most of the neonate's journey is anoxic. L. G. Frank, Weldele, and Glickman (1995) have documented the reproductive costs associated with female masculinization. Labor takes many hours, and the meatus must tear in the first birth. First babies frequently die from anoxia during birth; about 61% of them are stillborn. Maternal mortality is estimated to be 9% in the first birth.

Hyena males have more testosterone than females, but females have more androstenedione (usually thought to be a male hormone). Androstenedione is made in all mammalian ovaries and is converted to estrogen in the ovaries; it has been found to be related to aggressiveness in teenage girls (Burr, 1996). Testosterone rises in pregnancy until it is higher than in adult males, then drops sharply after birth, whereas androstenedione remains constant. This suggests that the hyena placenta produces huge amounts of male hormones. Measurements show that testosterone is the major product formed from androstenedione by the placenta.

The ovaries and placenta together produce high testosterone in fetal plasma, which is likely the cause of the virilization of the external genitalia. The fetus, unlike the mother, produces low levels of steroid binding globulin that normally mops up circulating androgens (L. G. Frank, 1994). At birth, cubs of both sexes have high levels of androgens: males are higher in testosterone and females higher in androstenedione.

Benefits of Masculinization and Dominance

Sons of the alpha female are the only males to dominate all other adult females. Cubs of higher ranking females are able to feed at kills in competition with adults more successfully than other cubs and are allowed to live longer in their natal group. Thus, the high reproductive costs associated with dominance-related adaptations are likely incurred as a response to intense feeding competition. Supporting this view is the observation that not all hyenas are communal hunters. The brown hyena (*H. brunnea*) and the striped hyena (*H. hyaenidae*) are solitary hunters and scavengers, and the females are not masculinized in these species. Intense feeding competition has caused female masculinization through the proximal mechanism of altering hormonal profiles of female hyenas. The costs associated with this adaptation are vivid illustrations of the trade-offs involved in natural selection.

Spotted hyenas are highly polygynous. One possibility is that sons of highly aggressive and thus dominant females are able to dominate other males because of their better juvenile nutrition (L. G. Frank, 1986). Adult males seldom fight with each other but do compete by whooping. Adult males whoop primarily in intersexual and intrasexual display; dominant males whoop more frequently and use a more effortful call than subordinate males (East & Hofer, 1991). Male dominance (over other males) is closely related to length of tenure in the clan. It has been argued that, because the relationship between the dominant male and clan females is dependent on tenure and is thus not transferable, intermale competition is lessened in intensity.

The reproductive success of the highest ranking females is 2.5 times that of lower. Fitness, as measured by interbirth interval or age at weaning, is closely related to rank.

Neonatal Facultative Siblicide

Siblicide is common among predatory birds, but spotted hyenas are the only mammals known to practice it. Hyena babies fight fiercely as soon as they are born. The fighting falls off rapidly as dominance is established (or the weaker baby dies), to be replaced by rough play. Death occurs from bite infections or through one twin's preventing the other from getting to the burrow entrance to nurse. Siblicide occurs only among female twins (not mixed-sex or male twins).

Because siblicide always involves a cost in terms of inclusive fitness, benefits must be great. High levels of neonatal aggressiveness, large size, and precocial development (in comparison with other carnivores) may be an adaptation to nursing competition. The cost of siblicide may be less or the benefits greater with female twins because females stay in the natal group and males disperse (East & Hofer, 1997; Holecamp & Smale, 1995).

from one to the other is still unclear. Is it that the drugs cause crime, that crime leads to drug use, or that both behaviors are caused by other factors? Elliott's (1994) longitudinal work with the National Youth Survey suggests that the use of alcohol and marijuana precedes serious offending but that the use of harder drugs often accompanies or follows serious offending.

In the same vein, prospective studies suggest that conduct problems and impulsivity often precede not only the development of delinquency but also alcohol and drug problems (Giancola & Parker, 2001; Hawkins, Catalano, & Miller, 1992). It appears that youth with a diagnosis of conduct disorder are at an increased risk for both juvenile delinquency and substance use disorders, and that the risk for both types of behavior is mediated through genetic and psychosocial risk factors associated with early externalizing disorders (Biederman, Mick, Faraone, & Burback, 2001).

The link between drug and alcohol use and delinquency is being actively investigated. Low executive functioning and a difficult temperament, which tend to precede the onset of antisocial behavior (e.g., Moffitt, 1993b; Windle, 1994), have recently been implicated in the relationship between early behavioral problems and later substance use (Giancola & Parker, 2001). Other researchers have suggested that behavioral disinhibition and undercontrol (impulsiveness, restlessness, distractibility) provide the link between delinquency and substance abuse (e.g., Caspi, Moffitt, Newman, & Silva, 1996). As noted earlier, recent findings suggest that a common set of genes convey a general predisposition to behavioral disinhibition and that these genes contribute to problems associated with behavioral disinhibition such as attention-deficit/hyperactivity disorder, conduct disorder, and oppositional–defiant disorder, and later to juvenile delinquency and substance abuse problems, and then to criminality and alcoholism (Iacono, Carlson, Taylor, Elkins, & McGue, 1999; Tarter et al., 1999). In a sample of over 1,000 youth, McGue, Iacono, Legrand, Malone, and Elkins (2001) found that externalizing disorders were risk factors for early age of first drinking. Taken together, these findings all seem to point to the conclusion that problems of behavioral disinhibition predate and predict drinking onset.

Comments

Events occurring early during development, even before birth, can affect neurodevelopment and steer a child onto a path of early behavior problems and juvenile delinquency. It is difficult, however, to distinguish the effect of neurodevelopmental insults from other factors. Many researchers have argued that problems in neurological functioning do not occur in isolation and may in fact be consequences of adverse environments (Aguilar, Sroufe, Egeland, & Carlson, 2000; Rutter, 1997). These problems may also interact with adverse environments. For example, Moffitt (1990) observed that children with low verbal ability who came from negative family environments had aggression scores four times higher than those with either low verbal ability or high family adversity alone.

Variables indexing neurodevelopment tend to lack a specific association with delinquency. White, Moffitt, Earls, Robins, and Silva (1990) examined the predictive power of a variety of characteristics (including measures of neurological functioning) at preschool for antisocial outcomes at ages 11 and 15, and concluded that neurocognitive problems are a general risk factor for later childhood and adolescent psychopathology. They reported that low IQ and delayed receptive language predicted not only antisocial problems but also attentional problems and hyperactivity. We return to the role of neurodevelopment in the development of delinquency in chapter 4 of this volume.

FAMILY AND PEER INFLUENCES

The enormous amount of research on the role family and peers play in the development of delinquency has produced fairly consistent results. This section begins with a consideration of the multiple developmental pathways to juvenile delinquency. The notion of pathways provides a useful framework for our discussion of familial and peer influences on delinquency.

Pathways to Delinquency

The pathway approach seeks to characterize the common developmental histories of delinquents and not just the individual delinquent acts. There is unequivocal support for a typological approach to antisocial behavior involving a focus on types of individuals rather than on type or frequency of delinquent acts. For example, Stattin and Magnusson (1989) described the relationship between teacher ratings of aggressive behaviors at ages 10 and 13 and official lawbreaking up to age 26 in a Swedish cohort. For both sexes, the relationship of childhood aggression was stronger with offenses against persons and property damage than with drug, traffic, and personal gain offenses. The strongest relationships, however, were with multi-offense categories for men (65% of the versatile men had been rated as highly aggressive children versus 25% of the nonoffenders). Similar results were found for females but only with the ratings from age 13 (79% of the versatile women had been rated as highly aggressive versus 21% of the non-offenders). Ratings of aggressiveness remained significant predictors of later offending after age and socioeconomic status were partialed out. The multiple correlation (intelligence, parents' education, and aggression ratings at either age 10 or 13) was .42 for boys and .27 (age 13 only) for girls. Stattin and Magnusson argue that because this and other studies have identified a small number of highly aggressive/delinquent children who exhibit a wide range of dysfunctional behaviors, research should focus on persons rather than variables. We adopt this approach in chapter 4 of this volume.

Loeber et al. (1993) identified a developmental sequence of disruptive behavior among boys in the Pittsburgh Youth Study that involves three distinct pathways to delinquency. The pathways are labeled Overt, Covert, and Early Authority Conflict. Starting at age 8, boys on the Overt pathway typically follow a developmental sequence of escalating behaviors from annoying or bullying others to fighting with individuals or gangs, and eventually to more serious interpersonal violence, such as attacking, strong-arming, or forcing sex on someone. Entry into the Overt pathway becomes less likely as children grow older. Overt boys tend to broaden the range of their disruptive behaviors to include those behaviors characteristic of the Early Authority Conflict or the Covert pathways.

The Covert pathway is characterized by a sequence of minor covert behaviors beginning at age 7, such as shoplifting, followed by property damage and setting fires, and ending with moderately serious forms of delinquency, such as joyriding, pickpocketing, stealing from a car, fencing stolen goods, writing illegal checks, using illegal credit cards, stealing cars, selling drugs, and breaking and entering.

Finally, the Early Authority Conflict pathway has the earliest age of onset, at age 3 (Loeber et al., 1993). It involves a developmental progression beginning with stubbornness and defiance, and ending with authority avoidance (running away, truancy, and staying out late at night).

Within each pathway, disruptive behavior and delinquency in the home later extends into the school and community, and infliction of harm to parents and peers changes to infliction of harm to strangers. In addition, for each pathway, a minority of individuals progress to its highest level, and they tend to be those who had the earliest onset. For this minority, desistence is unlikely. Tolan and Gorman-Smith (1998) presented additional empirical evidence to support the existence of these pathways but noted that it remains unclear what causes an individual to move from one level of the pathway to another.

Although this typology links specific pathways to specific types of delinquency, some (Moffitt, 1993a; Patterson, 1982; Tremblay, 2000) have argued that we can identify those at most risk for engaging in delinquency at a much younger age than suggested by Loeber's descriptive model.

The Early Starter Pathway

An alternative descriptive typology involves differentiating between those with an early age at first arrest (15 years old or younger) and those with a later first arrest. According to this model, early starters are responsible for the large proportion of crime and the more serious types of offending, whereas late starters engage in delinquency in adolescence but desist in early adulthood. In contrast to the multiple-pathways approach presented in the preceding paragraphs, this approach assumes that there is a single major pathway to chronic delinquency, the early starter pathway, and different mechanisms drive the delinquency committed by those with a later start (Caspi & Moffitt, 1995). However, as in the multiple-pathways approach, there is an orderly progression of the development of antisocial behavior in early starters that begins in toddlerhood and progresses with age to more advanced forms, moving through behavior problems, early arrest, chronic juvenile delinquency, and chronic adulthood offending.

The seminal work on the early versus late starter model has been conducted by Patterson and his colleagues (1989), and by Moffitt and her colleagues (Moffitt, 1993a, 2001). (Moffitt et al., 2001, refer to life-course-persistent versus adolescence-limited types.) The differences between these authors' typologies concerns the origins and the age at which they can best describe behavior. In fact, after birth, the differences between the typologies are primarily semantic. Both typologies focus on the importance of the continuity, severity, and frequency of antisocial behavior across time and context.

While Patterson (1982, 1986, 1992) emphasizes the social learning processes that unfold in social interactions and how negative and aversive behaviors in the family are inadvertently reinforced, Moffitt (1993a) identifies early neurological problems at birth or soon after birth as the origins of early starting delinquency. She posits that individuals who become delinquent are more likely to have neuropsychological deficits in verbal or executive functioning (i.e., reading and listening, problem solving, speech, writing, memory, attention, and impulsivity). Individuals with these risks may also live in environments that have significant adversity. Thus, over time, the individual risk factors may be exacerbated because of adverse environments (e.g., families with limited skills in parenting). Both Patterson and Moffitt describe similar transactional and social interactional processes and mechanisms that mediate the development of delinquency.

Aguilar et al (2000) prospectively followed high-risk families from the birth of the child to age 16. They found no differences in early neuropsychological functioning between early-starting-antisocial, adolescent-onset, and never-antisocial children. However, by grade 3, neuropsychological results did differentiate the groups. Also, the early starters had significantly more risk factors than either the never-antisocial or the adolescent-onset groups. Specifically, the early-onset children were more likely to have a single mother at birth, to have been physically abused by age 2, and to have a mother who was experiencing extreme life stress. The early-onset children were more likely to experience psychologically unavailable, neglectful, and physically abusive parenting across their childhoods and were significantly more likely to be avoidantly attached at 12 and 18 months.

The Aguilar et al. (2000) study provided evidence that the distinction between early-onset and adolescent-limited delinquency is a valid and important one. In fact, these results exactly replicate those presented by Moffitt (1993b) in data from middle childhood. However, instead of the expected pattern of neuropsychological differences very early in development, the factors that distinguished the groups very early in development were psychosocial adversity variables. Neuropsychological functioning in the first 4 years of life did not distinguish early-onset-persistent children from other groups of children. However, a recent review noted that the bulk of studies have documented a relationship between early-onset antisocial problems and markers of neuropsychological functioning (Moffitt & Caspi, 2001). Exhibit 3.2 describes research supporting the importance of age of

---

EXHIBIT 3.2
Early Onset and Persistence Among Adult Offenders

Patterson, DeBaryshe, and Ramsey (1989) posit that the developmental trajectory of early starters consists of overt antisocial behavior in childhood, early arrest in adolescence, chronic offending in adolescence, young adult offending, and chronic adulthood offending. Farrington (1991) found that family background and childhood factors predicted arrests in adulthood. Violent offenders, however, could not be distinguished from nonviolent offenders with these variables. Farrington concluded that although there was continuity in aggressive behavior, the continuity was not specific to violence. Capaldi and Patterson (1996) found, however, that violent and nonviolent offending were predicted by the same variables. In their sample, they found that aggression and family management practices (e.g., inconsistent parenting and lack of monitoring) measured in a sample of grade 4 children predicted both violent and nonviolent arrests in adolescence.

Harris, Rice, and Quinsey (1993) found that childhood antisocial history variables were among the best predictors of general and violent recidivism among correctional and mentally disordered offenders. They followed 618 adult male offenders who had been either treated in a maximum security psychiatric facility or briefly assessed there prior to imprisonment. Over an average time of 81.5 months at risk, 31% of these men committed a new violent offense.

Multivariate statistical procedures were used to select 12 variables for use in a prediction instrument. In descending order of the size of their relationship to violent recidivism, the 12 variables were: the Psychopathy Checklist (PCL-R), a 20-item checklist scored from file information that measures characteristics such as lack of empathy, proneness to boredom, impulsivity, and irresponsibility (Hare, 1991); elementary school maladjustment; age at index offense (older offenders less likely to commit a violent offense); diagnosis of personality disorder according to the American Psychiatric Association's *Diagnostic and Statistical Manual of Mental Disorders*, third edition (*DSM–III*); separated from biological parents before age 16; failure on prior conditional release; criminal history of property offenses; never married or lived common law; *DSM–III* diagnosis of schizophrenia (schizophrenics less likely to commit a violent offense); victim injury in index offense (greater injury associated with lower likelihood to commit a violent offense); history of alcohol abuse; and male victim in index offense. The violent recidivism rate for each value or range of values for each variable was determined following Nuffield's (1982) method. For every difference of more than 5% from the mean overall violent recidivism rate, a weighting of plus or minus 1 was added, depending on whether the value was associated with an increase or a decrease in recidivism from the mean. Each offender could then be scored on each variable, and the scores could be added to form a single risk score for each offender.

There was a linear relationship between risk score and likelihood of violent recidivism. The correlation between violent recidivism and risk score was .44. Choosing the 80th percentile of risk scores as a cutoff yielded 74% correct classification; the proportion of violent recidivists correctly identified (sensitivity) was .41, and specificity, the proportion of successes correctly identified, was .88. Quinsey, Harris, Rice, and Cormier (1998) similarly reported that sexual recidivism among child molesters and rapists is also linearly related to the actuarial risk scores of an instrument designed for sex offenders. In support of the early starter model, some of the predictors of violent recidivism in these follow-up studies pertain to childhood and teenage adjustment: separation from biological parents before age 16; elementary school maladjustment; and, from the PCL-R, early behavior problems and juvenile delinquency. The fact that these childhood variables are good predictors even among adults who are already serious offenders serves to underscore the importance of the early emergence of antisocial behaviors.

onset of antisocial conduct in explaining the persistence of men who have already engaged in adult criminal violence.

Role of the Family

Most researchers have observed that the social context of the family plays a critical role in the unfolding of juvenile delinquency. The influence of such early risk factors as neurological problems, parental criminality, socioeconomic disadvantage, difficult temperament, and marital conflict is mediated through the degree to which daily parent–child interactions are affected. According to this view, ineffective parenting practices foster antisocial behaviors and attitudes in the child that are then transferred to other contexts, such as the school, where they interfere with learning, academic achievement, and the development of positive relationships with peers. These interactional patterns in the home are also transferred and generalized to peer interactions. Antisocial peers actively support, reinforce, and reciprocate antisocial behavior. Thus, this model postulates the mechanisms and the processes through which the childhood forms of antisocial behavior (e.g., temper tantrums, stealing from the family) change into adolescent forms of delinquency. We now turn to a closer examination of the role of family characteristics and interactions.

Patterson and his colleagues (1984, 1989, 1991) argue that the family context and interactions within the family are both directly and indirectly related to the development of antisocial behavior. Family characteristics and family risk factors for juvenile delinquency can be classified into four domains: family characteristics (e.g., socioeconomic status); parental characteristics (e.g., antisocial personality); parenting techniques (e.g., lack of monitoring, inconsistent discipline); and parent–child relationships (e.g., parental rejection). Patterson and colleagues have provided evidence indicating that these family factors differentiate those individuals who are early starters (viz., who have arrests before age 14) from those who are arrested later. While the late starters may demonstrate some elevated scores on these variables compared to nondelinquents, their scores are significantly lower than those of the early starters.

Family Characteristics

As we discuss in chapter 2 of this volume, shared environmental factors have a modest influence on the prevalence of juvenile delinquency (Elliott, Huizinga, & Ageton, 1985). Low socioeconomic status is associated with a slight increase in the prevalence of juvenile delinquency (Rutter, Tizard, & Whitemore, 1970). Family stressors such as unemployment, family violence, marital discord, and divorce are also associated with a higher prevalence of juvenile delinquency (Farrington, 1987b; Pagani,

Tremblay, & Vitaro, 1998). Other risk factors in this domain include poor housing; poor parental job record (Farrington, 1991); single parenting (Webster-Stratton, 1990); domestic violence (Offord, Boyle, & Racine, 1991); and child abuse (Dodge, Bates, & Pettit, 1990; Widom, 1991). The presence of one or more of these family characteristics increases the risk for engaging in juvenile delinquency in an additive manner (Farrington, 1991).

The correlations among these variables and juvenile delinquency is informative but does not illuminate the process through which these variables contribute to juvenile delinquency. Capaldi and Patterson (1994) have suggested that these family characteristics are mediated through parenting practices or deviant peer associations. For example, a parent who is unable to hold a job contributes to the poor economic context in the family and in turn increases stress in the household. This stress contributes to an increase in the frequency of coercive interactions whereby family members inadvertently reinforce the child's coercive and antisocial behavior.

In support of this view, Capaldi and Patterson (1994) found that the effects of family demographics (and associated characteristics) on delinquency were mediated through family management practices. Laub and Sampson (1988) found a similar effect in the analysis of the well-known Glueck and Glueck (1967) longitudinal study. Pagani, Boulerice, Vitaro, and Tremblay (1999) presented evidence indicating that the effect of poverty is mediated by the family before the child enters the school system. It remains clear, however, that the majority of children from poor neighborhoods do not become delinquents.

In sum, family characteristics have consistent but small effects on delinquency in comparison to individual difference risk factors. The risks they pose are probably exacerbated by other factors, such as the characteristics of the parents.

Parental Characteristics

Longitudinal studies highlight the consistency of both aggressive behavior patterns over three generations and consistent use of punishment over two generations (Huesmann et al., 1984). This cross-generational continuity, like many findings we review in the following paragraphs, is consistent with both a genetic and a social learning account. Juvenile delinquents are more likely than nondelinquent youth to have depressed and irritable mothers (Forehand, Miller, Dutra, & Chance, 1997; Williams, Anderson, McGee, & Silva, 1990) or antisocial or drug-abusing parents (Offord et al., 1991). Capaldi and Patterson (1994) demonstrated that one characteristic distinguishing early-onset delinquent boys from late-onset delinquent boys was having depressed or antisocial parents.

Zahn-Waxler et al. (1988) followed a group of children whose mothers had been hospitalized with bipolar depression. Compared to matched comparison children, these children were more likely to have significant mental health and behavioral problems, including conduct disorder, by age 6. Depressed mothers tended to be less responsive to their children's concerns, less likely to use cooperative problem solving with their children, more likely to use hostile discipline, and less effective at teaching cooperative and compliant behaviors than nondepressed mothers (Downey & Coyne, 1990). The results of this study, however, may have been confounded by the mothers' inability to report on their children's behavior problems. In contrast, Frick et al. (1992) found that the father's psychopathology (including antisocial personality disorder and substance abuse), and not the behavior problems of the child or the mother's psychological adjustment, predicted future delinquency. Parent antisociality and psychopathology may either interfere with effective parenting practices or be transmitted genetically.

In a younger sample, Keenan and Shaw (1994) showed that parental criminality was related to boys' aggressiveness at age 2, after controlling for aggression at 18 months and maternal age. Furthermore, Capaldi and Patterson (1994) reported a mediational effect of maternal antisocial behavior (through family management practices) to antisocial behavior. Parenting practices of an antisocial parent may be similarly compromised as with depressed parents. In addition, antisocial parents may provide strong role models for antisocial behaviors.

Parenting Practices

Parenting practices are the best investigated proximal correlates of juvenile delinquency. In a review of family factors, Loeber and Stouthamer-Loeber (1986) concluded that lack of parental supervision was one of the strongest predictors of the development of conduct disorder and delinquency. Similarly, Loeber and Dishion (1983), in their review of prediction studies of delinquency, reported that the most consistent and powerful predictors of later delinquency were parenting variables related to harsh, inconsistent discipline, and poor supervision of the child. Patterson and his colleagues have described how the breakdown of parenting practices and family management may provide positive reinforcement for aggressive behavior problems (Patterson, 1982, 1986; Patterson et al., 1989).

Patterson's (1982) research indicates that families of aggressive children support the use of aversive and aggressive behaviors in their children by inadvertently reinforcing aggressive behaviors and by not adequately reinforcing prosocial behaviors. Parents of aggressive children also demonstrate coercive discipline practices involving high hostility, scolding, nagging, and threatening to use punishment without following through. There is also a lack of monitoring in these families (i.e., not knowing where the child is, who the child is with, what the child is doing, or when the child will be home). Monitoring becomes more important as children become older because they are increasingly likely to spend unsupervised time with their friends.

Thus, parents of aggressive children do not teach compliance and appropriate social problem solving, leading to coercive family interactions and the development of aggressive behavior. These coercive interactions occur many times a day. Over time, a stable system of coercive interactions becomes consolidated whereby children are reinforced for their aggressive behaviors, and aggressive behaviors are modeled and reinforced by the parents.

A significant body of research indicates that coercive parenting and lack of parental monitoring are related directly to juvenile delinquency as well as indirectly through associations with deviant peers (Conger et al., 1991; Patterson & Dishion, 1985). Capaldi and Patterson (1994) and Patterson, Capaldi, and Bank (1991) demonstrated that poor family management—particularly, poor discipline and supervision, inept parenting, physical coercion, and a low frequency of positive reinforcement—is associated with childhood antisocial behavior, which in turn is related to association with deviant peers and early arrest. Similarly, Loeber and Dishion (1983) have found that the inconsistency of parents' behaviors across disciplinary interactions and the severity of punishments are related to juvenile delinquency.

Similar coercive interactions may also characterize the relationship among siblings (Patterson & Bank, 1989). Although there is less research examining sibling relationships, there is both concurrent and prospective evidence that coercive processes among siblings are related to juvenile delinquency (Hetherington & Clingempeel, 1992; Patterson, Dishion, & Bank, 1984). In addition, researchers have reported that aggressive children tend to fight more frequently with siblings than nonaggressive children do (Loeber, Weissman, & Reid, 1983). This finding is even stronger when the older siblings are male. These coercive relationships need further investigation. Just as parents may model aversive and aggressive interactional styles, siblings may also be involved in similar interactional dynamics.

In addition to the high frequency of coercive interactions, there is also an absence of positive social exchanges, anticipatory guidance, and positive affective expression of the parents in families with aggressive children. Pettit and Bates (1989) observed 5 hours of parents' interactions with their 4-year-olds. They found that disruptive behavior was unrelated to the number of overt disciplinary interactions but was associated with the proportion of child initiations that were ignored by the mother. They concluded that the absence of positive parental behaviors is as important in the development of disruptive behaviors as the presence of negative parental behaviors. Furthermore, they argued that positive affective behavior creates a more positive bond between the parent and the child such that when control strategies are implemented, they will be more effective.

Positive parental involvement may also lower the incidence of problem behavior. Gardner (1987) observed preschoolers and found that children with behavior problems spent seven times as many minutes in conflict with their mothers as comparison children, and they spent half as many minutes in joint play and positive conversation. The overall interaction time was relatively similar across groups, but only 40% of it was positive in disruptive families whereas 90% of it was positive in comparison families.

Significant parental warmth (Werner & Smith, 1982) and a positive warm bond between parent and child lead to greater compliance and reciprocity (Crockenberg & Litman, 1990). Thus, research indicates that in addition to the presence of coercive interactions, the absence of a positive parenting style is also an important risk factor for juvenile delinquency.

Parent–Child Relationships

From an evolutionary viewpoint, the quality of the relationship between parents and their children reflects, at least in part, amount of parental investment. It would therefore be reasonable to expect children to be sensitive to the amount and quality of investment received. A large literature, much of it dealing with parent–offspring attachment, confirms this expectation. We review this literature in the following paragraphs and describe some complementary literature in Exhibit 3.3.

EXHIBIT 3.3
Variations in Parental Investment

Variations in the amount of parental investment received can have important psychological effects in humans. David (1994) has reported on a long-term study of the effects of compulsory childbearing in Prague. Two hundred and twenty children born to women twice denied an abortion for the same pregnancy were pair-matched on age, sex, number of siblings, birth order, and school class with 220 children born to women who had purposely discontinued contraception or had accepted unplanned pregnancies. The mothers were matched for age and socioeconomic status. All of the children were born into families in which both the mother and father (or father substitute) were present.

Differences between the two groups of subjects widened over time, always to the detriment of those born from unwanted pregnancies. For example, at ages 21–23, the subjects born to women twice denied abortions for the same pregnancy reported significantly more often than did the control subjects: less job satisfaction, more conflict with coworkers and supervisors, less satisfying relations with friends, and more disappointments in love. More were dissatisfied with their mental well-being

---

and actively sought or were in treatment. A larger proportion had had sexual experience with more than 10 partners, judged their marriages to be less happy, and more often expressed the desire not to be married to their current partner. There was considerable evidence that, in the aggregate, unwantedness and subsequent compulsory childbearing had a detrimental effect on psychosocial development. . . . In 1989, when the subjects were 26–28 years old, another study found that marital partners were very similar to their spouses. Families founded by men or women "born unwanted" were more problem-prone than families founded by individuals conceived in wanted or accepted pregnancies. (David, 1994, pp. 346–347)

Another example of the role of parental investment comes from a study by Bereczkei (2001), who reported that mothers modulate their investment as a function of the health of their children. In a study of 590 Hungarian mothers, low birth weight was associated with a shorter period of breastfeeding. Bereczkei suggested that mothers may attend to cues of survival prospect and modulate the amount and quality of investment accordingly. The same mothers reduced the interval between births when the health of the previous child was compromised. Daly and Wilson (1988) have provided an extensive discussion of variation in parental investment as a function of the characteristics of the parents and children. They found that children are much more likely to be abused and killed by stepparents than by natural parents. In fact, stepchild status is the most important risk factor for being a murder victim ever identified among children younger than 5.

Researchers have argued that the affective quality of the parent–child relationship is crucial in the development of antisocial behavior (e.g., Greenberg, Speltz, & DeKlyen, 1993). Longitudinal studies examining high-risk samples have reported that toddlers in high-risk environments with early insecure relationships (those in which children appear to lack confidence in their caregivers' responsiveness and availability) are significantly more likely than children with secure relationships to have problems with peer relationships, mood, depression, and aggression in later childhood (Lyons-Ruth, Easterbrooks, & Cibelli, 1997; Shaw, Owens, Vondra, Keenan, & Winslow, 1996). The effect is stronger for boys than for girls (DeMulder & Radke-Yarrow, 1991). It remains controversial, however, whether attachment security reflects an infant's temperament, the caregiver's responsiveness toward the infant, or both.

Shaw, Keenan, and Vondra (1994) have demonstrated that information about early attachment security and later parent–child and family relationships predict later externalizing behavior problems. They found a relationship between maternal behavior (i.e., unresponsiveness) at 12 months and both observed aggression at 24 months and maternal report of externalizing behaviors at 36 months. Maternal unresponsiveness is related to insecure attachment (Shaw et al., 1996). Among toddlers and preschool-aged children, other caregiving characteristics (e.g., parental involvement, hostility, inconsistency, and harsh discipline) are related to later aggressive behavior (Zahn-Waxler, Iannotti, Cummings, & Denham, 1990; Shaw et al., 1996). Thus, it is plausible that parental attachment reflects aspects of parental management techniques and socialization processes. However, Shaw et al. (1996) and others have argued that these are separate domains, and the observed interactions reflect not only the distal attachment history but also the proximal microsocial learning processes described by Patterson (1982). Furthermore, they view attachment not as part of a general theory of parenting but rather as a unique construct. The relationships between attachment styles and behavioral outcomes are not the same as the relationships between parenting characteristics and behavioral outcomes.

Child abuse is an extreme manifestation of a poor parent–child relationship. Widom (1998b) has critically reviewed research on the relationship of childhood abuse to violent behavior in adulthood. In a relatively well-controlled prospective study, Widom (1989b) performed a 20-year follow-up of 908 abused and/or neglected children whose victimization was documented by legal or child protection agencies before the age of 11. Seventy-three percent of these children were matched with nonabused/nonneglected children on sex, race, date of birth, and birth hospital (11 of the control participants were discarded because of documented abuse). Twenty-nine percent of the abused/neglected children and 21% of the control participants had an adult arrest. By sex, 16% of the abused/neglected females and 9% of the control females had an adult arrest, whereas 42% of the abused/neglected males and 33% of the control males had an adult arrest. A logit model based on age, sex, race, and group fitted these data quite well. Holding other characteristics constant, an abused or neglected child had 1.76 times the likelihood of being arrested as an adult compared to a control child. Abused/neglected males had higher frequencies than control males of violent, property, and sex offenses, whereas abused/neglected females had higher frequencies of property, order, and drug offenses than control females.

Similarly, Zinggraff, Leiter, Johnson, and Meyers' (1994) analysis of the North Carolina's central registry of child abuse and neglect found a positive relationship between the frequency of maltreatment and violent crimes in adolescence. Although there is a positive relationship between childhood maltreatment and subsequent violence, it appears to be small. In a meta-analysis, Hawkins et al. (1998) found that neglect was the best predictor of later violence in a meta-analytic review; the weighted mean correlation for child maltreatment and violence in adolescence was .06.

Comments

Parental characteristics and parenting behaviors shown to be related to the development of antisocial behavior are, of course, not necessarily environmental causes. They may either mediate the effect of parental genes, reflect the same genes present in parents and offspring, or both. For example, mediating effects have been found for alcohol expectancy effects. Brown, Tate, Vik, Haas, and Aarons (1999) found that amount of exposure to an alcohol-abusing family member mediates the relation between biological family history of alcoholism and adolescent alcohol expectancies.

Direct effects of genes have also been frequently observed. Neiderhiser, Reiss, Hetherington, and Plomin (1999) studied a genetically informative sample of adolescent siblings from 395 families. The associations between parental conflict/negativity and adolescent antisocial behavior and depression were explained primarily by genetic factors. In a study of parenting practice, adoptive parents reported more negative parenting of adoptive children ages 7 through 12 if the biological mothers of the children had reported antisocial behavior before their birth (O'Connor, Deater-Deckard, Fulker, Rutter, & Plomin, 1998).

The majority of the research reviewed in this section has been conducted with males. There are few studies examining the relationship between family variables and juvenile delinquency in both males and females. One exception is a study by Kolvin et al. (1988), who reported data on the relationship of social and economic deprivation to criminal behavior among 847 children from the Newcastle Thousand Family Survey. The usual difference between males and females in frequency of officially recorded offenses was observed. The relationship between the number of early vulnerabilities (marital instability, parental illness, poor care of children and home, social dependency, overcrowding, and poor mothering) and the frequency of offending was observed in both sexes. The parental care variables were the most important of these vulnerabilities. We examine female juvenile delinquency in greater depth in chapter 5 of this volume.

Although research on family variables has been fruitful, future studies may benefit from focusing on variables that are part of the nonshared environment rather than on variables that are part of the shared environment, because, as discussed in chapter 2 of this volume, nonshared environment contributes more than shared environment to individual differences in aggressive and delinquent behavior. For example, one might predict that family unemployment would be a weaker predictor of future delinquent behavior than the quality of parent–child interaction resulting from unemployment. In addition, a change in focus for the same type of variable may also produce larger effects. For example, quality of parent–child interactions measured at the family level (i.e., for all siblings) should be a weaker predictor than quality of parent–child interactions measured for the child being studied. Surprisingly, perhaps, researchers have not paid much attention to within-family differences in parent–child interactions and associated variables. Even in the most at-risk families, not all siblings become delinquents, but little is known about why some siblings become delinquents and some do not. It is quite likely that parents do not treat or interact with their children in the same way; differential parental solicitude is likely an important part of the non-shared environment (see chapter 2 of this volume).

It is clear that familial influences increase the risk for juvenile delinquency, sometimes through their effects on behavior at home, at school, or with peers. For instance, coercive behaviors and styles learned in the home are often transferred to the classroom and playground, where they begin to interfere with learning, putting children at increased risk for poor academic achievement and problematic peer relationships (Patterson et al., 1989). We now turn to the important role of peers in the development of juvenile delinquency.

Peer Influences

Misbehavior in school relates to poor school performance, and a lack of interest in school is associated with delinquent behavior (Hinshaw, 1992). Early disruptive behavior often precedes academic difficulties (Tremblay et al., 1992). Thus, individual behavioral problems may impede success in school, which in turn may result in the development of a negative and hostile attitude toward school and school-related tasks. At the same time, problems in school-related tasks may exacerbate aggressive behavior. School is also an important venue to meet and interact with peers who may inhibit or reinforce antisocial behaviors.

The importance of the peer group for the development of juvenile delinquency has long been established (Elliot et al., 1985; Thornberry & Krohn, 1997). Currently, the primary model in understanding peers' contribution to delinquency is the Peer Influence Model (Dishion, 1990). This model suggests that ineffective parenting leads to an association with deviant friends, which in turn leads to delinquency. According to this perspective, children develop friendships and networks that support antisocial behaviors, as suggested by the theory of differential association.

Peer influences start early. Among preschoolers, early peer rejection serves to isolate the aggressive child and may play an important role in the maintenance of aggression (Olsen, 1992). The rejection may be a function of the fact that aggressive children exhibit significantly more inappropriate play, and that they insult, threaten, hit, and exclude others more often than other children do (Dodge, 1983). They are less likely than other children to engage in social conversation or to participate in group activities (Coie & Kupersmidt, 1983; Dodge, 1983). In general, aggressive children have few prosocial skills and a wide range of aggressive and antisocial behaviors.

Once aggressive children are rejected by their classmates, their rejection and status are relatively stable and resistant to change (Bierman, 1990). For example, when aggressive children experience rejection from a peer, they escalate their aggressive behavior and as a result promote future rejection and increased marginalization from the mainstream peer group. Marginalization often results in association with similarly aggressive peers who positively reinforce and model aggressive behavior (Pepler, Craig, & Roberts, 1994). Repeated and reciprocal aggressive coercive interactions within the peer group at school escalate the development of aggressive behavior through processes similar to those within the family. Thus, training by antisocial peers may be an important extrafamilial cause in the development of antisocial behavior and juvenile delinquency.

In addition, being rejected by the mainstream peer group, aggressive children are attracted to each other based on behavioral similarity and then form antisocial cliques as early as middle childhood (Cairns & Cairns, 1991). Patterson et al. (1989) referred to this process as the "shopping" hypothesis. When aggressive children join antisocial cliques, their behavior problems tend to escalate and diversify (Dishion, French, & Patterson, 1995).

As mentioned earlier, social learning takes place within deviant peer groups whereby negative and antisocial behaviors are positively reinforced (Patterson, Dishion, & Yoerger, 2000). Dishion, Spracklen, Andrews, and Patterson (1996) reported that delinquent dyads react positively to rule breaking and deviant talk, whereas normative youth react positively to normative talk. Deviant talk predicted increases in delinquency after prior delinquency was controlled for. In addition, the relative rate of support for violent talk was significantly associated with serious adolescent violence after controlling for prior delinquency and coercive interactions in the home.

Association with deviant peers is highly correlated with peer conflict, indicating that interactions with deviant peers may reinforce coercive patterns of interaction and fail to teach the prosocial skills necessary for the development of close friendships (Dishion & Patterson, 1997). Deviant peer group friendships tend not to last very long (Dishion, Eddy, Haas, Li, & Spracklen, 1997). Furthermore, delinquent friends expedite the growth of delinquency by providing opportunities to learn, practice, and refine antisocial and delinquent behaviors. In their observational work, Dishion and Patterson (1997) found that early involvement with deviant peers (i.e., by grade 4) predicted increased deviancy training by grade 8 (i.e., higher relative rates of reinforcement for deviant talk, more time spent with peers, and a higher ratio of deviant to nondeviant peers). In turn, higher deviancy training rates predicted the simultaneous training of new forms of deviant behavior such as substance use and risky sexual behavior.

The effect of having antisocial friends is maintained over time. In longitudinal analyses comparing violent and nonviolent adults, Farrington (1991) reported that adolescent involvement in group violence and vandalism was associated with the maintenance of antisocial behaviors into adulthood.

Thus, there seems to be bidirectional processes whereby aggressive children actively select settings, activities, and individuals that provide maximum reinforcement for aggressive and delinquent behavior, and peers in turn socialize these individuals into new forms of antisocial behavior. Thus, heterotypic continuity—or the transformation of the antisocial acts from one kind to another (e.g., from insults to stealing)—may be caused by association with deviant peers.

Although deviant peer group friendships tend not to last very long, the stability of these groups does not seem to be an important factor for delinquency to occur. Brendgen, Vitaro, and Bukowski (2000) found that adolescents who had recently changed from nondelinquent to delinquent friends had the highest level of delinquency a year later and did not differ from adolescents who had stable delinquent friends over a 2-year period. Thus, even short-lived peer groupings contribute to delinquent behavior.

In the same vein, Zimring (1984) found that association with new deviant peers seemed particularly important. Individuals were more likely to engage in more extreme forms of aggression when they were with peers who were new to the group or with peers they wished to impress. This study also demonstrated the role of parental monitoring. Adolescents were less likely to engage in delinquency when their parents knew with whom they associated and in what activities they were involved. Patterson, DeBaryshe, and Ramsey (1989) argued that lack of parental monitoring and association with deviant peers are necessary conditions for moving individuals along the early starter pathway.

In summary, the research indicates that peer relationships contribute to the instigation and the maintenance of juvenile delinquency over the course of development. Peer influence is likely a significant part of the nonshared environment of siblings. The child–parent–family–peer contexts include multiple and reciprocal influences that affect each participant and the settings in which they operate. Early behavior problems such as aggressive or disruptive behaviors may become exacerbated in family, peer, and school interactions. These behaviors and interactions reciprocally influence each other, and negative consequences accumulate over time, resulting in the development, consolidation, and maintenance of juvenile delinquency.

Lack of parental monitoring and unsupervised time after school is correlated with children's exposure to deviant peers and susceptibility to peer pressure (Patterson, 1986). Aggressive children not only spend more time with their peers but are also less supervised by adults (Osgood, Wilson, Bachman, O'Malley, & Johnson, 1996). Thus, the conditions that precede the detrimental processes within the peer group are likely established within the family context early in a child's life and reinforced within the peer and school contexts.

Dishion (1990) described a process in which poor parenting practices are associated with peer rejection through two mediating variables: antisocial behavior and academic failure. Boys who were rejected by their peers had been exposed to more coercive and hostile family experiences compared to average children. Poor parenting practices led to poorly developed interactional skills in children, which in turn inhibited the development of positive peer relations. Dishion suggested that parenting skills such as arranging children's contact with peers, selecting safe neighborhoods, coaching children on initiating and maintaining friendships, and modeling peer relations are related to prosocial friendships during childhood. With development, children spend more time with peers, and more unsupervised time with peers than with adults. Thus, with development, peer interactions become more salient and the dwindling of adult monitoring and supervision can have a substantial impact.

COMMENTS

A recent review of the literature indicates that for children ages 6 to 11, the best predictors of delinquency are prior offending, substance use, male sex, low socioeconomic status, and an antisocial parent. For children ages 12 to 14 the best predictors are lack of strong prosocial ties, antisocial peers, and prior delinquent offenses (Lipsey & Derzon, 1998). Thus, predictors of delinquency are from the domains of individual behaviors; family history (i.e., living with criminal parents, harsh discipline, physical abuse and neglect, poor-quality family relationships, family attitudes that are favorable to violence); community factors such as poverty and community disorganization; and peer factors. It seems that individual, contextual, situational, and neighborhood factors need to be considered to fully understand the development of delinquency.

Most of the research on proximal factors relevant to delinquency has identified correlates or markers as opposed to causes. Theories to account for the patterns of these markers tend to focus on narrow domains. In the absence of a more general theory, the wealth of correlates of antisocial behavior that are themselves intercorrelated is somewhat of an encumbrance rather than a benefit. As Stattin and Magnusson (1989) have observed, there is a need to focus on individuals rather than on variables;

Moffitt's (1993a) distinction between adolescent-limited and lifelong persistent offenders provides a fruitful starting point for a more general theory. In the next chapter we develop a theory of delinquency that focuses explicitly on individuals rather than variables and that incorporates notions and findings from the fields of evolutionary psychology, behavioral genetics, and developmental psychology.

4

A TAXONOMY OF JUVENILE DELINQUENCY AND AN INTEGRATED THEORETICAL PERSPECTIVE

Empirical evidence presented in this book indicates that delinquency is disproportionately concentrated among young males; genetic variation underlies a significant amount of variation in delinquent propensities; and delinquency is associated with mating effort, neurodevelopmental problems, and a host of psychosocial factors having to do with the family and peers. How can these disparate findings be integrated in a single theory of delinquency? How can we reconcile conceptual approaches that assert that antisocial behaviors may have had adaptive benefits in ancestral environments, that delinquency and its associated characteristics are highly heritable, and that delinquency is caused by neurological pathology and deficient social environments?

The answer to these questions, we believe, lies in a taxonomy of delinquency in which different environmental trajectories result from different ultimate and proximate causes. As we explain in chapter 3 of this volume, developmental scientists have proposed a critical distinction between individuals who begin antisocial behavior early (often before puberty) and those who begin their antisocial behavior in adolescence. The purpose of this chapter is to further explicate this taxonomy and use it to integrate the empirical findings and theoretical perspectives presented in the first three chapters of this book.

Moffitt (1993b) proposed that, during adolescence, delinquent behavior is carried out by two distinct groups: a majority whose antisocial behavior is confined to adolescence, and a smaller group whose antisocial behavior begins earlier in life and continues through adulthood. As we discuss in chapter 3 of this volume, variations on this taxonomy of adolescence-limited and life-course-persistent antisocial behavior have been proposed by other researchers as well (e.g., Loeber, 1982; Patterson, 1992). In fact, age of onset for behavior problems is the single best predictor of adult criminal outcomes (Farrington, Loeber, & Van Kammen, 1990), and many researchers have commented on the remarkable continuity of serious antisocial behavior in different samples (Loeber, 1982; Loeber & Farrington, 1998; Robins, 1978).

We propose in this chapter that there are in fact three groups of adolescents who engage in delinquent behavior. The first is a group who begin engaging in delinquent behavior in adolescence and desist by early adulthood, termed *adolescence-limited delinquents* by Moffitt (1993b). The other two groups both begin their antisocial behaviors early in life and both persist throughout their lifespan. The first group of early-starting, life-course-persistent antisocial individuals (again to use Moffitt's, 1993b, terminology) are those whose antisocial and aggressive behaviors are associated with neuropathology resulting from prenatal, perinatal, and/or early postnatal problems, sometimes in combination with family and neighborhood adversity. The second distinct group of early-starting, life-course-persistent antisocial individuals show no neurodevelopmental pathology. This group appears to comprise a discrete class of individuals, or taxon, that is different in kind from other antisocial individuals, including other life-course-persistent individuals. In adulthood, we think these boys are properly considered to be psychopaths. Each of these three groups of individuals who engage in delinquent behavior during adolescence will be discussed in turn from a theoretically integrated perspective, drawing from evolutionary psychology, behavioral genetics, and developmental psychology.

ADOLESCENCE-LIMITED DELINQUENCY

Delinquent behavior during adolescence is normative (see Moffitt, 1993b, for a review). Self-report data document that it is statistically aberrant to refrain from crime during adolescence (e.g., Moffitt & Silva, 1988). More than 80% of adolescent boys and girls self-report engaging in delinquent behavior, including drinking under age, shoplifting, and committing assaults. Given that the large majority of youth engage in delinquent behavior, it is best viewed as a normal part of adolescence rather than a manifestation of some pathological process. By age 15, the boys in the New Zealand longitudinal study whose delinquent behavior began in adolescence equaled the early-onset boys in the variety of delinquent acts they engaged in and the frequency of these acts (Moffitt, 1990). However, their delinquent behaviors were temporally unstable and situationally inconsistent.

Moffitt (1993b) uses a developmental perspective to understand adolescence-limited delinquent behavior. According to Moffitt, these youth have little biological or environmental risk for antisocial behavior and engage in criminal behavior for the first time in adolescence. Specifically, she uses the principles of learning theory to explain both the emergence of antisocial behaviors and their desistence. With regard to emergence, adolescents mimic the behaviors of their life-course-persistent peers because these behaviors allow access to desirable resources and mature status, which entail power and privilege. Desistence occurs when the costs of antisocial behavior become higher than the benefits of more prosocial actions.

The desire for adult privileges among physically maturing adolescents is stymied by their prolonged childhood in modern societies. Moffitt (1993b) hypothesizes that with early physical maturity but delayed entrance into the adult workforce there is a role vacuum of 5 to 10 years, a maturity gap, with which modern teenagers need to cope. Delinquent behaviors are seen as statements of personal independence, and Moffitt suggests that these are in and of themselves reinforcing. Adolescence-limited antisocial youth mimic life-course-persistent offenders because they see that some delinquent behavior can achieve such adult goals as possession of property, sexual activities, and independence from parents. However, once they reach adulthood they revert back to their previously acquired prosocial skills because delinquency is costly and they can achieve their goals more easily without it.

Thus, motivational and learning mechanisms initiate delinquent behavior and changing contingencies extinguish it. The maturity gap theory anticipates desistence. As the teens get older, they have more adult roles available to them and antisocial behaviors actually limit access to opportunities to engage in these adult roles. For example, a criminal record interferes with finding a good job. Adolescence-limited offenders desist more easily than life-course offenders likely because they have had many opportunities in childhood to develop basic prosocial behavior and their academic records have usually not been affected by their limited delinquent behavior. Their social skills and academic achievements allow them to be eligible for postsecondary education, good marriages, and productive jobs. Furthermore, these adolescents are not constrained by enduring antisocial characterological traits and neuropsychological deficits.

As we discussed in chapter 3 of this volume, recent empirical findings support the position that adolescents who desist from crime in adulthood are physiologically and neurologically different from persistently antisocial adolescents. For example, Raine, Venables, and Williams (1995, 1996) found that adolescents who desisted from crime in adulthood had higher electrodermal and cardiovascular arousal and higher electrodermal orienting than the group who committed crimes in adulthood. Higher arousal and enhanced information processing of events with emotional content may protect some adolescents from moving on to criminal behavior in adulthood.

There should be variations in the timing of the adolescent crime peak if the maturity gap hypothesis is correct. Modernization and modernity should have increased the number of juveniles engaging in delinquent behavior because modernization lowers the age of puberty and increases the age of entry into the labor market, thereby extending the duration of adolescence. This increase has been shown to be true across time since the 1930s (see Moffitt, 1993a, for an overview). Farrington (1986) showed that the peak in crime during adolescence dramatically increased from 1938 to 1961 and from 1961 to 1983.

One life event that is expected to be associated with desistence from delinquent behavior is marriage (or its equivalent). In their comprehensive sociological review of desistence from delinquent behavior, Sampson and Laub (1993) emphasized the importance of marriage in decreasing antisocial behavior. They interpreted this finding in terms of social control theory. Desistence from delinquent behavior in early adulthood occurs because strong ties to conventional institutions such as marriage or to another person create an investment in conformity, thereby decreasing deviant behavior. Laub, Nagin, and Sampson (1998) found empirical support for the view that marriage directly leads to desistence, even after controlling for many other related factors.

Warr (1998), however, has argued that marriage affects criminal behavior not directly but rather by altering an individual's peer relations. In Warr's view, desistence is related to marital status specifically because the transition to marriage is followed by a significant decrease in the time spent with peers. Warr uses a differential association or a social learning theory of deviance as the explanation for desistence in early adulthood. Although both theories predict the same outcome—that marriage leads to desistence—the underlying mechanisms are quite different. It is thought that marriage marks a shift from a peer-oriented to a family-oriented lifestyle and that marriage alters the kinds of friends with whom one associates. Deviant peer exposure is reduced, and conventional peer exposure increased. Warr, in contrast to Laub et al. (1998), presents data showing that the effect of marriage on decreasing delinquent behavior works directly through its impact on exposure to peers; if measures of peer influence are held constant, the effect of marriage is for the most part nullified.

Moffitt (1993b) proposes that there is no biological basis for adolescence-limited crime. Instead, the origins lie in youngsters' best efforts to cope with the widening gap between physical and social maturity. In support of this position, behavioral genetic studies show that childhood aggression and adult crime are heritable, whereas the same is much less true for juvenile delinquency (Edelbrock, Rende, Plomin, & Thompson, 1995). Although Moffitt (1993b) uses the term *biological* in this context, it appears that she means *genetically caused*. In an ultimate sense, biology likely plays an extremely important role in the adolescence-limited type of antisocial behavior.

An evolutionary explanation of adolescence-limited delinquency explains variations in delinquent propensity across the life span as manifestations of intermale competition that has its ultimate roots in reproductive rivalry (e.g., Ellis & Walsh, 2000; Kanazawa & Still, 2000). Adolescence is a time when males compete intensely with each other for access to resources and for status, resulting in what Wilson and Daly (1985, 1993) have referred to as the young male syndrome of risk taking and violence. This competition is crucial to males because it is directly related to success in mating effort. Because of sex differences in minimal parental investment, as discussed in chapter 1 of this volume, it pays for males to exhibit their competitive abilities, either to increase their mating success or to prevent complete failure. (We will discuss female delinquency in chapter 5 of this volume.)

The proximal cause of the young male syndrome appears to be hormonal. A curve showing the number of male offenders convicted each year as a function of age looks like a testosterone output curve: It rises steeply with puberty and declines gently but systematically after young adulthood. And it is true for the majority of offenders that they are limited in their delinquent activity to the period of adolescence when testosterone levels are highest.

Delinquent behavior among adolescence-limited offenders may reflect either a display of competitive abilities or increased risk taking resulting from the losses and gains of competition. As explained by Lalumière and Quinsey (2000), delinquent behavior may act to signal qualities that are hard to fake. Fighting, committing robberies, and breaking rules display qualities such as physical strength, bravery, and willingness to incur risks. Being a gang leader displays social dominance. These and other delinquent behaviors may act as honest displays of good genes, a phenomenon referred to as the handicap principle (Zahavi & Zahavi, 1997; see Exhibit 1.3). Dominant males and gang leaders appear to reap many reproductively relevant benefits, including access to sexual partners (e.g., Mazur, Halpern, & Udry, 1994; Palmer & Tilley, 1995).

But in a competition not everyone can be a winner. Losing at male–male competition incurs important reproductive costs. Adolescent and young adult males who willingly accepted defeat, low rank, and female indifference are unlikely to have been our ancestors. Therefore, risk taking to achieve reproductively relevant goals can become the tactic of choice. Daly and Wilson have examined the link between indexes of competitive disadvantage and future prospects in studies of homicides (Daly, Wilson, & Vasdev, 2001; Wilson & Daly, 1997). Some of their work is described in Exhibit 4.1. Although more research needs to be done, especially using the individual as the unit of analysis, research to date supports the view that aggression, risk taking, and generally delinquent behavior are linked to competition for things that were historically associated with reproductive success.

From an evolutionary perspective, desistence from criminal behavior is expected to occur most frequently as a consequence of a shift from mating effort to commitment to a marital partner and parental investment

---

EXHIBIT 4.1
Competitive Disadvantage and Homicide

Daly, Wilson, and Vasdev (2001) found a very strong relationship between an index of economic inequality and the homicide rate in American and Canadian state and provincial aggregate data. Economic inequality as measured by the Gini index (which assumes a value of 0 when all households have equal income and a value of 1 when all income accrues to one household) was much more closely related to homicide rates than measures of economic prosperity, and this relationship held both in Canada, where economic inequality and prosperity are positively correlated, and in the United States, where they are negatively correlated.

M. Wilson and Daly (1997) also examined the relationships among average male life expectancy, economic inequality, reproductive timing, and homicide in aggregate data from 77 Chicago neighborhoods. Male life expectancy (with the effects of homicide removed) was very strongly negatively related to the homicide rate. The addition of economic inequality significantly improved the prediction of homicide rate, but adding median income did not. There was an inverse relationship between age at first motherhood and the homicide rate. Variations in the rates of death from accident, suicide, and homicide were similar over neighborhoods, but variations in rates of death from disease were not. Taken together, these data suggest that the amount of intermale competition, as assayed by economic inequality, increases risk taking and violence. Perceptions of longevity (i.e., short- vs. long-term horizons) influence risk taking among men and reproductive strategies among women.

(Kanazawa and Still, 2000). This transition is associated with changes in testosterone. Mazur and Booth (1998) report that male testosterone levels decrease after marriage, and increase following divorce. Similarly, P. B. Gray, Kahlenberg, Barrett, Lipson, and Ellison (2002) found that married men have lower testosterone than unmarried men and that married men with children who spend more time with their spouses and are more invested in them have lower testosterone than men less invested in their spouses. Within marriage, testosterone decreases with impending or new fatherhood (Storey, Walsh, Quinton, & Wynne-Edwards, 2000).

Such a shift in investment involves a reduction in interactions and competition with peers. Variables that make this transition less likely, such as the perception of a limited amount of time in which to make the investment pay off or a perception of lower return on investment, are expected to delay desistence. Thus, the ultimate reason why marriage is associated with desistence is a change in the costs and benefits associated with switching from mating effort to parental investment. These interpretations from evolutionary theory provide ultimate explanations for the effect of relative deprivation posited by Merton's (1938) strain theory, and the effects of short time horizons on self-control discussed by Gottfredson and Hirschi (1990) and in chapter 3 of this volume.

PERSISTENT ANTISOCIALITY AS PATHOLOGY

As discussed in chapter 3 of this volume, Moffitt (1993a, 1993b) hypothesized that the origins of early-starting persistent antisociality lie in the interaction between children's neuropsychological vulnerabilities and their criminogenic environments. Neurodevelopmental disruptions, brain injuries as a result of birth complications, and postnatal neurological problems are all related to antisocial behavior (Moffitt, 1993b). These neurological problems are thought to result in two main types of neuropsychological deficits in childhood: deficits in verbal functioning and deficits in executive functioning (Moffitt, 1990; Moffitt & Henry, 1989; Moffitt & Silva, 1988).

Moffitt and her colleagues (Moffitt, 1990; Moffitt & Henry, 1989; Moffitt & Silva, 1988) have shown that both poor verbal and poor executive functioning are associated with early-starting persistent antisocial behavior. In their studies of New Zealand boys, neuropsychological problems at ages 3 and 5 were related to extreme antisocial behavior at age 15. Below-average test scores on language measures and measures of self-control—such as inattention, overactivity, and impulsivity—were linked with early antisocial behavior and its persistence into adolescence. It appeared that even subtle neurological deficits influenced temperament and behavior, making affected children more difficult to rear and increasing the likelihood of behavioral problems in later childhood.

Neurologically disadvantaged children were put at further risk for early-starting antisocial behavior because they were also more likely to come from environments formed by parents with similar difficult temperaments and personalities (Moffitt, 1993a). Typically, these parents lacked the necessary psychological and physical resources to deal constructively with a difficult child. It is this combination of a vulnerable child and an adverse rearing environment that Moffitt argues initiates the risk for a life-course-persistent pattern of antisocial behavior. For example, several studies have found that birth complications and maternal rejection early in life form a particularly dangerous combination that is associated with violent criminal behavior in early adulthood (Raine, Brennan, & Mednick, 1994; 1997).

As described in chapter 3 of this volume, the risk for life-course antisociality is exacerbated later in childhood by the failure of high-risk children to learn conventional prosocial alternatives to antisocial behavior. The failure to master social and academic skills in childhood makes it very difficult to profit from prosocial life opportunities. The lack of prosocial skills also contributes to ensnarement in a deviant lifestyle created by the consequences of offending. In this model of the origins and maintenance of antisocial behavior, there is an ongoing process of reciprocal interactions between neurological traits and environmental reactions to them.

Based on this model and the evidence amassed to support it, some scientists (e.g., Moffitt, 1993a; Moore & Rose, 1995; Raine, 1993; Robins, 1966) have concluded that early-starting antisociality reflects pathology. The antisocial behaviors are statistically unusual and their pattern fixed. This fixed pattern is considered to be maladaptive (in a social science sense) because it does not change in response to changing circumstances. Furthermore, it is argued that there is comorbidity with psychological problems such as mania, depression, and anxiety (Cloninger, Bayon, & Przybeck, 1997; Fergusson & Woodward, 2000; Kasen et al., 2001; Langbehn & Cadoret, 2001; McGlashan et al., 2000; Pine, Cohen, Cohen, & Brook, 2000).

Early-starting persistent antisociality has a long history of being viewed as a pathological condition. Robins (1966) argued that lifelong persistent antisociality is a psychiatric disease:

> It occurs in children whose fathers have a high incidence of the disease and whose siblings and offspring also appear to have an elevated incidence. The symptoms follow a predictable course, beginning early in childhood with illegal behavior and school discipline problems and continuing into adulthood as illegal behavior, marital instability, social isolation, poor work history, and excessive drinking. (pp. 302–303)

The question naturally arises of whether behavioral patterns that are to an appreciable extent heritable and follow a predictable course are de facto diseases or disorders.

Wakefield (1992a, 1992b) has conceptualized the term *disorder* as "harmful dysfunction." A person is considered to have a disorder when there is a failure of his or her internal mechanisms to perform their natural function and this failure impinges harmfully on the person's well-being as defined by social values and meanings. In Wakefield's view, a condition is a mental disorder if (a) the condition causes some harm or deprivation of benefit to the person as judged by the standards of the person's culture (the value criterion), and (b) the condition results from the inability of some mental mechanism to perform its natural function, wherein a natural function is an effect that is part of the evolutionary explanation of the existence and structure of the mental mechanism (the explanatory criterion).

The proximal mechanisms that underlie early-starting persistent antisociality include psychological, neurological, and behavioral processes, and differences in these processes lead to antisocial behavior. Most researchers implicitly or explicitly view these differences as deficits, and it is this constellation of deficits that constitutes a disorder and, more specifically, a disorder of personality (e.g., Hare, 1996; Moffitt, 1993a, 1993b; Raine, 1993; Robins, 1966; Zinger & Forth, 1998). Abundant research makes it clear that some early-starting, persistently antisocial individuals suffer from some sort of brain disorder due to any of a variety of prenatal, perinatal, or postnatal problems, injuries, or medical conditions. Neurodevelopmental pathology appears to make both direct and indirect contributions to antisocial behavior. Direct contributions involve interference with learning prosocial skills and emotional regulation. Indirectly, neurodevelopmental pathologies are likely to contribute to disadvantage in intermale status competition.

Despite the well-documented association between persistent antisocial behavior and neurodevelopmental pathology, there is evidence for the existence of a separate group of life-course-persistent antisocial individuals whose antisocial behaviors reflect a genetically caused life-history strategy rather than a pathological condition. A life-history strategy is a genetically organized pattern for allocation of time, energy, and other resources to survival, growth, and reproduction during different periods of an organism's life. Before discussing this possibility further, it is necessary to consider whether persistent antisociality lies on a continuum or whether some early-starting persistent antisocial individuals constitute a discrete natural class of individuals. It has been unclear whether early-starting lifelong-persistent antisocial individuals should be construed as a discrete class who differ in kind from other antisocial individuals or whether people simply differ in the degree to which they exhibit antisocial tendencies. This question has previously been discussed theoretically (e.g., Lykken, 1995; Moffitt, 1993a) but has not been specifically addressed empirically.

A DISCRETE NATURAL CLASS OF
CHRONICALLY ANTISOCIAL MALES

A *taxon* has been described as an "entity, type, syndrome, species, disease, or more generally, a nonarbitrary class" (Meehl & Golden, 1982). Biological sex and species are examples of some generally accepted taxa. There is growing evidence within the field of psychopathology that a number of disorders are taxonic. For example, an impressive amount of evidence is accumulating that there is a "schizotypy" taxon underlying schizophrenia (Blanchard, Gangestad, Brown, & Horan, 2000; Golden & Meehl, 1979; Korfine & Lenzenweger, 1995; Lenzenweger & Korfine, 1992; Tyrka et al., 1995); a dementia taxon (Golden, 1982); an endogenous depression taxon (Grove et al., 1987; Haslam & Beck, 1994); a dissociation taxon (Waller, Putnam, & Carlson, 1996; Waller & Ross, 1997); and a taxon underlying bulimia nervosa (Gleaves, Lowe, Snow, Green, & Murphy-Eberenz, 2000). However, not all discrete taxa associated with behavior reflect psychopathology. For instance, Gangestad, Bailey, and Martin (2000) used self-report data concerning sex-linked childhood behaviors to identify a taxon. This taxon consisted of men who had heterosexual preferences as adults and who reported stereotypical male behaviors in childhood. Members of the complement class reported fewer typical male childhood behaviors, and some of them were homosexual in adulthood.

Taxometric analyses provide an empirical method of determining whether discrete taxa underlie continuously distributed trait scores. Taxometric methods are described in Exhibit 4.2. Two studies (Harris, Rice, and

---

EXHIBIT 4.2
Taxometric Analyses

Taxometric techniques are logically straightforward. If a taxon exists, then it is conjectured for bootstrapping purposes that, within that taxon and within its complement class, the chosen indicators are relatively uncorrelated with each other. Greater covariation between the indicators results from mixing individuals from the taxon and complement together.

The Maxcov-Hitmax method (Meehl & Golden, 1982; Meehl & Yonce, 1996; Waller & Meehl, 1998) is one of several taxometric procedures. This method is often performed using continuous indicators but can be performed with a set of construct valid dichotomous items. The Maxcov-Hitmax method can be applied to multi-item scales by removing two of the items from the scale and constructing a subscale from the remaining items. The total sample of individuals is then divided into subsamples. These subsamples are devised by dividing the range of subscale scores into intervals (e.g., one for each possible score on the subscale). The covariance between the two items set aside is then plotted against the sum of the remaining six items. If a taxon exists, then the resulting graph should be peaked, with a maximal value where individuals from both classes are mixed together nearest a 50–50 mix, and much lower values at the extremes.

The mean above minus below a cut (MAMBAC) method is a taxometric procedure that can be used with two quasicontinuous variables that are thought to discriminate a taxon from its complement class. The mean of subjects on one variable above versus below a series of cut scores on a second variable is evaluated in the MAMBAC procedure (Meehl, 1992; Meehl & Yonce, 1994). This mean difference reaches a maximum at that cut-point where the taxon and its complement class are best discriminated, while the difference becomes progressively smaller as the cutoff moves toward higher or lower scores. An inverted U–shaped graph therefore indicates a taxon. By contrast, if there is no taxon, and scores on each scale are unimodally distributed along a continuum, the MAMBAC graph will show an upright U–shaped curve.

The Goodness of Fit Index (GFI) is one type of consistency test that allows one to assess whether the covariation between indicators generated by the taxonic model fits the observed pattern of covariation (Waller & Meehl, 1998).

Base rate estimates of the underlying taxon also allow one to assess the consistency of the taxometric results. Base rate estimates of the taxon can be obtained from each of the assumed taxon indicators. If the estimates are not similar in magnitude, it suggests that one or more of the indicators do not conform to the taxometric model (Golden, 1982). However, if the base rate estimates are similar, it increases confidence in the taxonic model. It is unlikely that different nonredundant methods would provide consistent estimates if actual base rates corresponding to real empirical classes did not exist (Gangestad & Snyder, 1985).

If various taxometric methods indicate that a taxon exists, and parameter estimates derived within and across taxometric procedures were numerically consistent, then there would be strong grounds for believing the taxon exists (Meehl, 1995; Waller, personal communication, February 7, 2000; Waller & Meehl, 1998), and it would be a "damn strange coincidence" otherwise (Meehl, 1990a; 1990b; Salmon, 1984).

Quinsey, 1994; Skilling, Harris, Rice, & Quinsey, 2002) have presented taxometric evidence that some men who exhibit lifelong-persistent antisociality in fact form a discrete class, differing from other adult offenders in kind, not just in degree. These studies of 684 adult male offenders demonstrated that a single discrete natural class underlies scores on a measure of psychopathy (the revised Psychopathology Checklist or PCL-R; Hare, 1991) and a measure of antisocial personality disorder (the Antisocial Personality Disorder criteria in the American Psychiatric Association's *Diagnostic and Statistical Manual of Mental Disorders,* fourth edition (*DSM–IV*; APA, 1994). Eight other variables reflecting aggressive and antisocial behavior in childhood—such as elementary school maladjustment, teen alcohol abuse, and childhood aggression—also proved to be clear indicators of the underlying taxon.

Subsidiary analyses suggested that the optimal classification of taxon membership can be accomplished by a combination of items from the adult antisociality measures and from indicators of aggressive and antisocial behavior evident in childhood. These taxon indicators are presented in Table 4.1. Note that none of the taxon indicators, with the possible exception of impulsivity, reflect neuropathology.

Apart from this research, there is little or no scientific evidence addressing the issue of the discreteness of lifelong-persistent antisociality. However, if persistent antisociality is a discrete natural class and it begins early in life, the class should be demonstrable in children. Skilling, Quinsey, and Craig (2001) addressed this issue by conducting taxometric analyses on a community sample of boys who were nearly 12 years old on average. Taxometric analyses were applied to several measures of antisocial behavior among children and adolescents. These measures were similar in content to the *DSM–IV* Conduct Disorder criteria (APA, 1994), the Psychopathy

TABLE 4.1
Point-Biserial Correlations for Multivariate Logistic Predictors of Taxon
Membership for Adult Male Offenders

Predictor	Correlation
Impulsivity	0.69
Callousness	0.64
Irresponsibility	0.64
Lack of remorse	0.63
Conning and manipulative	0.55
Shallow affect	0.51
Early behavior problems	0.48
Violent adult behavior	0.48
Lying	0.42
Parasitic lifestyle	0.36
Sexual promiscuity	0.33
Elementary school maladjustment	0.32
Criminal history	0.29
Separation from parents under age 16	0.25
Ran away from home	0.23

Note. All *p* < .05. From "Identifying persistently antisocial offenders using the Hare Personality Checklist and the DSM antisocial personality disorder criteria," by T. A. Skilling, G. T. Harris, M. E. Rice, and V. L. Quinsey, 2002, *Psychological Assessment, 14,* 27–38. Reprinted with permission of the authors.

Checklist Youth Version (PCL-YV; Forth, Hart, & Hare, 1990), and the Childhood and Adolescent Taxon Scale (CATS; Quinsey, Harris, Rice, & Cormier, 1998). Participants were 1,111 boys from a community sample of students. The results from this study provided evidence of a discrete entity underlying scores on three different measures of serious antisocial behavior in boys. A distinct class of boys (9% of the total sample) who are already engaging in serious antisocial behavior were identified in childhood as taxon members. The indicators that most accurately identified membership in the taxon are presented in Table 4.2. As in the adult case, only one item, poor behavioral controls, arguably reflects neuropathology.

These findings, and especially the finding that some persistent adult offenders are members of a discrete group, support the view that there is a group of life-course-persistent offenders who are qualitatively different from other persistent offenders. The developmental pathway leading to life-course persistence may be quite different among these offenders.

LIFE-COURSE-PERSISTENT ANTISOCIAL BEHAVIOR AS AN ADAPTIVE LIFE-HISTORY STRATEGY

As we have seen, criminality has been linked to a variety of neurodevelopmental difficulties, supporting the view of persistent antisociality as a pathology. There is, however, an alternative pathway for the origin of early-onset persistent antisociality, one that involves a different adaptive life-history strategy. As discussed in chapter 1 of this volume, adaptations are characteristics of organisms that arose in ancestral environments because of

TABLE 4.2
Point-Biserial Correlations for Multivariate Logistic Predictors of Taxon Membership in a Community Sample of Boys

Item	Taxon
Criminal versatility	0.68
Stolen while confronting a victim	0.64
Stolen without confronting victim	0.58
Need for stimulation/proneness to boredom	0.58
Often lies	0.51
Often bullies, threatens, intimidates	0.47
Suspended or expelled from school	0.44
Destroys others' property	0.44
Physically cruel to people	0.40
Conning and manipulative	0.38
Poor behavioral controls	0.35
Irresponsibility	0.33

Note. All correlations are significant at $p < .001$.

their natural or sexual selection benefits. Adaptations would have increased the relative fitness of organisms that possessed them. A nonpathological, adaptive interpretation of the development of early-onset persistent antisociality among taxon members is feasible because there are characteristics associated with this group of individuals that could easily be imagined to contribute to an individual's fitness under a wide variety of conditions.

In a recent literature review, Bugental (2000) has conceptualized the domains of social behavior as social algorithms used in life-history strategies. Bugental suggests that there are five domains of social behavior: attachment; hierarchical power (social dominance); coalitional groups; reciprocity (negotiation of matched benefits); and, overlapping with these four, mating. The degree to which these domains are independent of each other is not yet established. To the extent that the correlates of persistent antisocial conduct are organized into traits that have functional significance in the sense of plausibly conferring fitness benefits in ancestral environments, support is given to the notion that such conduct reflects genetically based life-history design rather than pathology. We might expect that, if persistent antisociality represents a life-history strategy, it would be reflected in a particular pattern of social algorithms.

Krueger, Hicks, and McGue (2001) have provided evidence consistent with a social algorithm perspective from an adult twin study of self-reported altruistic and antisocial behaviors. Several statistical approaches provided compelling evidence of the independence of altruistic and antisocial behavioral traits. Variations in altruism appeared to result from both shared or within-family processes and unique environmental effects, whereas antisocial tendencies were linked to genes and unique environmental effects.

Certain antisocial traits, such as relative fearlessness and risk taking, while sometimes problematic within kinship groups, could provide important benefits in competition and conflict occurring between groups. This is particularly clear in the widespread practice of raiding other groups for wives so extensively documented in the historical and ethnographic literature (for a review, see Lalumière, Quinsey, Harris, & Rice, in press).

The remarkable life of Egil Skallagrimsson (910–990) compellingly illustrates the interaction of early-starting and persistent antisocial traits with the historical opportunities provided by the Viking age. (See Palsson & Edwards, 1976, for a translation of the anonymous 14th-century saga, and Byock, 1995, for a fascinating medical-archeological postscript.) Certain traits appear to have direct fitness consequences, as Dunbar, Clark, and Hurst (1995) have documented in a study of revenge versus compensation for murders among the Vikings of Iceland and the Orkneys.

> Vikings recognized certain individuals as being particularly dangerous. Such an individual was labeled a berserker (from which we get the word berserk). Berserkers were renowned for their fearlessness in battle, their

great strength, their willingness to take on all odds, their uncompromising tendency to kill first and ask questions afterwards, and their ability to fight on, unhindered by any wounds received. Berserkers were much feared throughout the Viking world, and at the same time much in demand among raiding crews. The involvement of a berserker in a murder clearly increased the costs involved in a revenge killing, because these individuals could not be easily overpowered by a single avenger acting alone. . . . [W]hen the murderer was a recognized berserker, the victim's family was more likely to settle for blood-money than a revenge killing. (p. 241)

We (Lalumière, Harris, & Rice, 2001; Quinsey, 1995; Quinsey et al., 1998; M. E. Rice, 1997; also see Mealey, 1995) have suggested that early-starting life-course-persistent antisociality could represent a genetically determined life-history strategy. The hypothesized elements of this strategy are short-term mating tactics, selfishness, nonreciprocating and duplicitous tactics in social exchange, and an aggressive and risky approach to achieving social dominance. This social algorithm is remarkably similar to that described by Bugental (2000). Evidence for the latter comes from a study of maximum security forensic psychiatric patients in England (Morrison & Gilbert, 2001). Using self-report methodology, Morrison and Gilbert found that primary psychopaths (highly antisocial individuals who are lacking in social anxiety, low self-esteem, social withdrawal, and moodiness) viewed themselves as socially dominant and that the perception of social dominance bore a strong positive relationship with responding aggressively to interpersonal provocation. We consider primary psychopaths to be members of the discrete class of persistently antisocial offenders described here (see Skilling, Harris, Rice, & Quinsey, 2002).[1]

It is likely that the majority of ancestral humans belonged to a cohesive, mutually supportive (i.e., reciprocally altruistic) group that cooperated with each other to survive and reproduce (see, e.g., Dawkins, 1978; Ridley, 1993). This cooperative strategy opens up the possibility of a niche for an alternative cheating strategy, in which one could take advantage of others. To do this effectively, one would need to lack empathy and be especially selfish, callous, and superficially charming. If many people were cheaters, though, the strategy would lose its effectiveness because of the difficulty in finding cooperators to exploit and because of the increased vigilance cooperators would employ. Thus, these two strategies would be expected to be

---

[1] The PCL-R is currently the best instrument to assess psychopathy in forensic populations. It contains 20 items: glibness/superficial charm; grandiose sense of self-worth; need for stimulation/proneness to boredom; pathological lying; conning/manipulative; lack of remorse or guilt; shallow affect; callous/lack of empathy; parasitic lifestyle; poor behavioral controls; promiscuous sexual behavior; early behavior problems; lack of realistic, long-term goals; impulsivity; irresponsibility; failure to accept responsibility for own actions; many short-term marital relationships; juvenile delinquency; revocation of conditional release; and criminal versatility.

frequency dependent, with life-course-persistent antisociality being maintained at low prevalence.

The low incidence of psychopathy in the general population (Hare, 1993) is consistent with the hypothesis of frequency-dependent selection. As would be expected with frequency-dependent selection, the prevalence of antisociality in general is necessarily low when the relative gain from behaving antisocially toward a cooperator is much smaller than the relative loss to the cooperator (Colman & Wilson, 1997). Heino, Metz, and Kaitala (1998) provide examples of ecological scenarios in which frequency-dependent selection might occur, including predator–prey relationships, rare-type advantages in acquiring mates, and the use of mimicry. Frequency-dependent selection typically results in the evolution of stable polymorphisms (the existence of multiple genotypes). If life-course-persistent antisociality reflects a stable polymorphism, then affected individuals would have to be members of a genetically discrete class.

This view of early-starting persistent antisociality as a life-history strategy is consistent with the fact that these individuals exhibit traits quite different from other people and that these differences are especially evident in childhood. Substantial heritability and subtle neuroanatomical and neurochemical differences—not reflecting pathology or deficits—are expected for these individuals. It would also be expected that taxon members would act relatively impulsively, fearlessly, and unempathically. These traits should be associated with differences in autonomic responsivity as found in a variety of psychophysiological studies. Recently, for example, Herpertz et al. (2001) reported that psychopaths showed a pronounced lack of fear of aversive, frightening events. The selectionist hypothesis departs from the pathological interpretation in that this hypothesis asserts that, while many adverse medical conditions cause antisocial, violent behavior, they do not cause this adaptive, early-starting lifelong-persistent taxon.

Thus, we propose that there are in fact two quite different paths to serious and chronic criminality: a path associated with the taxon with nonpathological determinants and another path associated with less extensive criminal histories, developmental neuropathology, and competitive disadvantage. Longitudinal studies of high-risk children (e.g., Aguilar et al., 2000) have not been decisive in this connection, in part because taxon members may have been mixed with those who have neurodevelopmental difficulties.

Empirical Tests

The adaptive life-history view suggests that taxon members should show few (if any) signs of neurodevelopmental problems. This prediction has received some support. Adults with psychopathic disorders show fewer signs of neurodevelopmental instability than other violent offenders. Coid (as cited in Coid, 1993) found that indicators or correlates of neuropsychological abnormality—such as perinatal trauma, developmental delay, and history of seizures—did not correlate with a *DSM* diagnosis of Antisocial Personality Disorder but did correlate with schizotypal and schizoid personalities. Schulsinger (1972) reported that psychopathics (defined in his study as men with a consistent pattern of "impulse-ridden, or acting-out behavior" without psychosis or neurosis) did not differ from matched controls (with no mental disorder) on a composite measure of obstetrical complications. Lalumière, Harris, and Rice (2001) found that psychopathic violent offenders scored lower on a measure of obstetrical complications than nonpsychopathic violent offenders.

Fluctuating asymmetry (FA) is another way to assess whether an organism has experienced instability in its development. It reflects "the imprecise expression of underlying developmental design due to developmental perturbations" (Gangestad & Thornhill, 1997, p. 72). High FA is associated with higher resting metabolic rates (Manning, Koukourakis, & Brodie, 1998); schizophrenia (Mellor, 1992); birth prematurity (Livshits & Kobyliansky, 1991); mental retardation and developmental delay (Naugler & Ludman, 1996); lower IQ among university students (Furlow, Armijo-Prewitt, Gangestad, & Thornhill, 1997); left-handedness (Yeo, Gangestad, & Daniel, 1993); genetic homozygosity (Livshits & Kobyliansky, 1987); and relatively poor health (Thornhill & Moller, 1997). Lalumière et al. (2001) found that persistently antisocial offenders (psychopaths) were lower in FA than other violent adult offenders. Indeed, the FA levels of adult psychopaths were similar to healthy, noncriminal nonpsychopaths.

Harris, Rice, and Lalumière (2001) tested the distinction between nonpathological and pathological etiologies of chronic violent offending among 868 adult violent male offenders who were assessed at a maximum-security psychiatric institution. They examined measures of neurodevelopmental insults, antisocial parenting, and psychopathy. As shown in Figure 4.1, structural equation modeling indicated that neurodevelopmental insults and psychopathy were each linked to violent offending but were independent of each other. Psychopathy had a much stronger link to violent offending than neurodevelopmental insults did. Antisocial parenting was related to both neurodevelopmental insults and psychopathy but had no independent relationship with violence.

There are observations of apparently advantageous traits associated with psychopathy. For example, Venables (1981) found, in a longitudinal study of 1,800 Mauritian children, that those who were at risk for psychopathy on the basis of their skin conductance responses measured at age 3 and assigned at random to a nursery school condition were much more likely to engage in positive interactions, including cooperative play, than any of the other at-risk or control children. In an event-related potential study, Raine

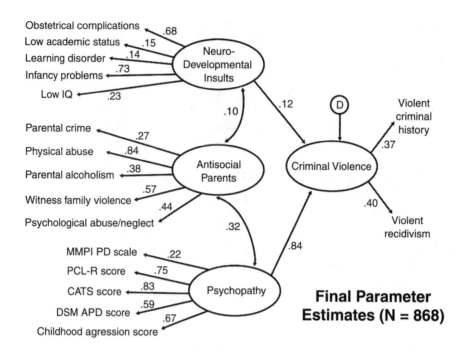

Figure 4.1. Neurodevelopmental insults, antisocial parenting, and psychopathy as predictors of violent offending. From "Criminal Violence: The Roles of Psychopathy, Neurodevelopmental Insults, and Antisocial Parenting," by G. T. Harris, M. E. Rice, and M. L. Lalumière, 2001, *Criminal Justice and Behavior, 28*, 402–426. Copyright 2001 by Sage Publications. Reprinted with permission.

and Venables (1987) found that antisocial children exhibited a heightened capacity to attend to events of immediate interest in comparison to prosocial children. Similarly, Raine and Venables (1988) found that psychopathic adult offenders showed better parietal function as measured by evoked potentials from parietal (but not temporal) sites and by Wechsler Intelligence Scale Block Design and Object Assembly tests. Finally, in a small study, deVries (1984) observed that Masai infants of the sub-Sahara who were rated (on an adapted version of the Child Temperament Questionnaire) as having difficult temperaments at age 4–5 months were more likely to survive a severe drought than infants rated as having easy temperaments.

One would predict that the development of life-course-persistent taxon members would be different and affected by different factors than the development of other life-course-persistent males. For example, the quality of parenting seems to increase the vulnerability of life-course-persistent males (those described by Moffitt, 1993a, 1993b, as neurologically impaired), whereas taxon members might not be influenced by this environmental factor. Wootton, Frick, Shelton, and Silverthorn (1997) reported that children ages 6 to 13 classified as callous and unemotional (features linked to psychopathy by Frick, O'Brien, Wootton, & McBurnett, 1994) differed from other children with regard to the impact of ineffective parenting on their conduct problems. Specifically, the number of conduct problems was not linked to the effectiveness of parenting among callous/unemotional children, whereas it was negatively linked among other children. In fact, there was a nonsignificant tendency for callous/unemotional children to have more conduct problems when parenting was more effective.

These findings concerning differential effects of parenting are highly reminiscent of early work on the development of psychopathy that are worth quoting at length. Robins (1966) described the characteristics of adult "sociopaths" identified in a follow-up study of persons referred to a child guidance clinic as follows:

> Almost every sociopath had a poor work history, had been financially dependent on social agencies or relatives, and had marital problems. Three-quarters of them had multiple arrests leading to prison terms. They drank excessively, were impulsive, sexually promiscuous, had been vagrant, were belligerent, delinquent in paying their debts, and socially isolated. . . . The symptoms that best distinguished them from all other diagnostic groups were their poor marital histories, their impulsiveness, vagrancy, and use of aliases. . . . Sociopaths had a higher rate of injuries and deaths by violence than had other subjects. Children resulting from their unions had a high rate of problem behavior and failure to graduate from high school. (p. 296)

Robins found that the best predictors of "sociopathic personality" were the variety, number of episodes, and seriousness of childhood antisocial behaviors. Future sociopathy was also strongly related to having an alcoholic or sociopathic father. It was not related to social class; the stigma of childhood mental health clinic involvement; or parental divorce, rejection, or disciplinary practices. If our taxonomy of persistent delinquency is correct, future research will uncover that different etiological factors operate for these two groups of persistently antisocial individuals.

Finally, and perhaps of greatest importance, the view that persistent antisociality is an adaptation predicts that membership in the antisociality taxon should not have incurred a fitness penalty in the ancestral environment (it could in current environments, yet still be part of an adaptation). Indirect evidence for this proposition comes from a study of university undergraduates and low-socioeconomic-status men recruited from the community in which it was found that age of first intercourse loaded on an antisociality factor (Quinsey, Book, & Lalumière, 2001). Among adolescents, Rowe and his colleagues (Rowe & Rodgers, 1989; Rowe, Rodgers, Meseck-Bushey, & St. John, 1989) have found precocious sexual behavior of one sibling to be positively correlated with the antisocial conduct of the other. This finding suggests a genetic link between antisociality and precocious sexual behavior, particularly because a twin study indicates that age at first intercourse is genetically influenced (Dunne et al., 1997). Direct evidence comes from a positive correlation between degree of delinquency and the likelihood of fathering children at a young age. As covered in chapter 1 of this volume, Stouthamer-Loeber and Wei (1998) found in a longitudinal study of inner-city public schools in Pittsburgh that 12% of 506 males fathered a child before age 19. These men were more than 200% more likely than other men in the sample to have committed serious criminal acts. Delinquency did not decrease after fatherhood. Fagot et al. (1998) found that high-risk boys in the Oregon Youth Study who became fathers had more arrests and abused substances more frequently than boys who did not become fathers. Moreover, by the time their offspring averaged 2 years of age, 40% of these adolescent fathers had no contact with them.

Primary Versus Secondary Psychopathy

Mealey's (1995) distinction between primary and secondary psychopathy (she uses the term *sociopathy* in her review) provides a useful heuristic for reconciling a pathological view of early-starting antisociality with our three-group approach. Mealey argues that similar phenotypes may develop from different genotype–environment interactions. Our description of early-onset persistent antisociality as a class of individuals executing an adaptive life-history strategy is informed by Mealey's description of primary psychopathy.

Primary psychopaths could have an extreme polygenic genetic distribution. They seem to have a genotype that results in inborn temperament or personality and patterns of autonomic arousal that design them to be selectively unresponsive to the environmental cues necessary for prosocial socialization and moral development, to actively seek more deviant and arousing stimuli, and to pursue high-risk and aggressive interpersonal strategies. Mealey describes primary psychopaths as having a theory of mind but using only the cognitive aspects of this tool without access to the emotional aspects. She notes that there are significant heritabilities for temperament and for traits such as empathy, inhibition, negative affect, anger, impulsivity, and aggression. Primary psychopaths are physiologically insensitive, hypoaroused, sensation and novelty seeking, low on harm avoidance, and low on reward dependence (e.g., Raine, Venables, & Mednick, 1997). Correspondingly, they would be high on measures on dopamine activity, low on measures of serotonin activity, and low on measures on norepinephrine activity (L. Ellis, 1991; Zuckerman, 1989). It is theorized that these hypoaroused individuals would have (a) difficulty inhibiting their behavior when both reward and punishment are possible outcomes and (b) a reduced ability to be socialized by the standard techniques of reward and punishment typically used by parents of young children. They might also have a diminished ability to experience anxiety, be unable to appreciate the consequences of punishment, and be unable to progress through the normal stages of moral development.

Mealey (1995) argues that secondary psychopaths or pseudopsychopaths would be a result of an adaptation of the psychopathic lifestyle in response to evolutionarily relevant environmental cues. These individuals will be competitively disadvantaged with respect to obtaining resources and mating opportunities. Unlikely to outcompete other males, they adopt a cheating strategy. Competitive disadvantage could be related to a variety of factors, including age, health, physical attractiveness, intelligence, and social skills. Environmental risk factors could include inconsistent discipline, parental use of punishment, father absence, family violence, an alcoholic parent, a mentally ill parent, and low socioeconomic status—similar to the risk factors found in Moffitt's (1993a) descriptions of early-onset life-course-persistent antisocial individuals.

In contrast to Mealey's (1995) division of psychopaths into primary and secondary, we postulate two groups of early-starting and persistently antisocial individuals: one group composed of individuals with neurological problems and another composed of individuals who pursue a genetically determined life-history strategy involving a risky and aggressive interpersonal strategy. Future research is needed to confirm the heterogeneous nature of the early-starter group. We predict that a subset of them are the fledgling lifelong-persistent antisocial types, or primary psychopaths (cf. Lynam, 1996), while others may follow the developmental course postulated by Patterson (1992) and Moffitt (1993b).

SUMMARY

We propose a taxonomy of juvenile delinquency comprises three groups. The first group is composed of adolescence-limited delinquents. As the term implies, these adolescents engage in delinquent behavior for a limited time. Adolescence is a period of intense competition for resources, status, and mates. Most males engage, at this time of their lives, in risky behaviors that are sometimes illegal. Many of these risky behaviors are displays of hard-to-fake qualities that may reflect good genes. The ultimate cause of their risk taking is differential reproductive success in ancestral environments, and the proximate causes include all the factors that help them gain access to the things that were statistically related to reproductive success in ancestral environments.

The second group is composed of lifelong-persistent offenders who have a history of early neurodevelopmental problems, unstable early environment and parental support, school failure, and exposure to deviant peers. The causes of the delinquent behavior of this group are thus pathological and do not have much to do with the selective history of our species, except perhaps that these causes create disadvantages in social competition. Members of this group can be identified with neuropsychological tests and other markers of developmental instability.

The third group also consists of lifelong-persistent offenders, but the causes of their behavior are not pathological. These offenders, often referred to as psychopaths, are pursuing a lifelong evolutionary adaptive strategy of defection, manipulation, dominance, coercion, aggression, and high mating effort. The evolution of this life history probably occurred through frequency-dependent selection, in which a small group of men was able to fill a niche created by the fact that most people are social cooperators. Although much empirical work remains to be done, studies show that those in this third group do not show the signs of developmental instability suggested by a pathological view of persistent offending. These offenders form a distinct class in taxometric studies of antisocial behavior. Unfortunately, there are as yet no behavioral or molecular genetic studies of psychopathy as defined in the modern literature.

The implications of a life-history strategy conceptualization of persistent antisociality pertain primarily to identifying its most likely proximal causes. The social policy implications of whether it is an adapatation or a disorder are less straightforward. Descriptively, the persistence of the antisocial behaviors of psychopaths is well established, as is the ineffectiveness of current interventions designed to reduce antisocial manifestations among adult psychopathic offenders. Indeed, there are data suggesting that treatment programs that reduce recidivism of non-psychopathic offenders actually increase the recidivism of psychopathic offenders (Rice, Harris, & Cormier, 1992; for related findings, see Seto & Barbaree, 1999, Ogloff, Wong, and Greenwood, 1990). Similarly, there is an interaction between psychopathy and phallometrically measured deviant sexual interest that is associated with uniquely high rates of recidivism among both adult (Harris, Rice, Quinsey, Lalumière, Boer, & Lang, in press; Rice & Harris, 1997) and juvenile sex offenders (Gretton, McBride, Hare, O'Shaughnessy, & Kumka, 2001). None of these observations or their policy implications are affected by whether persistent antisociality is a disorder or not. The direction of investigations designed to develop future interventions and prevention programs, however, is likely to be critically affected by this distinction. We deal with interventions in Chapter 6 of this volume. Before turning to these concerns, however, we consider how our integrated theory applies to female delinquents.

5

SEX DIFFERENCES IN AGGRESSION
AND FEMALE DELINQUENCY

One of the most well-documented individual differences in the study of antisocial behavior is that men are more aggressive than women. This finding occurs across cultures and holds true whether sex differences are measured categorically or on a continuum (Moffitt, Caspi, Rutter, & Silva, 2001). This sex difference emerges during development. During infancy and toddlerhood there are few differences between girls and boys in their rates of aggression (Keenan & Shaw, 1994; Rose, Rose, & Feldman, 1989); temperament; activity level; and compliance (Prior, Smart, Sanson, & Oberklaid, 1993). However, sex differences in aggression emerge at about age 4 (Prior et al., 1993; Rose et al., 1989) and, by the time of school entry, there are stable sex differences in the frequency of externalizing behavior problems that persist into adulthood (Offord et al., 1991). During the peripubertal period for girls, in which girls are more physically developed than boys, sex differences in aggression decline (Moffitt et al., 2001). Aggression varies over age in a similar manner in males and females. For example, both males and females are more likely to commit violent crimes between the ages of 14 and 24 than at other ages, although the onset for females tends to be 2 years earlier on average (Campbell, 1999). There are also sex differences in the seriousness of aggression: Men are more likely than women to commit more serious acts of aggression, such as serious violent crimes. Meta-analyses have shown that the sex difference in noncriminal aggressive behavior is greater for physical aggression than verbal or psychological aggression (Bettencourt & Miller, 1996; Eagly & Steffen, 1986). Hyde (1984) demonstrated a moderate effect ($d = .50$) for the sex difference in aggression, larger than the sex difference in verbal or mathematical abilities. Similarly, Eagly and Steffen (1986) found a moderate effect ($d = .40$) across all studies on sex differences in aggression, again finding males to be more aggressive than females. There was only one form of aggression in which women scored higher than men: indirect aggression (e.g., gossiping and spreading rumors). The goal of this chapter is to explain these sex differences in aggression in light of the integrated theoretical perspective presented in chapter 4 of this volume.

DEFINING AGGRESSION

Because the vast majority of studies of aggression have focused on boys, current models of the development and consequences of aggressive behavior, such as those presented in earlier chapters of this volume, are based on male data (e.g., Loeber, 1990; Moffitt, 1993b; Patterson et al., 1989). Very little attention has been paid to the risks and long-term consequences of aggression for girls, presumably because their problem behaviors are less prevalent and less violent than those of boys. Recently, a different perspective for understanding the problems of aggressive girls has been recommended. In particular, the use of gender-specific assessment methods (Keenan & Shaw, 1994; Serbin, Moskowitz, Schwartzman, & Ledingham, 1991; Zoccolillo, 1993) that focus on the type of aggression that is more typical of females than males, indirect aggression (Frick, 1995). Indeed, it has been suggested that rather than comparing the problems of girls to those of boys, girls should be assessed and evaluated relative to other girls in their age group.

Consider the diagnosis of conduct disorder, the second most common psychiatric diagnosis among girls (Zoccolillo, 1993). Current criteria of conduct disorder comprise behaviors that may be more typical of boys than girls, such as cruelty to animals, physical attacks, and getting into fights (APA, *DSM–IV*, 1994). Because the diagnostic criteria for conduct disorder were not validated with female samples, they may not accurately assess the conduct problems in girls, such as lying, skipping school, running away, using substances, and engaging in prostitution (Zoccolillo, 1993). However, there is evidence that females diagnosed as conduct disordered are as antisocial in their behavior as similarly diagnosed males—because fewer females exhibit antisocial behavior, fewer of them meet the criteria for a conduct disorder diagnosis (Moffitt et al., 2001).

Three types of aggression have been discussed in the literature: physical, verbal, and indirect. Indirect aggression usually involves verbal behavior but can also refer to manipulation or third-party aggression. Unfortunately, distinctions among these three types of aggression are not always made, and until the late 1980s researchers used the term *aggression* to mean only physical aggression. In addition, aggressive behavior was collapsed across all contexts and ages in the earlier studies, possibly obscuring important contextual effects. Recent studies indicate that girls are just as likely as boys to engage in verbal aggression and are more likely than boys to engage in indirect aggression (Lagerspetz, Bjorkqvist, & Peltonen, 1988). This research suggests that females and males may not differ in quantity of aggression but rather in type. Boys' antisocial behaviors, unlike those of girls, are often overt public displays. Indirect aggression, however, is also likely to be important. Cowan and Underwood (1995) found that indirect aggression is perceived by children of elementary school age to be as harmful as physical aggression. There is no evidence, however, that the long-term negative outcomes associated with indirect forms of aggression are the same as those linked with physical aggression. The extent to which indirect aggression is a risk factor for subsequent antisocial conduct remains to be determined.

Women report more aggression toward their partners than men in both dating and marital contexts. For example, DeMaris (1992) found that 7% of men and 42% of women acknowledged using violence toward a dating partner. Men reported that violence was initiated by their partner twice as often (39% versus 20%) as by themselves, and women confirmed this—they were twice as likely to report they had initiated the violence (49% versus 24%). An examination of aggression in dating contexts revealed that adolescent girls were just as likely as boys to have been aggressive toward their partners (Hilton, 1996). However, the aggressive acts committed by females were less severe than those committed by males. Durdle (1998) similarly found that adults rated the same interspousal aggressive acts as more severe when perpetrated by men than by women.

Findings in the literature on female delinquency are in part determined by the method used to measure delinquency. In some respects self-report and official statistics present similar results (e.g., the male–female differences in delinquency are largest for violent crimes), and there is no self-reported delinquent behavior in which girls are significantly more involved than boys (Chesney-Lind & Shelden, 1992). However, in contrast to official statistics, self-report measures indicate that the rates are similar for less serious crimes. Finally, according to official statistics, girls are more likely to commit acts of prostitution and to run away. Not surprisingly, self-report data demonstrate that female delinquency is more prevalent than official reports suggest. The picture of female delinquency given by official and self-report data is that girls commit a variety of offenses but are less likely than boys to engage in serious and, especially, violent delinquency. Self-report data suggest that most delinquency is not serious and that for nonserious offenses boys and girls do not significantly differ. Although the results do suggest that there is a real difference between boys and girls in the extent and frequency of delinquent activities, these differences are smaller than official statistics suggest. These findings are congruent with the recent research examining sex differences in aggression in a noncriminal context, which indicates that males engage in more physical aggression of a serious nature than females from adolescence onward (Leschied, Cummings, Van-Brunschot, Cunningham, & Saunders, 2000).

DEVELOPMENTAL COURSE AND OUTCOME

Despite sex differences in aggression, there are similarities in developmental outcomes for aggressive girls and boys. A longitudinal study found that early aggressiveness of both girls and boys predicted later aggression scores, harsh punishment of their own children, and criminal acts (Huesmann et al., 1984). Once established, aggression predicts later aggressive tendencies as accurately in girls as it does in boys over several developmental transitions (Cairns, Cairns, Neckerman, Ferguson, & Gariepy, 1989; Campbell et al., 1994; Pulkinnen, 1987).

Robins (1986) reported that the types of conduct problems experienced by girls and boys were ranked in a similar order according to how frequently they occurred, but girls had significantly fewer conduct problems overall than boys. Although the types of conduct problems reported were similar, the outcomes for girls and boys with conduct disorder differed in adulthood. In a follow-up of children referred to clinics for antisocial behavior problems, Robins (1966, 1986) noted that the girls were somewhat less likely than the boys to be diagnosed with antisocial personality as adults. However, both the girls and the boys were at increased risk for drug and alcohol abuse. The girls were more likely than the boys to experience internalizing disorders such as anxiety and depression in adulthood. Robins (1986) noted that "an increased rate of almost every disorder was found in women with a history of conduct problems" (p. 399).

Given that there are some differences in aggressive boys' and girls' long-term outcomes, it seems logical to search for the long-term sequelae of aggressive behavior problems in somewhat different areas for males and females. Proportionately more aggressive boys than girls develop into adults who engage in violent crimes (Magnusson, 1988). Girls, however, seem to express their aggressive tendencies within the confines of the family and close relationships. Official statistics indicate that most violent women were convicted of attacks on their own families or neighbors (McClintock, 1963).

In a comprehensive review of aggression among female adolescents, Leschied et al. (2000) concluded that girls' risk factors for engaging in aggression are similar to boys'. The criminogenic risk factors identified in their review for both girls and boys included family interactions; parental violence; poor family management; parents' proviolent attitudes; family conflict; and certain social cognitive processes, such as hostile attributional bias and selective attention to aggressive cues. In addition, there were unique correlates among girls, such as self-harm, suicidal ideation, and physical and/or sexual victimization. Loeber (1999) has also suggested that early onset of puberty, lack of empathy, sensitivity to rejection, and assortative mating (i.e., selecting similarly aggressive mates) may be important risk factors for girls that require future research attention.

Finally, Moffitt et al. (2001) reported that the same individual and family risk factors predicted antisocial behavior in males and in females. There is some evidence to suggest that boys have higher rates of important risk factors, such as more compromised neurological functioning, hyperactivity, and peer problems, and that these increased levels of risk account for one half to two thirds of the sex differences in antisocial behavior (Moffitt et al., 2001). Family adversity contributes to individual differences in antisocial behavior, but not sex differences. Thus, it is not the type of risk factor but rather the greater level of exposure to individual and peer risk factors that account for sex differences in antisocial behavior. We still need more research on the developmental correlates of aggression in girls, as well as the relationship of aggression to developmental outcomes, and the list developed by Loeber (1999) provides a good starting point.

Most aggressive girls in the longitudinal study by Cairns and Cairns (1995) engaged in serious antisocial acts with family members or other girls. Early aggressiveness in both sexes predicted later problems. Girls who were physically or verbally aggressive were less motivated to attend school, had poorer school performance, and completed fewer grades than nonaggressive girls. The education of the aggressive girls was often interrupted by low school motivation, early heterosexual activity, and young motherhood (Pulkkinen, 1992). More than 50% of these seriously antisocial girls had dropped out of school by grade 11.

Other studies have shown that women who were aggressive as girls are less likely than men to be arrested for a violent crime but have severely dysfunctional lives, including incidents of spousal and child abuse (D. O. Lewis et al., 1991). Severely antisocial females are also more likely to have unstable work careers and to experience job loss (Pulkkinen, 1992). These studies also showed that, although men are more likely than women to exhibit aggressive behaviors after childhood, the women who do are extremely antisocial. These women also have problems as parents (Serbin, Moskowitz et al., 1991). They demonstrate lower emotional and verbal responsivity and use fewer appropriate play materials, and their children display early signs of psychosocial difficulties. Even more disturbing are frequent visits to emergency rooms and elevated rates of accidents and acute infections among their children, possibly due to child abuse.

Two other longitudinal studies support the notion that aggressive girls are at risk for negative outcomes as defined in a social science sense. First, Serbin, Peters, McAffer, and Schwartzman (1991) found that women who were aggressive in childhood showed elevated levels of sexually transmitted diseases and their gynecological sequelae, more visits for prescription of birth control, and a higher pregnancy rate during their teen years. Thus, although aggressive outcomes were not the primary focus of this study, there is evidence that aggressive girls are reproductively precocious and risk accepting. Similarly, Underwood, Kupersmidt, and Coie (1996) conducted a 10-year follow-up of girls who were aggressive in childhood. They reported that 50% of the aggressive girls had become teen mothers, compared to 26% of comparison girls. As we noted in chapters 1 and 4 of this volume, this association of early reproduction with the severity of antisocial conduct is also found in boys (Stouthamer-Loeber & Wei, 1998). There is converging evidence to suggest that antisocial behavior has sex-differentiated outcomes in adulthood. Specifically, males are more likely to experience work, substance abuse, and legal problems, while females are more likely to experience relationship problems such as depression, suicide attempts, and poor physical health (Moffitt et al., 2001).

Antisocial behavior among the children of antisocial mothers appears to reflect the effects of both maternally provided genes and environments. A recent study (Loucks, 1995) established that more than 70% of women in a Canadian prison were mothers and that women diagnosed as psychopaths had more children on average than nonpsychopathic women. From an evolutionary viewpoint, it is apparent that precocious and risky reproductive behavior, while considered negative from a societal perspective, may promote the fitness of the females involved by reducing the intergenerational interval and perhaps increasing offspring number, underscoring the idea that ultimate reproductive causes can produce societally devalued outcomes in the current environment.

Cloninger and colleagues (1978) have developed a two-threshold polygenic model of antisociality. In this model, the genes for antisociality are located on the autosomes of both sexes but are triggered by androgens (they are said to be sex linked, as opposed to sex limited where the genes would be located on the sex chromosomes). The threshold is determined by the number of active genes for the expression of the trait. Females who express the trait thus have a higher genetic loading than males, and the risk is higher for the relatives of persistently antisocial females than for males with similar characteristics. Therefore, the heritability of antisociality is expected to be higher in females and environmental responsivity higher among males (e.g., Cloninger, Christiansen, Reich, & Gottesman, 1978). The threshold model assumes greater importance in the context of assortative mating.

There is strong evidence for assortative mating for both antisocial males and females. Such cross-trait assortative mating contributes to increased risk of engaging in adult crime (Moffitt et al., 2001). Moffitt et al. (2001) reported that one fifth of their conduct disorder cohort associated with antisocial mates and accounted for two thirds of the offspring in their teenage years. Research clearly needs to take into account the role of assortative mating and selective reproduction if we are to understand the persistence of antisocial behavior.

In summary, both official statistics and self-report data indicate that males commit larger numbers of physically aggressive acts than females do. Official reports of aggressive behavior in females underestimate its incidence because they reflect primarily physical aggression. There are well-documented continuities in conduct problems from childhood to adulthood in both sexes. Girls with conduct problems generally exhibit less antisocial conduct as adults than boys; however, the behaviors typically measured are less common in women than men (Robins, 1986). In searching for the sequelae of aggressive behavior problems for girls and boys, researchers should expand their outcome variables to include indicators appropriate for women, such as depression and serious aggression within close relationships. Accumulating evidence suggests that individual and environmental risk factors for antisocial behavior in males and females are more similar than different.

SEX DIFFERENCES IN JUVENILE DELINQUENCY AND RECENT TRENDS

Sex differences in aggressive behavior lead us to expect sex differences in juvenile delinquency more generally. Canadian youth crime statistics indicate two important trends. First, and contrary to public opinion, between 1994 and 1998 the overall number of charges declined. Second, there was an increase in charges against females for violent crimes during the same period. The ratio of male to female young offenders over all categories of Canadian Criminal Code violations was 3.4:1 (Leschied et al., 2000). Violent offenses accounted for 21% and 24% of all charges against girls and boys, respectively; the ratio of boys to girls for all violent offenses was 2.9:1. However, for the most serious violent offenses—such as homicide, sexual assault, and armed robbery—the ratio was 7:1.

These data indicate that, while boys commit more violent crime than girls overall, the proportion of girls charged with violent crimes increased twice as fast as that of boys over the last four years. Only four female youths were charged with homicide and nine for attempted murder (0.01% and 0.03%, respectively) in Canada from 1994 to 1998. The increasing number of girls proceeding through the juvenile justice system no doubt fuels the perception that adolescent girls are becoming more aggressive. Gabor (1999) has argued that the increasing rate of violence among Canadian youth may reflect a growing intolerance for youth violence reflected in zero tolerance policies in schools and communities. Reittsma-Street (1999) suggests that the trend to process more females than males is likely a heightened fear of "girl crime," despite what are actually relatively low rates of female delinquency. These figures parallel the statistics for adult crimes, in which men outnumber women in all crime categories except prostitution, in which women outnumber men 7 to 1.

Canada shares the increasing violent crime rate among adolescent girls with other countries. Hennington, Hughes, Cavell, and Thompson (1998) reported that in the United States the general crime rate for adolescent girls has increased at a much higher rate than for any other segment of the population. In particular, the percentage of girls involved in violent crime increased by 103% from 1984 to 1993. However, it should be remembered that male adolescents continue to commit the majority of violent crime, with a prevalence ratio of male to female adolescents of 3:1 to 12:1, depending on the type of violent offense reported (Borduin & Schaeffer, 1998).

FEMALE JUVENILE DELINQUENTS AND THE JUVENILE JUSTICE SYSTEM

There is a significant literature on the effects that variations in the definition of crimes have on officially recorded crime rates. The fact that police do not arrest everyone who has committed an offense makes it possible that police statistics present a biased picture of female juvenile delinquency (e.g., Horowitz & Pottieger, 1991). Chesney-Lind and Shelden (1992) provide a historical overview that demonstrates that sexism has pervaded the juvenile justice system in the United States since its inception in 1899. After the establishment of this system, girls were referred to juvenile courts for immorality and waywardness in large numbers and a tremendous number of girls were detained, tried, and institutionalized for these offenses. During the 1950s and 1960s the "crime" of immorality was replaced by status offenses like running away. Despite gains in diverting and deinstitutionalizing girls for these offenses, Chesney-Lind and Shelden argue, females are still discriminated against. The bias against girls is largely due to status offenses because the vague language around these statutes permits differential treatment of adolescents who come into the system. This vague language has allowed the system, with the notion of the state as parent, to become involved in monitoring girls' behavior, particularly sexual behavior that would be condoned or ignored in boys. For reviews of the history of interventions for the "girl problem" in America and England at the turn of the 20th century, see R. M. Alexander (1995) and Bartley (2000), who document parental and societal efforts to control young women's reproductive careers.

Running away, skipping school, exhibiting incorrigibility, and so on account for one third of all official female delinquency, compared to one fifth for boys. Girls are also 170% more likely than boys to be referred to juvenile court for status offenses. We know from self-report data that this difference is not due to an overrepresentation of females committing these types of offenses (Chesney-Lind & Shelden, 1992). Why is it then that this discrepancy exists? Biases in policing and the court system seem to be operating. In addition to these biases, there appears to be a bias in parental use of the status offense category. A majority of status offenders are committed by relatives; and, because they set different standards of compliance for girls and boys, parents are more likely to refer their daughters to court for troubling behaviors.

There are few attempts in the existing literature to explain why the criminal justice system and parents would take more of an interest in girls' behavior than in boys' and why this bias would involve sexual behaviors in particular. An evolutionary perspective, however, provides insights on why this intense interest exists. Early and or promiscuous sexual behavior in females could lead, from the parent's point of view, to a decline in the value of a female as a mate; possible early marriage to a low-status male; and, historically, a low probability of infant survivorship. The fitness interests of female adolescents and their parents are not identical.

Although there are undoubtedly differences in the way with which societal authorities deal with girls and boys, these biases appear to predominate only with status offenses. Therefore, it does not seem plausible that biases in the juvenile justice system account for the sex differences seen in serious juvenile delinquency. Theories that attempt to explain female juvenile delinquency must be able not only to account for delinquency in girls but also to explain the sex difference observed in serious violent offenses.

EXPLANATIONS OF FEMALE DELINQUENCY

Early Biological Theories

Medieval explanations of female delinquency were characterized by the view that female offenders were possessed by the devil and were wicked. This view remained common until the late 1800s, when Lombroso and Ferrero (1895) published *The Female Offender*. This work set the stage for biological perspectives that would remain strong well into the 20th century. Lombroso's female offenders (typically prostitutes) were "born criminals," their delinquency caused by innate tendencies. Lombroso concluded that female criminals were rare because generally women were weak, had an underdeveloped intelligence, and had a biological role as caretaker of children. Women were thought to be passive by nature and therefore less inclined to crime than men. However, when women did deviate, they were believed to be extremely vile because their "wickedness must be enormous before it could triumph over so many obstacles" (see Highlight 1 in Siegel & Senna, 1981).

Criminals were thought to be less highly evolved than normal law-abiding citizens and could be distinguished by their "primitive" body traits. Lombroso and Ferrero's (1895) book is filled with figures on the weight of women's lower jaws and on the size of their hands, noses, and so on. This focus on anatomy and sexuality set the tone in discussions of female criminality for many years to come.

Glueck and Glueck (1934) also believed in the inborn nature of female delinquency. However, these researchers also believed in the role of the environment, acknowledging that poverty was related to delinquency. The Gluecks investigated a wide range of physical and social variables, but the sexual history of each girl was included, regardless of the offense, keeping female delinquency firmly in the arena of sexuality.

Pollack (1950) elaborated on the theme of sex but also contended that female crime was accounted for by women's biological nature. He argued that it was women's natural tendency to conceal and misrepresent and that therefore "female" offenses such as shoplifting, fraud, and theft were "natural" crimes for women. Menstruation, pregnancy, and menopause also seemed to bring about increases in crime: "The menopause finally seems to bring about a distinct increase in crime, especially in offenses resulting from irritability such as arson, breaches of the peace, perjury and insults" (see Highlight 2 in Siegel & Senna, 1981). Pollack also believed that female delinquency went unrecorded because of misplaced chivalry on the part of officials, in addition to women's unusually cunning and deceitful nature.

Cowie, Cowie, and Slater (1968) examined the characteristics of girls in a juvenile institution in Britain. They found that most of the girls were incarcerated for sexual delinquencies. They explained this finding with reference to the role played by the female anatomy and the earlier maturation of girls versus boys. They also concluded that the nature of delinquent offenses among girls was different from that of offenses committed by boys. Cowie et al. accounted for the lower rate of delinquency among girls by suggesting they are less genetically inclined than boys to be antisocial and require an extreme push from the environment to overcome this relative immunity. This same approach was taken by American researchers such as Vedder and Somerville (1973).

Early Sociological Theories

Biological theories and their emphasis on female sexuality began early and remained strong well into the 1960s. However, sociologists began actively searching for nonbiological causes of delinquency early in the 1920s. This work, especially early on, focused on males, specifically in relation to gang involvement. These theories were not developed to explain female delinquency, and some early theorists dismissed girls as completely unimportant in their analysis of delinquency (Chesney-Lind & Shelden, 1992, p. 68). Like the early biologically oriented investigators, these theorists thought that female delinquents were fundamentally different from male delinquents, that delinquent girls had "psychological" problems, whereas delinquent boys were affected by strain or subculture deviance. It is of interest to examine whether these sociological theories can in fact explain female delinquency. Because this literature is covered in chapter 3 of this volume, only a brief examination follows.

Strain theories suggest that delinquency results from the discrepancy between an acceptance of the goals of a materialistic society and an inability to achieve these goals through legitimate means. Applying this logic to females, it seems reasonable to assume that the female crime rate should be higher than the male crime rate. Females should experience more strain because they strive to achieve these same goals as males but have even less opportunity to achieve them (Morris, 1987). Because the female crime rate is lower than the male crime rate, this theory appears to be inadequate. Furthermore, the female crime rate should have decreased as increases in equality with males were achieved; again, this has not been the case.

Subcultural deviance theory posits that a distinct subculture exists within the lower class that generates high rates of delinquency because it opposes working-class norms. However, there is very little literature on female subcultures, so it is difficult to assess whether this theory applies to female delinquency.

Differential association theory is based on the assumption that criminal behavior is learned and a person becomes delinquent when exposed to behaviors that are deviant. Given that males and females share the same neighborhoods and the same families, it might be argued that their patterns of crime should be similar. Traditional sociology and psychology emphasized the importance of delinquent peers in male delinquency, and research on female delinquency and gangs suggests that delinquent peers are also important for girls. Relationships of girls to their girlfriends are strong predictors of both gang membership and delinquency (Bowker & Klein, 1983). A. Campbell's (1984) book *Girls in the Gang* also stressed the powerful influence that "sisterhood" had on female delinquent behavior. The delinquent behavior of peers has been shown to be one of the most important predictors in explaining delinquency in both sexes. Differential association theory finds some empirical support in these data but is not completely sufficient because the differing patterns of violent crime in the two sexes is left unexplained. It is necessary to identify more specific mechanisms that cause juvenile delinquency in females.

Early Psychosocial Theories

Sociological theories have maintained a strong presence throughout the decades. The study of sociodemographic factors in offender populations became commonplace in the second half of the 20th century. This second, newer school of thought argued that the same factors were important in both male and female delinquency; that is, similar structural factors and economic conditions lead both sexes to abandon traditional expectations of success and resort to delinquency. However, male offender populations were almost exclusively studied, and females were mentioned only in relation to findings extrapolated from the male studies. Not until recently, when the extent and nature of female delinquency was better understood, were sociological theorists in a position to explain delinquency in both sexes.

Konopka (1976) suggested that female delinquency was an expression of emotional problems in which young women were driven by loneliness and dependency. She also emphasized the influence of peers and socialization in causing deviant behavior through their effects on emotions. The focus on sexuality was still present, as was the notion of individual pathology. This notion of an emotionally unbalanced girl was picked up by many in the literature and has remained ever since. The "troubled" adolescent girl was a continuation of the early biological perspectives that viewed female delinquency, unlike male delinquency, as a psychopathology, although family and other social variables were given more weight in these updated versions.

Statistical descriptions of female offenders began in earnest at this point, painting a picture of the female delinquent as being poor, young, and undereducated; lacking social and vocational skills; and coming from abusive, assaultive, neglectful, alcoholic, or otherwise disruptive family backgrounds. This profile was very similar to that of the male offender at that time as well as currently (Joel, 1985).

Although themes from the past continued into the 1970s, the women's movement began to exert some influence on theories in this field. Some feminist writers, such as Adler (1975), suggested that with an increase in opportunity more women would commit crimes. Adler also thought that the liberation of women in the 1970s was directly linked to increases in the amount of female crime: "The female criminal knows too much to pretend or return to her former role as a second rate criminal confined to feminine crimes such as shoplifting and prostitution" (see Highlight 3 in Siegel & Senna, 1981).

The feminist movement shifted the theoretical focus of explanations for female aggression and female crime to socialization. Hoffman-Bustamente (1973) suggested that the lower rate of female crime should be viewed within a socialization framework. The female sex role stressed conformity and supervision for girls; these factors in turn limited the opportunity and access for girls to engage in antisocial behavior. Girls and boys were taught to deal with aggression and conflict in different ways, and this different socialization was reflected in the types of crimes they committed. An equalization of the crime ratio was expected to result from the equalization of sex roles. At the time, official statistics appeared to provide some support for this idea. Both the American and Canadian data demonstrated dramatic increases in the number of girls arrested during the 1960s and 1970s. The American data, for example, showed that from 1960 to 1975 there was a 250% increase in the number of girls arrested and a large increase in the number of arrests for violent offenses (Chesney-Lind & Shelden, 1992). These statistics supported the feminist view that the women's movement had triggered a crime wave among young women and the view that female aggression was unleashed when "liberated" from societal constraints.

However, with a longer perspective, it becomes apparent that the change in juvenile arrests was not accounted for by this liberation hypothesis but was affected by demographic shifts. Arrests fell off after 1976, coinciding with a dramatic drop in the number of people under the age of 18. It appears that the increase in arrest rates occurred as the baby boom generation moved through adolescence. The increases in crime from 1960 to 1975, however, can be explained by the increase in the adolescent population. The fact that these changes were not sustained after 1975 diminishes the likelihood that the liberation hypothesis is valid.

Contemporary Psychosocial Theories

Much of the contemporary research on girls' delinquency has been on girl gang members. An examination of factors related to gang membership (Bjerregaard & Smith, 1993) indicated that social disorganization and poverty were not related to gang membership or delinquency for either sex. This finding supports the earlier assertion that sociological theories concerned primarily with socioeconomic status and other societal factors have little empirical support. Peer delinquency was significantly associated with delinquency in both males and females, although this relationship was not large in either sex. Low school expectations was also a significant variable for both sexes, but its relationship with gang membership was much stronger in boys than in girls. Lack of perceived educational opportunity was the only predictor significant for boys but not for girls. Early sexual intercourse was associated with gang membership in both sexes as well, although this relationship was stronger in boys than in girls.

A prospective study of 11,764 Finnish males and females (Rantakallio, Myhrman, & Koiranen, 1995) found that 532 men (8.9%) and 60 women (1.0%) up to the age of 25 had committed at least one officially recorded crime. The sex difference in the incidence of delinquency could not be explained by any demographic, social, educational, or health factors. The predictors of delinquency were very similar for females and males. An IQ of 50–84 was most highly correlated with delinquency, as was poor school performance. Poor school achievement was associated with an increased incidence in delinquency for both males and females. Similarly, Moffitt and Caspi (2001) found the same childhood risk factors to identify persistently antisocial males and females, although fewer females than males were so identified.

Rowe, Vazsonyi, and Flannery (1995) examined sex differences in 18 psychosocial and personality trait variables and their relationship to self-reported delinquency in 407 boys and 425 girls. The variables associated with delinquency were nearly identical for the two sexes. The male and female correlations were very similar in magnitude and did not differ significantly from one another. The variables across both sexes that were significantly related to delinquency were early sexual experience, a lack of affection from both mother and father, poor school achievement, anger problems, impulsivity, deceitfulness, rebelliousness, and peer delinquency.

A meta-analytic review of published and unpublished studies done over 30 years examined female youths on a wide range of delinquency correlates (Simourd & Andrews, 1994). Eight general risk categories were identified after reviewing the 60 studies that qualified to be included in the meta-analysis: low social class; family structure or parental problems (broken home, marital problems); personal distress (anxiety, low self-esteem, apathy); personality variables (lack of empathy or moral reasoning); poor parent–child relations (attachment, supervision); educational difficulties (poor grades, dropout); temperament or misconduct problems (psychopathy, impulsivity, substance use); and antisocial peers or attitudes.

The results indicated that, for females, the most important correlates of delinquency were antisocial peers or attitudes, temperament or conduct problems, educational difficulties, poor parent–child relationships, and personality variables. Personal distress, family structure or parental problems, and low social class did not appear to be strongly related to delinquency. A similar pattern of results was found for male youths; there were no statistical differences in the risk correlates across sex.

These findings suggest that theories postulating different influences on boys and girls leading to delinquency are on weak empirical ground and that a unitary explanation could account for both sexes' delinquency. In 1981, Anne Campbell began her book *Girl Delinquents* with the following passage:

But this conjunction [the feminist movement and the study of female crime] was also unfortunate in its consequences. The rush of enthusiasm galloped straight past even the most fundamental need to define its own subject matter. It sped past the massive body of available data on males, blinkered to the possibility of its relevance to females. Dizzy with monomania, women became obsessed with their total uniqueness— their alienation, their frustration, their powerlessness. (p. 1)

Twenty years later, with evidence from contemporary research, the similarities of the sexes can no longer be ignored. Any theory that is put forth must not only account for the similar correlates of delinquency in boys and girls but also explain the sex differences that exist in patterns of male and female crime. It is clear that the risk factors for delinquency are similar in boys and girls and that for less serious offenses, such as status offenses and petty theft, the participation rate of the sexes is about equal. Differences between the sexes exist only for the more serious crimes, crimes that in general involve violence or physical aggression. When seeking to account for sex differences in more violent crimes, an examination of sex differences in behaviors that are related to delinquency, such as aggressiveness and risk acceptance, may be useful.

As we discuss in chapter 4 of this volume, the most serious and chronic offenders follow a persistent criminal pathway, a pathway beginning in childhood and continuing through their entire lives. Taking a developmental perspective, researchers such as Moffitt (1993a, 1993b), Patterson and his colleagues (Patterson, 1986; Patterson et al., 1989), and Loeber (1990) have clarified some of the early prenatal, neurological, and familial factors that put boys at risk for delinquency. In discussing her lifelong-persistent group, Moffitt (1993a) identifies neuropsychological risk factors within the individual that may occur prenatally or in infancy that predispose a child to have a difficult temperament and certain behavioral problems. These problems interact with parental characteristics to produce a series of interactions likely to result in antisocial behavior.

Patterson et al. (1989) have identified parental and social factors that are involved in the developmental progression to delinquency. This progression begins with poor parental discipline and monitoring, leading to child conduct problems; these conduct problems in turn lead to rejection by normal peers and academic failure. At this point there is involvement with a deviant peer group and commission of delinquent behaviors. Patterson's theory is based on his work with boys, but there is little reason to assume that this model would not work as well for girls. Combining Moffitt's (1993a) neuropsychological data with Patterson's family interaction model gives us a more complete picture of the risk factors associated with delinquency and how they interact over the life span. These theories combined with other evidence on risk factors, such as the importance of delinquent peers in adolescence (Rowe et al., 1995; Simourd & Andrews, 1994) and early puberty in females in mixed school settings (Caspi, Lynam, Moffitt, & Silva, 1993), appear to offer sound explanations to account for both male and female delinquency.

The use of Moffitt's (1993a) neuropsychological perspective and its relationship to conduct disorder also provides an insight into a possible explanation of the sex ratio difference in serious crimes favoring males. Moffitt and Caspi (2001) report that life-course persistence is extremely rare in females (the sex ratio is approximately 10 males to 1 female). The majority of females who engage in antisocial behavior do so in adolescence. One of the distinguishing features of the lifelong persistent pathway is conduct disorder in childhood. Conduct disorder is much more prevalent in boys (6–16%) than in girls (2–9%; Zoccolillo, 1993). Given this, and the relationship between conduct disorder and delinquency, it is possible that there are fewer girls than boys involved in serious delinquency because there are fewer girls with conduct disorder and therefore less of a predisposition to a life of serious crime.

What is needed is an explanation for the sex differences in the prevalence of conduct disorders. Gualtieri and Hicks (1985) noted that males are selectively afflicted with neurodevelopmental and psychiatric disorders of childhood, including conduct disorder. As we discuss in chapter 3 of this volume, they suggested that there might be something about the male fetus that evokes an inhospitable uterine environment (e.g., maternal immunoreactivity), leading to fetal brain damage and associated behavioral problems. As we discuss in chapter 4 of this volume, however, a pathological explanation of conduct disorder and life-course persistence does not apply to all persistent men. If the adaptive life-course-persistent path is relevant for men only, then we would expect conduct disorder and other childhood precursors to be less prevalent in females.

These considerations are premised on the fact that conduct disorder is seen less frequently in females than in males, a fact that has recently been questioned by Zoccolillo (1993), who believes that the sex difference reflects diagnostic bias. Moffitt et al. (2001) tested Zoccolillo's theory by comparing the outcomes of females with subclinical conduct problems (three or four symptoms) with those of males with diagnosed conduct disorder (five or more symptoms). They found that for 23 out of 35 measures related to conduct disorder, the diagnosed boys were significantly worse than the subclinical girls. Where the outcomes were similar, they mainly concerned problems differentially associated with women, such as teenage pregnancy, early cohabitation, problems in partner relationships, anxiety, suicide, and depression. They also tested the reverse hypothesis by comparing the outcomes for subclinical males and diagnosed conduct disorder females. They found that on 21 measures the diagnosed girls were significantly worse off. The outcomes where they were similar were those typically associated with men, such as problems in work, disability from work, substance use, and self-reported violence. Thus, adjustment was negatively associated with number of conduct symptoms for both sexes. These data indicate that if the criteria were to be relaxed for females, they should be for males as well. Furthermore, there is no special predictive utility for subclinical problems for either sex, and those with diagnosed conduct disorder usually have poorer outcomes.

The idea that the expression of conduct disorder may take different forms has also been noted in the literature on sex differences in aggression. There are sex differences in aggressiveness, in that boys demonstrate greater physical aggression than girls (Rutter & Giller, 1984). However, as we discuss earlier in this chapter, recent studies indicate that girls are more likely to engage in indirect aggression (Lagerspetz et al., 1988). This research suggests that females and males may not differ in the frequency of aggression but rather in the type of aggression that they use. This finding may also be true of conduct disorder. If this is the case, the question then becomes why: Why is it that females and males express their aggression in different ways?

The feminist movement focused attention on the idea of socialization differences. Hoffman-Bustamente (1973) suggested that the lower rate of female crime should be viewed within a socialization framework. From an evolutionary perspective, however, the use of socialization as the cause of differences in male–female aggression and thus serious violent crime is inadequate because it does not explain why we socialize girls and boys differently. What are the ultimate causes of sex differences in aggression?

ULTIMATE CAUSES OF SEX DIFFERENCES IN AGGRESSION AND JUVENILE DELINQUENCY

At the beginning of this chapter, we describe some of the findings that a theory of sex differences in aggression needs to explain. The association between youth and heightened crime rate holds constant regardless of historical period, country, race, type of crime, and sex (Hirschi & Gottfredson, 1983). While males far exceed females in the amount of serious crime they commit, females show a similar rise during their teen years. With respect to aggression, many similarities exist between the sexes during childhood, but although the frequencies differ, the trend is the same in both sexes: Aggression falls consistently from age 4. While researchers such as Daly and Wilson (1982, 1983, 1988) have compiled a significant body of research supporting an evolutionary perspective of male aggression, there is a paucity of theory or research on understanding female aggression from an evolutionary perspective.

Recently, however, A. Campbell (1999) suggested that the lower rates of aggression by females compared to males indicate a female adaptation. She notes that personal survival was particularly critical to reproductive success; the infant's survival is closely linked to the mother's survival. Among the Ache of Paraguay, for example, maternal death increases age-specific child mortality by a factor of 5, whereas paternal death is related to a threefold increase (K. Hill & Hurtado, 1996). If the mother died during the infant's first year of life, infant mortality was 100%. It makes evolutionary sense for females to be more risk averse than males.

Males engage in more severe forms of aggression than females. Males' higher rate of involvement in violent aggressive behavior reflects their greater fitness variance and their consequent willingness to engage in risky tactics. Women have lower fitness variance and a lower ceiling of reproductive output. Consequently, even though women compete, and may even kill one another, they generally have little to gain (given their lower fitness variance) and more to lose (i.e., their own survival) by engaging in dangerous tactics. That is, the cost/benefit ratio of direct physical aggression is higher for females than males with respect to reproductive success.

Early accounts of mate choice depicted women's sexual strategy as passive—women used their physical qualities to attract mates, whereas men competed with each other for mates. However, as A. Campbell (1995) has noted, this view does not account for the adolescent peak in female aggression. It is quite likely that this peak reflects intrasexual competition among adolescent females, albeit in a less severe form than that among males. Given that females' fitness variance is relatively low, and that they are sure of their maternity, it may not be worthwhile for females to risk their life and future offspring for the remaining half of the genes they need. Burbank (1987) found that, although physical attacks are more often directed against other women (intrasexual competition), when females do fight with each other, they seldom use weapons and the damage inflicted is usually slight.

The peak in delinquent behavior coincides with the development of sexual maturity and the developmental task of mate selection (A. Campbell, 1999). There are few data on physical aggression in adolescent girls, but those that exist indicate that many of the fights in which girls engage concern sexual reputation, competition over access to desirable partners, and jealousy. A. Campbell (1981) found that among juvenile delinquent females, 89% had been involved in at least one fight and 25% had been involved in more than six. Of these fights, 73 percent were against another girl but only 10% involved weapons. Almost half of the fights were over personal integrity issues such as accusations of promiscuity and gossiping. Thus, in keeping with an evolutionary perspective, females behave in a manner that would have increased reproductive success in an ancestral environment. Males compete for dominance and status, whereas females compete in order to secure highly resourced and devoted mates.

Symons (1979) argued that intramale competition is advantageous to females, that the winner of this competition is the female's best choice. But A. Campbell (1995) argued that because females all desire the same qualities in males (their investment and their genes) and males prefer partner novelty, it is unlikely that a passive strategy will optimize mate selection. Because male commitment is a limited resource, suboptimal mate choice has fitness consequences for females. In species that have low male paternal investment, females do not need to compete with each other for men. If all women wanted the one genetically optimal male, they could all have him. He is likely more than willing to comply. However, in species with high male paternal investment, such as our own, the ideal course of action for females is to monopolize the best mate and his resources, making female competition for males inevitable (R. Wright, 1994).

Thus, there may be situations that require females to engage in risky strategies in order to secure a male partner, such as a high ratio of females compared to males or a low proportion of men with resources. In cases where there is a high mortality rate for male youth, such as in war-torn countries, aggression among females may be high because males can be more selective when females outnumber them. Similarly, if resource-rich males are scarce, females may be willing to engage in risky behavior in order to obtain mateships with them. Gang girls represent one segment of the population in which more aggressive behavior in females is common. Based on interviews with female gang members, M. G. Harris (1994) illustrated that girls participate in violence and drug use in contemporary gangs. Taylor (1993) interviewed many gang girls concerning their impressions of female gang life. From their accounts, females are involved in all aspects of gang life including drugs, violence, carrying weapons, and competition for males:

> Girls fight, shoot and do things the same as boys. . . . [V]iolence is a part of what's out here, it's just life. (p. 107)

> It's simple, girls is gangsters just like fellas. . . . [W]e can do anything the fellas can do, and anybody that think we can't is ignorant and dumb. (p. 119)

> It's hard to get a good man and girls grab any fella that treat you special. . . . [W]e ain't got nothing but girls, girls, girls, girls and the guys got their pick. We just start fighting each other over the same guys. (p. 130)

There also may be individual differences with regard to aggression in females. Although female fitness variance is lower than that of males, aggregate data may obscure individual differences in fecundity among women. Females who believe they are less attractive to males may be more willing than other females to engage in risky tactics. For example, shoplifting is consistently the most common property offense committed by girls (e.g., Chesney-Lind & Shelden, 1992; A. Campbell, 1981). Usually the items stolen are worth less than $50 and are for personal use; examples are cosmetics and clothes. From an evolutionary perspective, it may be that girls who shoplift are at a competitive disadvantage and are acquiring items that they think are necessary to compete for mates.

Females are less aggressive than males because they are the reproductive resource for which men compete and because they show less variability in fitness than men. However, because male parental investment is an important limiting factor on female reproductive success, women at a competitive disadvantage may risk displaying aggressive competitive behavior in order to obtain it.

As summarized in Exhibit 5.1, research on nonhuman female primates similarly indicates that they adopt aggressive strategies that carry lower risk than those adopted by males.

EXHIBIT 5.1
Female Aggression in Nonhuman Primates

Most monogamous groups of primates are territorial and have only one breeding female. In these species, females participate in intergroup conflicts because production and rearing of offspring appears to depend on excluding competitors from the territory's resources. Aggression is mostly directed toward animals of their own sex, perhaps due to potential mate competition. In the monogamous tamarins and marmosets, fights between opposite-sex animals are rarely observed. When fights do occur they are between same-sex animals, with the resident female or male driving away an intruder. Fights including males often take on overt forms, whereas female conflicts may be more subtle. High-ranking females may interfere with other females getting access to alpha males, but rarely does the interference result in physical aggression. Even though female–female fights are more frequent, serious injury occurs infrequently, unlike the outcomes of conflicts between males (Hrdy, 1981).

In species where the females emigrate, such as howler monkeys and hamadryas baboons, a female's long-term survival and reproduction depend on her achieving a position within the new group—in this case the females are aggressive because aggressive females rise in the hierarchy and are more reproductively successful. Similarly, when a female common chimpanzee transfers into a new group, the resident females are highly competitive with her. Interactions among females are generally characterized as antagonistic (Parish, 1994).

Bonobo or pygmy chimpanzees live in large multifemale, multimale communities; and, as in common chimpanzees, female bonobos disperse from natal communities (Parish, 1996). Although not related to each other, the females of this species form bonds with the other immigrant females. It appears that strong female–female bonds thwart sexual coercion by males. Bonobo females appear to establish strong affiliative bonds with each other despite being unrelated. Moreover, they control access to highly desirable food and share it with each other more so than males. Food control may translate into the ultimate payoff of enhanced reproductive success. In captivity, earlier reproduction is seen in this species as compared to common chimpanzees—bonobo females begin their reproductive careers 1.5 to 4 years earlier.

In species characterized by male dispersal, such as rhesus macaques, female hostility toward other groups is common. Female bonded groups defend "their" territory. However, aggression is not usually directed toward neighboring males. Several factors influence rates of female aggression in these species: The most intense aggression is displayed when defending territory or dependable resource; female–female aggression frequently concerns defense of territorial boundaries or food resources, while female aggression against males more often involves resistance to migrants (Smuts, Cheney, Seyfarth, & Struhsaker, 1987). However, these intergroup encounters rarely escalate into physical attacks.

COMMENTS

Empirical progress has been made that can inform proximal theories of female juvenile delinquency. We know much more now than in 1984, when Rutter and Giller expressed their concern that so little was known about antisocial behavior in females. With respect to aggression, it is now clear that girls do engage in aggressive behavior but that they more frequently engage in low-risk strategies, such as indirect aggression (where the aggressor can often remain unidentified), than do boys. However, researchers still need measures sensitive to the types and domains of aggression and more gender-specific indicators across the developmental phases through to adulthood so that they can assess the manifestations and consequences of aggression in girls more accurately than they have to date.

The correlates of juvenile delinquency are similar in males and females. What remains unknown, however, is the extent to which the outcomes of early externalizing problems are the same for both sexes. The developmental trajectories of aggressive girls may involve processes similar to those of boys but may result in different outcomes. For example, girls' trajectories to delinquency indicate that there is strong comorbidity with depression and suicidal ideation, as well as physical and sexual victimization (Moffitt et al., 2001). The developmental trajectories of aggressive girls exemplify the joint processes of cumulative and interactional continuity: They are maintained by individual characteristics of the girls themselves and by their interactions within the family, school, peer, and marital systems. There is emerging evidence that the risks experienced by aggressive girls may be transferred to the next generation through their ineffective parenting practices as well as their genes.

The available data on aggression in humans and the comparative data from primates suggest that sex differences in level and type of aggression are related to differences in sex-typical mating strategies. In terms of ultimate causation, males are on average more aggressive than females because their fitness variance is greater, making risky behavior a more viable option. However, females are also aggressive when the benefits of aggression outweigh its costs. An example of such situations is when resources or good men are scarce. Female aggression, however, tends to be more subtle or indirect, in keeping with the aversion to risk associated with lower fitness variance and the demands of motherhood. Nevertheless, the ultimate roots of indirect aggression likely lie in the differential reproductive success of ancestral females who adopted strategies that diminished the fitness of rival females while elevating their own through the acquisition of desirable mateships, as well as social and material resources.

The juxtaposition of the growing applied literature on female delinquency with recent attempts to discern its ultimate cause throws our theoretical ignorance into sharp relief. It is much less clear in the case of females how much or what kinds of antisocial behavior are the result of pathology and how much or what kind is the expectable result of environmentally sensitive variations in reproductive and social strategies. Similarly, it is unclear whether the three-group taxonomy we propose in chapter 4 of this volume validly applies to females. There is no doubt that female delinquents can be divided into an adolescence-limited group and a life-course-persistent group (e.g., Mazerolle, Brame, & Paternoster, 2000; Moffitt & Caspi, 2001), but is not clear whether the latter group contains, like males, a subgroup of female delinquents who are engaged in an adaptive life-history strategy. Our consideration of fitness variance and risk aversion strongly suggests that such a strategy is unlikely to have evolved in females. However, it is quite possible that this male-oriented strategy may occur in females as a result of partial masculinization of the brain and/or a strong dose of the genes associated with taxon membership. Studies of signs of early developmental perturbations among life-course-persistent females along with taxonomic studies will provide answers to this important question.

6

PREVENTION AND INTERVENTION

Efforts to prevent juvenile delinquency are of most interest when informed by our understanding of its proximate causes and evaluations of these efforts can provide tests of causal theories. If an intervention has been successful in changing a hypothesized cause of delinquency, a resulting reduction in juvenile offenses supports its causal status.

In this book we argue, as others have argued (e.g., Rowe, 1994), that the proximal causes of delinquency can be found in both an individual's genetic history and his or her developmental history. This view raises issues concerning the malleability of antisocial behaviors. For example, it is often believed that antisocial behaviors are resistant to modification to the extent that they are heritable or inherited. There are, however, three reasons why this commonly held view does not bear close examination. First, because the heritability of a trait is estimated in a particular environment for a particular group, a change in that environment can alter the heritability of the trait. The development of a new intervention, such as a cure for some condition, changes the effect of heritable variations in the propensity to develop the condition.

Second, genes exert their effects during development through long causal chains resulting in particular traits. Once these causal chains are identified, interventions to modify a trait are possible at any link in the chain. One can imagine a variety of interventions that could accomplish the same result: prescribing drugs to remedy chemical deficiencies associated with the expression of a particular gene, suppressing the expression of particular genes, providing particular experiences that modify a genetically controlled developmental sequence, and so forth. Similarly, our brains are constructed so as to be modifiable by experience. But experiences exert their effect through the modification of neural structures, and it is these that are the contemporaneous causes of behavior, not the experiences themselves. Thus, it is theoretically possible to modify the effects of learning not only through providing certain experiences but also by altering their neural effects. Third, and most important, an empirical demonstration of the efficacy of a particular intervention trumps any claim about the immutability of a behavior it targets.

Developing theories of juvenile delinquency offer the promise of developing interventions on the basis of a causal analysis instead of a mindless focus on altering empirically identified risk factors. However, it must be acknowledged that the promise of this approach is as yet unfulfilled. We hope that this book will encourage such efforts. Raine and Dunkin (1990) provided an early example in which they attempted to identify the implications that psychophysiological laboratory studies have for counseling and therapy. In particular, they recommended that programs for antisocial individuals should focus on rewards rather than punishments (antisocial individuals are less affected by the latter than by the former) and on occupations that capitalize on the strengths of antisocial individuals. Such occupations include tasks involving manipulospatial ability (because of antisocial individuals' enhanced parietal lobe functioning) and sales tasks (to take advantage of their glibness and superficial charm—caveat emptor).

At the most general level, the integrated theory we present in chapter 4 suggests that interventions would be effective to the degree that they place particular emphasis on enhancing maternal health, increasing the proximal benefits of parental investment and decreasing those of mating effort; reduce apparent competitive disadvantage by decreasing inequality in access to resources; reduce family adversity and increase conflict resolution skills; and foster prosocial peer influence. Interventions to reduce serious or violent antisocial behavior should differentially target young males. Special efforts to identify and treat members of the persistently antisocial class of males and females early in development are particularly likely to produce good results. This chapter reviews the prevention and treatment outcome literature and interprets its findings in terms of our integrated theory.

PREVENTION

Developmental prevention science is best represented by three major complementary and sequentially organized strategies: the identification of risk factors, the development of screening procedures to identify children at risk, and the implementation of preventive intervention for changing risk factors and reducing children's probability of engaging in antisocial behavior (Loeber & Dishion, 1987).

These strategies have different implications depending on the level of prevention chosen. Following Caplan (1964) and Mrazek and Haggerty (1994), the three levels of prevention in the field of juvenile delinquency can be conceptualized as (a) primary or universal prevention, which attempts to prevent all children in a geographical setting, without any further selection criteria, from being at risk (e.g., prevention of child abuse and neglect); (b) secondary or targeted selective prevention, which attempts to prevent antisocial behaviors in those at risk (e.g., children who are aggressive at a young age); and (c) tertiary or indicated prevention, which attempts to prevent further antisocial behaviors by known delinquents. The first two approaches identify children who have not been referred for treatment or adjudicated by the criminal justice system.

Offord, Chimura-Kraemer, Kazdin, Jensen, and Harrington (1998) recently published a critique of the advantages and disadvantages of universal and targeted preventive strategies. There is general agreement in the literature that universal primary prevention could be the most effective approach for reducing antisocial behaviors in the future (Leitenberg, 1987). At present, however, there are difficulties in implementing primary prevention programs. These difficulties include a lack of consensus on the optimum screening methods used to identify who is at risk and lack of knowledge concerning the long-term effects of interventions (reducing the influence of risk factors).

There is also a lack of resources. Despite accumulating evidence to support the high cost of delinquency in our society, it is challenging to convince the public and politicians that a universal approach is required. Primary prevention may have a greater impact and be more palatable to society as a whole when implemented in a more global context of prevention, that is, when aimed at general health promotion. The results of two large-scale efforts currently under way—the Fast Track Program of the Conduct Problems Prevention Research Group and the Chicago Metropolitan Area Child Study of the Metropolitan Areas Research Group—may improve the prospects of primary prevention efforts (Lorion, Tolan, & Whaler, 1987).

At present, secondary (selective targeted) prevention is more likely than primary prevention to have a greater impact on juvenile delinquency. Secondary preventive interventions target individuals by measuring risk factors that are specifically related to delinquency in order to identify a select group of individuals: the most persistent future delinquents. Offord et al. (1998) have pointed out that broad and accessible criteria for inclusion, such as poverty or rate of unemployment in the community, can be used to determine the level of risk within a population. These relatively inexpensive indicators could be combined with more expensive measures to improve specificity. The discovery of a discrete class of persistently antisocial individuals lends strong theoretical support to this approach, particularly inasmuch as offenders in the antisociality taxon have been shown to respond very differently to interventions designed to reduce recidivism than offenders who are not taxon members (e.g., M. E. Rice et al., 1992).

The most commonly used type of prevention, tertiary prevention, has major limitations. First, it can focus only on the very small group of individuals who have been caught by authorities, thereby leaving out a much larger group of juveniles who engage in an important number of antisocial behaviors. Second, currently available preventive interventions are less likely to succeed when targeting individuals who have been involved in delinquency for a long time and who have had many opportunities to develop and consolidate sophisticated patterns of antisocial behavior. In other words, intervention is more likely to succeed when implemented early in the development of problem behaviors. Ideally, preventive interventions would target individuals who are usually targeted at the tertiary stage, but it would do so before they get to that stage. Note that this statement does not contradict the risk principle of effective interventions, that interventions are more likely to be effective when applied to high-risk individuals (Andrews et al., 1990a).

Offord et al. (1998) pointed out that a criticism of tertiary prevention is the labeling or stigmatization of individuals who are identified as high-risk, although there is limited empirical evidence to support the deleterious effects of such identification. In addition, Offord et al. noted that a potential disadvantage of targeted prevention approaches is that they ignore macrosocial variables that may contribute to delinquency. In our view, the magnitude of this disadvantage is likely to be small. As we have seen, macrosocial variables, such as socioeconomic status, are not good predictors at the individual level and their effects may reflect selection rather than causation. Moreover, relative socioeconomic disadvantage at the individual level appears to be more important than the absolute aggregate level. None of this is meant to argue that socioeconomic inequities are unimportant, or that societies have no ethical obligation to reduce them, only that the effects on the level of crime from these sorts of interventions in themselves is likely to be small. Social justice does not need crime reduction as a rationale.

The best approaches can only be identified empirically, using an approach like Program Development Evaluation (Gottfredson, 1984), in which outcome research is combined with theory testing. The basic ideas in Program Development Evaluation are to formulate program elements in terms of a proximal theory of the phenomenon to be changed, develop measurements of program elements as instantiations of the theory, monitor implementation, and measure program outcomes. The outcomes are then used to evaluate both the program and the underlying theory in a cyclical iterative process. From what we know, this approach is likely to involve a combination of universal and targeted strategies. Targeted strategies can be aided by a number of standardized assessment instruments, such as the Youth Level of Service/Case Management Inventory–Revised (Hoge & Andrews, 2001). These instruments are designed to measure specific criminogenic needs, because the Program Development Evaluation approach involves determining the degree to which program elements change these needs and relating these changes to outcome. If, for example, a program was successful in changing particular criminogenic needs but these changes were unrelated to outcome, the program would be judged unsuccessful and the theory on which it was based contradicted.

Identification of Risk Factors

In this section we revisit the large literature on risk factors, already discussed in chapter 3 of this volume, but in a more applied context. Where the literature permits, our concern is with identifying particular individuals who become persistently antisocial, rather than with predicting crime frequency. Study findings are likely to vary according to the type of prediction on which they focus (general delinquency, recidivism, etc.), and according to how antisocial behaviors are defined and indexed (self-report, arrest, conviction, etc.). These variations need to be taken into account when comparing studies of prediction. Despite these causes of variations in study outcomes, some consistent findings have emerged. In particular, age of onset is a consistently good predictor (Tolan, Perry, & Jones, 1987; Tolan & Lorion, 1988).

In the Cambridge Study of Delinquent Development, Farrington, Gallagher, Morley, St. Ledger, and West (1988) found that the five best nonbehavioral predictors of delinquency for boys between the ages of 8 and 10 were low family income, large family size (greater than five children), parents with criminal conviction records, low intelligence, and poor quality of parental child-rearing behavior. The best behavioral predictors were the combined teacher and peer ratings of troublesomeness, peer ratings of dishonesty, and parent/teacher ratings of daring.

Loeber and his colleagues (Loeber, 1982, 1990; Loeber & Dishion, 1983; Loeber & Stouthamer-Loeber, 1987) found that the best predictors of official male delinquency, in descending order of importance as defined by the mean relative improvement over chance (RIOC) statistic, were drug use (.53); composite measures of parental family management techniques (.50); child problem behavior and aggressiveness (.32); stealing, lying, and truancy (.26); criminality or antisocial behavior of family members (.23); poor educational achievement (.23); single measures of parental family management techniques (.23); separation from parents (.20); and socioeconomic status (.18).

The best predictors of official recidivism were stealing, lying, and truancy (.46); child problem behavior (.38); criminality or antisocial behavior of family members (.37); prior delinquency (.36); and socioeconomic status (.14). The absence of family management variables as a predictor of recidivism is likely due to a lack of research as opposed to a lack of predictive power.

In a review of the longitudinal research on predictors of violence in adolescence, Lipsey and Derzon (1998) identified the strongest predictors from both the ages 6–11 and the ages 12–14. For the younger group, the best predictors were committing general offenses and substance use. The second group of predictors for the younger group were male sex, family socioeconomic status, and antisocial parents. The strongest predictors for the older group were lack of social ties, antisocial peers, and having committed an offense.

Hawkins et al. (1998) examined a wide variety of risk and protective factors related to violence. Individual predictors of violence included pregnancy and delivery complications, hyperactivity, concentration problems, restlessness, risk taking, aggressiveness, early initiation of violent behavior, involvement in other forms of antisocial behavior, and attitudes favorable to antisocial behavior. Family predictors of violence were a parent with a criminal record, harsh discipline, physical abuse or neglect, poor family management practices, low levels of parental involvement, high levels of family conflict, and parental attitudes favorable to violence. School factors included academic failure, truancy, and frequent school transitions. Social relationship predictors included delinquent siblings, delinquent peers, and gang membership. Predictive accuracy of these variables increased with age. Finally, the community predictors were poverty, disorganization, availability of drugs, exposure to violence, and racial prejudice.

The probability of violent offending increases with the number of risk factors. Based on a vulnerability index created by Farrington (1997) involving low family income at age 8, large family size (four or more biological siblings up to the 10th birthday), low nonverbal IQ, and poor parental child rearing (harsh and inconsistent parenting and parental conflict), Hawkins et al. (1998) examined the relationship between vulnerability and serious offending. They found that 3% of individuals with none of these risk factors were convicted for violent crime, whereas 31% with four or five risk factors were convicted. The conclusion of this review was that violent behavior is a function of complex interactions of context, individual factors, and situational factors. If these risk factors were independent of each other and causal, interventions to reduce violent offending would need to be multifaceted.

There are therefore two major categories of risk factors identified in retrospective and longitudinal studies: family factors and child behaviors (Hawkins & Catalano, 1990). Although the delinquency risk factors show impressive consistency, there have been few demonstrations of their causal status. Moreover, although many family and child variables are considered dynamic variables suitable for treatments designed to reduce delinquency, the possibility that they are proxies for static causal variables can be ruled out only by treatment outcome studies. Recent research has developed scales that combine static risk, dynamic risk, and need factors for use in such studies (Hoge, 2002).

Indicators of Chronic Offending

Wolfgang et al. (1972) reported that 5% of the delinquent males of their sample were responsible for about 40% to 50% of all crimes. After examining the proportion of the group identified by Wolfgang et al. as chronic offenders, Weitekamp, Kerner, Schindler, and Schubert (1995) noted that, although a small proportion of the sample committed the majority of crimes, most of the serious and violent offenders were a small subset of the repeat offending population. The important question is: Can this specific group be distinguished ahead of time from those who do not persist in delinquent behaviors? Moffitt's (1993b) developmental taxonomy suggested that persistent offenders can be identified early in childhood. Loeber's (1982, 1990) reviews suggested that persistent offenders have a different pattern of offending than nonpersistent offenders. Using data from studies based on official data, Loeber (1990) proposed that those who are more likely to persist have a higher frequency of antisocial behaviors at a given point, a greater propensity to exhibit antisocial behaviors in multiple settings, a greater variety of antisocial behaviors, and an earlier onset.

Elliott, Dunford, and Huizinga (1987) surveyed, under the National Youth Survey, 1,494 youths ages 11 to 17 for 5 years, starting in 1977. The sample was representative of the population of teenagers in the United States. They categorized the youths into four groups according to the frequency and seriousness of self-reported delinquent acts: nonoffenders (0–3 self-reported delinquent acts, no index offenses); exploratory offenders (4–11 delinquent acts, 0–1 index offenses); nonserious career offenders (12 or more delinquent acts, 0–2 index offenses); and serious career offenders (3 or more index offenses).

Of the participants, 13% were classified over the 5-year period as nonserious career offenders and 6% were classified as serious career offenders, for a total of 19% career offenders. In the first year of classification, 1977, there was a linear relationship between group membership and various indicators, such as attitudes toward crime, perceived sanctions against crime, perceived negative labeling by others, and exposure to delinquent friends. The same relationship was found for sex (male), age (older), and urbanization (urban higher than rural) but not for race or social class. Career offenders also had a higher number of self-reported nonserious and serious crimes, greatly exceeding the number needed for classification in the last two categories. Ten percent of offenders in the 1977 sample accounted for 57% of all self-reported offenses, 50% of all reported index offenses, and 36% of all serious offenses (assault and robbery only). Serious offenders had more nonserious offenses as well. There was also a direct relationship between classification category and number of arrests, but only 24% of the serious career offenders were ever arrested.

The predictors for meeting the career offender criteria over a 4-year period were, in descending order of importance, as follows: sex, peer involvement/exposure to delinquent peers, perceived family sanctions, age, occupational aspirations, and negative labeling by the school. These variables led to a correct classification of 70% and an RIOC of 12%. The predictive accuracy was 90% if all participants were predicted to be noncareer offenders.

When prediction of career offenders from first arrest was investigated, 81% were correctly classified, yielding a RIOC of 62% (in this case the base rate was 22%). Sixteen percent were false positives. Six variables—peer involvement/exposure to delinquent peers, negative labeling by family, school involvement, family strain, seriousness of the offense, and family involvement—increased the accuracy by 40% over the base rate.

Findings that a minority of offenders commit the majority of antisocial behaviors and that only a minority of those engage in violent offenses (Elliot et al., 1987) naturally suggest that selective incapacitation may be an effective means of reducing crime. However, it is unlikely that this type of prevention will appreciably reduce the incidence of antisocial behaviors based on data from the National Youth Survey. Only 14% of juveniles who have committed three or more index crimes 2 years in a row were arrested (Elliot et al., 1987). In addition, this type of prevention, unless serious offenders were to be permanently incarcerated, does not prevent the transition to adult criminality.

However, identification, prediction, and intervention focusing on the most dangerous offenders (i.e., the most repetitive and violent) are likely to be critical if we are to reduce delinquent behaviors. Secondary preventive efforts (other than incapacitation) for these future dangerous youth have many advantages: (a) the focus of scarce resources on individuals who are most likely to benefit from them; (b) the increased probability of observing intervention success, especially on the incidence of delinquent behavior; and (c) a favorable public response to intervention efforts.

The identification of the most serious future offenders is technically difficult because of their rarity. The smaller the proportion of serious future offenders, the greater the proportion of false positives, those individuals falsely identified as potentially violent. A balance must be struck between the number of youths who will receive a comprehensive preventive intervention without needing it (false positives), and the number of true positives who may be positively affected by the intervention. The balance is determined by the intrusiveness and cost of the intervention. The ideal outcome, of course, would be a successful intervention aimed only at those who need it. We are still far from this ideal, but the application of existing predictive technology could bring us closer. The remainder of this section discusses issues related to the technology involved in the identification of risk factors and the development of screening methods. But first we say a few more things about false positives.

Protective Factors

In all studies of prediction of juvenile delinquency there are a substantial number of false positives, that is, some youths at risk do not become delinquents. To what extent are these false positives a necessary consequence of measurement error and fallible predictors and to what extent are these youths actually different from other vulnerable youths who do become delinquent? A program of research, originating in the field of child psychopathology, has investigated factors related to resiliency among vulnerable children (Anthony & Cohler, 1987).

Protective factors generally "refer to influences that modify, ameliorate, or alter a person's response to some environmental hazard that predisposes to a maladaptive outcome" (Rutter, 1985, p. 600). Rutter points out that (a) protective factors do not necessarily mean positive experiences (e.g., the animal literature indicates that acute stress in early life sometimes prepares the animal to better cope with later stress); (b) protective factors are detectable only for high-risk individuals; and (c) protective factors can be nonenvironmental and part of the biological makeup of the individual.

Protective factors should not be considered to be merely flip sides of risk factors. Protective factors operate only under conditions of risk. That is to say, protective factors operate to prevent delinquency under high-risk conditions or among high-risk individuals. Because both biological and environmental factors have been identified as potential protective factors, it is not always clear what factors protect against vulnerability and what factors create vulnerability. This is a conceptual, as well as an empirical, problem. For example, if biological father criminality is a risk factor for future general criminality (Mednick et al., 1983), and if intelligence modifies that risk (Kandel et al., 1988), is intelligence a risk factor or a protective factor? One solution to this problem is to consider higher intelligence to be a protective factor if it reduces the probability of criminality among biological sons of criminal fathers, and lower intelligence to be a risk factor if it increases the probability of criminality in general. That this is not an entirely satisfactory solution is shown by the example of schizophrenia. Schizophrenia is a small risk factor for violent offending in the general population, but it appears to be a protective factor for recidivism among violent offenders simply because of the high risk of the nonschizophrenic offenders (G. T. Harris et al., 1993).

Werner (1987, 1989a, 1989b) reported a prospective study of a multi-racial cohort of 698 children from birth to adulthood. The study was originally aimed at investigating the influence of prenatal and perinatal factors, as well as the caretaking environment, on the development of the children living on the Kauai Island of Hawaii. Approximately 15% of participants had contacts with the police before age 18. Werner identified poverty, exposure to perinatal stress, family distress, and a mother with less than grade 8 education as risk factors. For vulnerable children, factors protecting against the commission of delinquent acts were being the firstborn; being perceived by the mother as active, affectionate, cuddly, good-natured and easy to deal with; and being perceived by psychologists as autonomous and positively socially oriented. Vulnerable adolescents who did not become delinquent had, in comparison to those who did become delinquent, better verbal skills; a more internal locus of control; higher self-esteem; and higher scores on the California Psychological Inventory scales of responsibility, socialization, achievement, and femininity (for both sexes). Finally, the age of the opposite-sex parent (younger mother for males and older father for females), being from a family of four or fewer children, having more than 2 years' spacing to the next sibling, and being surrounded by alternate caretakers within the household were also found to be protective factors. Werner (1987) remarked that "structure and strong social bonds were absent in the lives of most high-risk children who had a delinquent record in adolescence" (p. 30). These findings lend themselves to an interpretation involving the amount and quality of parental investment, suggesting that interventions maximizing parental investment—including income support, education concerning birth control, availability of day care, and parenting education—could have positive effects.

In the Cambridge study, Farrington and colleagues (1988) identified having few or no friends, being shy or withdrawn, having no siblings with behavior problems, having parents with no criminal convictions, and being rated low on daring as protective factors among 63 vulnerable youths. "The most protective factor [for juvenile delinquency] may be the avoidance of contact with other boys in the neighborhood, with siblings, and with fathers, who may exert undesirable influences" (p. 130). Unfortunately, vulnerable boys who were not convicted were also less successful in other aspects of their lives.

There are other protective factors worth further investigation; these include parental monitoring, which decreases association with deviant peers (Patterson & Dishion, 1985); attending preschool, which increases probability of school success and which in turn might decrease the probability of rejection by prosocial peers (Berrueta-Clement, Schweinhart, Barnett,

Epstein, & Weikart, 1984; Berrueta-Clement, Schweinhart, Barnett, & Weikart, 1987); and intelligence, which seems to protect against the involvement in criminal behaviors (White et al., 1989). Protective factors, once identified, may not only increase predictive accuracy, and hence increase correct identification of individuals at risk, but may also suggest targets of intervention.

Screening Methods

The identification of risk and protective factors permits the determination of risk status and potential targets of intervention. However, the individual who receives the preventive intervention must first be identified. One way to pursue prevention is to target all youth at risk of becoming delinquent (e.g., everybody from age 6 to age 17). This approach is very costly unless the intervention is minor, and minor interventions are unlikely to produce useful results (e.g., McCord, 1978), at least with the most serious offenders. It should be remembered, however, that the best preventive intervention will minimize the amount of intervention received by each child and will concurrently maximize efficacy. An example of a successful preventive intervention applied to a whole target population is Olweus's (1992) bullying prevention program in Norwegian schools.

Screening methods are used to target individuals according to the level of risk being considered. One way to make a prediction about a particular youth is to look at the base rate of a reference group that possesses similar characteristics related to a high probability of engaging in antisocial behaviors, such as sex or ratings of aggressiveness. The use of individual predictors separately has many shortcomings: It is not very powerful, and it is difficult to subjectively combine individual predictors because of an absence of information about correlations among and interactions between predictors. A better approach is to use the relevant characteristics of the youth in a combined fashion. Multivariate prediction resolves most of the limitations regarding the use of individual predictors.

One method uses a hierarchical approach to prediction in which predictors are evaluated in a sequential fashion. Loeber and his colleagues (Loeber, Dishion, & Patterson, 1984) recommend a sequential method, the multiple gating technique, for the screening of chronic offenders. This technique attempts to minimize the cost of screening for high-risk individuals (mainly the cost of assessment) while maximizing the power of prediction. First, individuals of a given age range at low to moderate risk are identified using low-cost assessment techniques (e.g., teacher ratings). In the second stage, the subsample is screened using more elaborate assessment techniques (e.g., phone interviews with parents), a smaller subgroup of individuals who present higher risk is identified, and so on. Loeber et al. (1984) reported that the increase of predictive accuracy from 37.6% for the first gate to

74.2% for the third gate and an increase of valid positives from 25% to 56%. There are other validated examples of similar multiple gating strategies, such as the one developed by August, Realmuto, Crosby, and Mac-Donald (1995). Although this approach appears promising and was developed long ago, 15 years after Loeber's demonstration, most prevention programs still implement a single-gate procedure.

LeBlanc (1998) summarized the state of affairs of screening instruments with these observations: (a) Validation studies need to be conducted to delineate the appropriate screening instruments for secondary and tertiary preventions; (b) multistage, multi-informant, multimethod strategy and multivariable domains are needed for secondary prevention screening, whereas tertiary prevention could rely on single-stage screening with multivariables and multi-informant approaches; and (c) with respect to universal prevention, current instruments have methodological difficulties, mostly due to the lack of consensus concerning the best predictors, despite consensus on the domains to be assessed. In summary, despite the considerable number of instruments with strong face validity, the challenge is to demonstrate their accuracy under field conditions. From our perspective, the lack of consensus regarding individual predictors simply reflects their interchangeability, reminding us of the many different methods that can be used to measure the g factor in intelligence testing, an equivalence summarized by the phrase "the indifference of the indicator" (Jensen, 1998). For more on the development of predictive instruments, see Quinsey et al. (1998).

Preventive Intervention Strategies

Leitenberg (1987) remarked, "What is most likely to be done in the name of delinquency prevention is least likely to be effective, and what is most likely to be effective is least likely to be done" (p. 312). He added that what is not likely to work for preventing delinquency is "individual and group counselling, recreation, social casework, street work with gangs, vocational programs that contain no chance of advancement, scared-straight programs, diversion programs [unless carefully implemented], remedial education, Outward Bound wilderness programs, residential programs, tougher law enforcement, community involvement programs . . . and incapacitation of career offenders" (p. 320). This pessimistic conclusion does not mean that these programs cannot achieve other important aims (e.g., higher levels of education). It seems clear, however, that the prevention of delinquency requires addressing targets and problems specifically related to delinquency based on theory and empirical support.

Behavior-oriented and communication-skills-oriented parent training—such as Patterson's parent management training model (Dishion, Patterson, & Kavanagh, 1992; Patterson, 1997) and, in interventions with adolescents, behavioral family-system therapy, such as Alexander's functional family therapy model (J. F. Alexander & Parsons, 1973, 1982)—show promise in interventions with children. More effective interventions seem to be ones that use pragmatic, case-specific, broad-based but problem-focused strategies provided in multiple settings (Gordon & Arbuthnot, 1987; Henggeler, 1989; Kazdin, 1987; Michelson, 1987; Miller & Prinz, 1990; Shore & Massimo, 1979; Tremblay, Pagani-Kurtz, Vitaro, Masse, & Pihl, 1995). From a secondary prevention point of view, interventions are more likely to produce positive outcomes if they are implemented during the preschool and elementary school age period (Loeber & Stouthamer-Loeber, 1987).

Social learning approaches that focus on teaching relevant skills such as child management, communication, social reinforcement, and contingency contracting appear to be the most promising, especially for children referred for minor offenses (Barth, 1990; Kazdin, 1985, 1987). Not much is known about the efficacy of these techniques with more serious youthful offenders; the techniques seem to work better when the child is young. The rationale behind interventions directed at families is supported by empirical studies that have concurrently and predictively related family variables with antisocial behaviors (see Snyder & Patterson, 1987), even after controlling for age at delinquency onset, social class, and other demographic characteristics (Tolan, 1988).

Although family interventions have become the psychological treatment of choice for reducing problem/antisocial behaviors in children and adolescents (Gordon & Arbuthnot, 1988; Gordon, Arbuthnot, Gustafson, & McGreen, 1988; Hazelrigg, Cooper, & Borduin, 1987), there are still unresolved problems with these interventions. One of the major problems is implementation, especially with high-risk families. Indeed, single-parent families, black families, and families of low socioeconomic status show high dropout rates and gain the least from treatment (Dumas & Wahler, 1983; Webster-Stratton, 1985).

The family preservation model (see Whittaker, Kinney, Tracy, & Brooth, 1990) and other similar models appear to provide a method that may overcome implementation and maintenance problems. Briefly, programs using this model, such as Homebuilders, provide services in the home. Providing services in the home has many advantages for assessment, permits greater involvement of the family, and may increase the success of intervention in terms of generalizability and maintenance of changes (Gordon et al., 1988; see Kelly, Embry, & Baer, 1979, for a nice scientific demonstration of treatment efficacy along these lines).

The family preservation model also responds to a variety of presenting problems and needs. Importantly, it is based on a treatment technology as well as empathy and warmth, which makes this model quite different from other models that have been found to be ineffective (e.g., the casework approach). In addition, the intervention is brief and intense. The goals are to stabilize the family during crises and to provide formal and informal resources. Unlike other individualized approaches, the family preservation model attempts to avoid dependency.

An example of this family preservation model of service delivery is multisystemic therapy (MST). MST is a mental health intervention that adopts a social-ecological philosophy toward understanding antisocial behavior. It is a flexible intervention that is tailored to each client. Interventions are designed to target specific and well-defined problems and to decrease these problem behaviors while promoting positive social behaviors. The underlying philosophy of MST is that criminal conduct is multicausal and therefore treatment must address the multiple sources of criminogenic influence. Interventions focus on the youth (values and attitudes, social skills, etc.) and on other sources of criminogenic influence such as the youth's family, school life, peer group, and neighborhood. MST therapists work in the home with families in order to empower parents to be able to parent their children more effectively (Henggeler, Schoenwald, Borduin, Rowland, & Cunningham, 1998).

In follow-up studies of serious juvenile offenders, MST has proven effective in reducing long-term rates of criminal offending and in reducing rates of out-of-home placements. Graduates of MST have documented re-arrest rates 25% to 70% lower than among control youths. MST was found to be equally effective with youth and families of divergent backgrounds—effectiveness was not moderated by demographic characteristics such as race, age, or social class—and with varying strengths and weaknesses (Borduin et al., 1995; Henggeler, 1999; Henggeler, Melton, & Smith, 1992; Henggeler, Melton, Smith, Schoenwald, & Hanley, 1993). Moreover, as discussed in the following paragraphs, MST has been found to be an extremely cost-effective treatment approach. The twin issues of dissemination and treatment fidelity have been discussed in detail by Henggeler, Melton, Brondino, Scherer, and Hanley (1997), and Schoenwald, Henggeler, Brondino, and Rowland (2000).

Prevention Programs

The interested reader can find recent comprehensive reviews of prevention programs in Kazdin (1987, 1993a); Tremblay and Craig (1995); Tremblay, LeMarquand, and Vitaro (1999); Yoshikawa (1994); and Zigler, Taussig, and Black (1992). In this section we briefly present two recent evaluations of primary and secondary prevention programs, as well as a new program, Fast Track.

Hawkins, Von Cleve, and Catalano (1991) recently attempted to break the link between childhood aggressiveness in class and at home and future delinquency and drug use. The program was based on the social development model (Hawkins, Farrington, & Catalano, 1991) and an integration of social control theory and social learning theory. Hawkins, Von Cleve, et al. randomly assigned 285 first-grade children to a 2-year intervention program targeting parent and teacher management skills (see Hawkins & Weis, 1985, for a presentation of their approach to prevention). They also assigned 173 first graders to a control condition (both between and within schools). The two groups did not differ at pretest on 20 self-report items, and the control group was slightly more "prosocial" on 8 other items. At posttest, control boys were rated by teachers as more aggressive on Achenbach's (1991) Child Behavior Checklist (CBCL); control girls were rated as more self-destructive. No other difference was found on other components of the CBCL. Unfortunately, this effect was obtained for white children only. The authors are now investigating the effects of these improvements on future delinquency.

The Perry Preschool Project, begun in 1962, was designed to prevent educational failures and future behavior problems among 3- and 4-year-old high-risk children (IQ between 60 and 88, predominantly from low-income black families). This study was not designed to prevent juvenile delinquency. Fifty-eight children were randomly assigned to a preschool program, and 65 others were randomly assigned to a control condition (no preschool). The impacts of the program on school achievement and delinquency are reported in Schweinhart, Barnes, and Weikart (1993); Schweinhart and Weikart (1983); and Berrueta-Clement et al. (1987). Briefly, 31% of preschool children and 51% of control children were later arrested or charged as juveniles or adults. Other statistically significant differences in favor of the preschool group were found for total number of arrests, seriousness of offenses, and nature of case dispositions as adults. The differences in arrests were primarily for adult arrests (misdemeanors and drug-related arrests). There were no differences in self-reports of general misconduct.

D. J. Johnson and Walker (1987) reported on a home-based program, the Houston Parent–Child Development Center, targeting behavior problems of low-income Mexican American children starting at age 1. A 3- to 6-year follow-up showed that "mothers who had participated in the program, compared with randomly assigned controls, were more affectionate, used more appropriate praise, used less criticism, used less restrictive control, were more encouraging of child verbalization, provided a more stimulating home environment, and held more modern values" (p. 377). A 5- to 8-year follow-up showed that randomly allocated control participants ($N = 88$), compared to program children ($N = 51$), were rated by teachers as more impulsive, obstinate, restless, disruptive, and prone to fight. Program children of both sexes were also rated in comparison to control participants as more considerate and less hostile, and program boys were rated as less dependent.

One of the best examples of the current generation of multimodal prevention programs is the Fast Track Program (Conduct Problems Prevention Research Group, 1992). The goal of this program is to promote the competencies of children at risk for conduct disorder. Children with behavior problems are identified in kindergarten by parents and teachers and are randomly allocated to a control or prevention group in grade 1. The intervention takes 6 years and involves parent training, home visiting, parent–child relationship enhancement, social-cognitive skills development, academic tutoring, emotional regulation training, and interpersonal skills training. The content of this program is described more in depth in Bierman, Greenberg, and the Conduct Problems Prevention Research Group (1996) and McMahon, Slough, and the Conduct Problems Prevention Research Group (1996). There is an extensive ongoing evaluation of this program, and we will have to wait and see if the program is effective in the long term.

The following is a short list of evaluations of primary and secondary prevention programs that are often referred to in the prevention literature: Denno and Clelland (1986); Infant Health and Development Program (1990); Jaffe, Suderman, Reitzel, and Killip (1992); Jones and Offord (1998); Kellam and Van Horn (1997); Klein, Alexander, and Parsons (1977); Kolvin (1981); C. Lewis, Battistich, and Schaps (1990); McCarton et al. (1997); Olds et al. (1997); Peters and Russell (1996); Tolan, Perry, and Jones (1987); Tremblay, Pagani-Kurtz, et al. (1995); and Webster-Stratton (1997).

Tremblay and Craig (1995) summarized the delinquency prevention experiments literature with the following observations:

1. When interventions target more than one risk factor, there are significant differences between treated and untreated groups. Thus, intervention in multiple contexts is likely more effective than intervention in a single context.
2. Successful interventions are implemented long before adolescence.
3. Interventions need to last for a relatively long period of time.
4. Programs need to be implemented with integrity and consistency.
5. And finally, preventive interventions should be evaluated with long-term follow-ups that employ sound experimental designs.

Tremblay et al. (1999) argued that adolescent mothers should be an important focus of prevention efforts, an observation indicating that interventions promoting pregnancy delay among high-risk adolescents are extremely important. Indeed, babies born to adolescent mothers with histories of behavior problems are at a very high risk for many developmental problems (Serbin, Peters, & Schwartzman, 1996). Adolescent mothers with behavioral problems tend to mate with males who also have a long history of behavior problems and tend not to provide adequate care to their developing fetus (Rowe & Farrington, 1997). Thus, improving the quality of care for the adolescent mother, as well as providing parenting support, may be effective in reducing the lifetime risk of delinquency of the offspring (Carter, Kirkpatrick, & Lederhendler, 1997). The effect of the intervention would likely be strongest on the next generation.

INTERVENTIONS FOR YOUNG OFFENDERS

Deterrence Theory

Deterrence theory does not offer an explanation of the development of delinquency, unless an explanation is contained in the assumption that people would commit crimes if there were no costs. Deterrence theory argues that criminal behavior is deterred to the extent that punishment is swift, sure, and aversive. Note that the time scale of swiftness is of a different order of magnitude than that ordinarily employed in conditioning studies. *Specific deterrence* refers to the effect on the behavior of the person punished, and *general deterrence* refers to the effect on people in general.

In the late 1960s and early 1970s, a number of reviews concluded that treatment and rehabilitation efforts failed to reduce the recidivism rates of identified offenders (e.g., Martinson, 1974). At the same time, a number of studies were published that appeared to give strong support to the effectiveness of deterrence (Schneider, 1990). The original research on deterrence was conducted primarily by economists who used an expected utility model. It was not long, however, before these studies were shown to have fatal methodological problems inherent in their use of cross-sectional aggregate data. The fundamental difficulty was that variation in victim reporting, police processing, and/or prosecutorial discretion simultaneously reduces the number of offenses, increases the apparent clearance rate, and increases the apparent incarceration rate. Thus, in two cities with the same true certainty of punishment but with one having half the victim reporting rate, the apparent rate of punishment will be twice as high in the city with half the reporting rate. There will thus be a spurious negative correlation between certainty of punishment and crime frequency (Schneider, 1990).

Schneider (1990) conducted an ambitious study of deterrence using interview and officially recorded data on 876 adjudicated delinquents in six juvenile courts. This number represents 63% of the intended number of offenders at the end of the court's jurisdiction or 1 year of sentence, whichever came first. Official arrest data were gathered 3 years after offender disposition. Offenders were randomly assigned (with less than perfect adherence) to restitution, probation, or incarceration. The sample participants averaged 16 years of age, and 87% of the offenders were male. Sixty-one percent had at least one prior offense. Only 2% had only status or victimless crimes.

Restitution programs usually reduced recidivism and never produced a negative effect or one that was less pronounced than the dispositional alternative against which it was compared (57% of restitution participants recidivated versus 64% for other dispositions). Overall, restitution programs produced an estimated decline of 18 offenses per year for every 100 juveniles (each offense cost an average of $600). This effect was found only with planned and organized restitution efforts, not with ad hoc arrangements. Incarceration had a suppressive effect of about the same size as restitution, but probation had no effect. The quality of implementation of each of the intervention types was important.

The best predictor of intentions to desist from criminal activity was the respondents' image of themselves as good citizens, followed by the degree of remorse for the crime and the perception that the sanction was fair. Victim empathy was unrelated to intentions to desist. Surprisingly from a deterrence perspective, young offenders who believed that they were likely to be caught if they reoffended were more likely to recidivate, as were those who believed that they would be punished severely if arrested. In contrast, a sense of citizenship and remorse were related to lower recidivism rates.

Restitution programs increased the sense of citizenship but had no effect on remorse, whereas incarceration increased remorse but had no effect or reduced the sense of citizenship. Ad hoc restitution programs and probation failed to give youths a sense of success and thus failed to increase a sense of citizenship.

Social Learning Theory

Andrews (1980) found support for a social learning or behavioral formulation of differential association in a series of experimental treatment studies of adolescent and young adult offenders. It will be recalled that differential association theory asserts that criminal behaviors are learned in intimate association with persons who reward procriminal attitudes and behaviors. This theory was tested by measuring the effects of variations in the warmth and interpersonal rewardingness of different social groups and the degree to which their members espoused procriminal sentiments on the recidivism rate and procriminal attitudes of adjudicated offenders.

In the first of five studies, it was found that community volunteers who discussed topics such as rationalizations for law violation, self-control, and the function of rules with prisoners had lower procriminal attitudes than the prisoners but that their attitudes become more procriminal over the course of eight sessions. Prisoners' attitudes became less procriminal over the same period. In the second study, volunteers and prisoners were randomly assigned to discussion or recreation groups. The results of the first study were replicated, but no effects on attitudes were found in the recreation groups.

In the third study, prisoners were randomly assigned to discussion groups with volunteers who had similar pretreatment levels of procriminal sentiment but who had been rated as high or low in interpersonal skill (warmth, openness, and understanding). Greater anticriminal attitude shift was found in groups with high-interpersonal-skill volunteers.

In the fourth study, prisoners were randomly assigned to a community discussion group or a prisoner-only discussion group. Evaluation of the discussions as open, frank and warm were associated with decreasing criminal attitudes in the community group and increasing criminal attitudes in the prisoner-only group.

In the fifth study, 190 probationers were randomly assigned to either a volunteer or a professional officer. The interpersonal skills (empathy scores) of more anticriminal officers and volunteers (high on Gough's, 1969, Socialization Scale) were negatively correlated with recidivism; however, the empathy scores of less anticriminal officers were positively correlated with probationer recidivism. The highest recidivism rate was found among probationers assigned to low-empathy/high-socialization (austere and moralistic) officers. The proportion of offenders who recidivated in each group were: officers high in empathy and socialization (.15); low in empathy and high in socialization (.42); high in empathy and low in socialization (.30); and low in both empathy and socialization (.16).

Because empathy was positively correlated with another measure, identification with criminal others, high-empathy/high-socialization officers were split on criminal identification. The lowest recidivism rate was found among high-empathy/high-socialization/low-criminal-identification officers. Changes in probationer procriminal attitudes paralleled the recidivism findings. A multiple correlation of .48 was found between measures of criminal attitude change and recidivism.

In conclusion, it can be seen that the tests of etiological theories of delinquency are clearest when individual data are used, when longitudinal studies are employed, and when theoretically derived variables can be experimentally manipulated.

The Importance of Evaluating Intervention Efficacy

The quality of the prevention programs presented so far is certainly not representative of the quality of prevention programs in general, especially with regard to the evaluation of the short- and long-term effects. Although there are increasing numbers of sophisticated and rigorous evaluations of innovative programs (e.g., Metropolitan Area Child Study

Research Group, 2002), the frequent lack of systematic evaluation of intervention efficacy is troublesome. Psychologists have an ethical obligation to provide interventions that are effective, as demonstrated by controlled outcome studies (Canadian Psychological Association, 1988). The importance of outcome study cannot be overstated, especially because some programs can have serious deleterious effects.

McCord (1978) reported data from the Cambridge-Somerville Youth Study on 253 male individuals who received, between the ages of 5 and 13, a combination of the following components: vocational counseling; medical or psychiatric attention; a sojourn in summer camps; and referrals to the Boy Scouts, YMCA, and other community programs. Another 253 boys matched for risk (age, delinquency-prone histories, family background, home environment) and randomly assigned to a control group did not receive any intervention. Both groups contained "average" and "difficult" children. All participants were followed for about 30 years (an extension of previous follow-up reports: McCord & McCord, 1959a, 1959b). Official offense records and personal contacts were used to provide outcome data. Ninety-five percent of living participants were relocated (9% had died).

There was no significant difference in juvenile and adult official and unofficial records between the two groups, and no difference between difficult and average participants. Nineteen percent of the treated participants committed a serious crime; the comparable value for the untreated participants was 17%. There was also no significant difference between the number of serious crimes committed or the age when the first crime (serious or not serious) was committed. However, more treated participants than nontreated participants committed more than one crime. No difference was found in the number of men subsequently treated for alcoholism, but more treated participants reported problems with drinking. Treated participants tended to report more stress-related diseases and tended to die younger. More control participants were professionals (43% vs. 29%). Although a majority of treated participants reported satisfaction with the program, no attempt was made to relate level of satisfaction to outcome.

A substantial portion of treated participants reported having developed a strong attachment to their counselors. McCord (1978) speculated that the deleterious outcome of treated participants might be due to a development of harmful dependency on counselors. Whatever the cause of these iatrogenic effects, we can conclude that long-term evaluation of programs is critical in order to ensure the effects of the program are at least not harmful to the individuals.

Dishion, McCord, and Poulin (1999) conducted a review of several controlled intervention studies (including the Cambridge-Somerville Youth Project discussed earlier in this section) examining the hypothesis that peers contribute to escalating problem behavior among adolescents. They concluded that in the case of the Cambridge-Somerville study, the negative 30-year effects were associated with repeated experiences in summer camp. It seemed that aggregating peers with similar problems produced short- and long-term iatrogenic effects on problem behavior. In both of the intervention studies reviewed, the older, more deviant adolescents were the most susceptible to the iatrogenic effects from peer aggregation. They proposed that youth actively reinforce deviant behavior through laughter and social attention and suggest that it may be important to avoid aggregating high-risk youth in intervention groups (Dishion et al., 1997). There is some evidence (e.g., Tremblay, Pagani-Kurtz et al., 1995) that mixing antisocial youth with prosocial youth is an effective strategy to reduce deviancy training by peers. Dishion et al. (1999) speculate that the prosocial youth do not get negatively influenced because they are less likely to respond and thereby reinforce the antisocial behavior of their peers (but see Andrews, 1980). The lesson from this analysis is that it is important to conduct both short- and long-term evaluations of interventions. Good intentions may inadvertently lead to harm. For a recent demonstration of both intended positive and unintended adverse treatment effects in programs designed to reduce aggression among high-risk children, see Metropolitan Area Child Study Group (2002).

Meta-Analytic Evaluations of Interventions for Juvenile Delinquency

The effectiveness of interventions directed toward reducing the recidivism rates of identified juvenile offenders has been the subject of vigorous and often pointless controversy. As in other areas of psychological treatment, the appropriate question is: "What treatment, by whom, is most effective for this individual with that specific problem under which set of circumstances" (G. Paul, 1967, p. 111). Although the literature on treatment efficacy has markedly improved in recent years, most studies fall short of ideal scientific standards (Basta & Davidson, 1988). These standards include random assignment of participants to treatments, demonstrably high levels of program integrity, theoretically relevant measures of client characteristics, multiple measures of process and outcome, and long follow-up periods. Tremblay et al. (1999) noted that only 20 studies in the literature on oppositional defiant disorder (ODD) and conduct disorder (CD) met the criteria of at least a 1-year follow-up, outcome measures related to ODD and CD, and the use of random assignment or quasi-experimental designs.

Because individual studies are not scientifically ideal, narrative reviews of the literature have come to markedly different conclusions about the effectiveness of treatment for juvenile delinquents. Compounding the problem of interreviewer disagreement is the tendency of many reviewers to address the issue of effectiveness in completely general terms, that is, to assume that one can draw general conclusions about treatment effectiveness that apply to offenders with different characteristics, widely different treatments, and varying settings.

Meta-analysis has emerged as an alternative to narrative literature reviews. The difficulty with narrative reviews is that they are not quantitative, although they may provide a box score tally of studies that do or do not find particular effects. Reviewers often disagree in their interpretation of a given literature because they may not assign the same weights to different studies, they often disagree on methodological criteria, and they can only make subjective interpretations of what factors account for variations in outcome over studies.

Meta-analysis is a way of combining data over studies. It can be used to investigate differences among groups of individuals, differences within individual participants over studies, covariation among variables, or test validity. In order to obtain credible and accurate results, considerable attention must be given to the method of dealing with variations in study quality such as the methodological criteria determining study inclusion or quantifying methodological rigor (Bangert-Drowns, Wells-Parker, & Chevillard, 1997). Meta-analyses apply statistical techniques to account for the variation in study outcomes by measuring outcome with a standard measure of effect size as described in Exhibit 6.1.

Effectiveness of Cognitive Behavioral Treatments for Children

Because the empirical evidence shows that juvenile delinquency is often a continuance of early behavioral problems, the literature on the effectiveness of treatments for children with externalizing or conduct disorders is of great importance. Durlak, Fuhrman, and Lampman (1991) have conducted a meta-analysis of the effectiveness of cognitive behavioral treatments for children that addresses this issue and provides an example of a well-done meta-analysis.

Cognitive behavioral treatment (CBT) seeks to teach children cognitive strategies to guide their behavior. Narrative reviewers have concluded that CBT is an effective treatment for children but have noted variation in its effectiveness over studies. It could be that CBT is less effective for children with serious clinical problems, particularly of the externalizing variety. Because CBT contains a variety of techniques, such as self-instructions, problem solving, role playing, imagery, and a variety of reinforcement procedures, the specific combination of techniques might be responsible for variations in treatment effectiveness. Additional factors could be methodological rigor, type of comparison condition, and type of outcome measure. Theoretically, CBT should be differentially successful depending on the children's cognitive stage of development. Children with more advanced cognitive skills ought to benefit more from CBT.

EXHIBIT 6.1
Meta-Analytic Effect Sizes

The discussion of meta-analysis below generally follows Hunter and Schmidt (1990). A concise presentation can be found in Durlak and Lipsey (1991) and an example of the approach in Durlak et al. (1991). The steps in conducting a meta-analysis include specifying the question to be addressed, defining a population of studies, searching for the studies, coding outcome and relevant variables, and computing the standardized outcome measure.

The most common measure of standardized ES is d, $(Mean_t - Mean_c)/SD$. In treatment studies, the SD of the untreated control group's posttreatment scores is sometimes used to eliminate reactivity effects. Where two treatments are employed and in nonintervention studies, the pooled SD is used to reduce sampling error. Pearson rs can also be computed, and d can be converted to r.

In treatment studies of clinical samples, one can also compute the normative effect size (NES), calculated as $(M_{t/c} - M_n)/SD_n$. $M_{t/c}$ is the mean of the treatment or control group and SD_n is the standard deviation of the normative group (Durlak et al., 1991). There is no definitive answer to whether studies should be weighted by sample size. Sample size can be correlated with ES to determine if it is of importance.

If sampling error accounts for 75% or more of the observed variation in ESs, then one concludes that there are no variables moderating the effects of treatment. An alternative approach involves computing Q_t to identify if the ESs from all the studies are homogeneous. Q_t is distributed as chi-square with $K - 1$ df, where K is the number of ESs. If Q_t is significant, then the ESs are heterogeneous and other models incorporating potential moderators should be tested. In these tests, categorical models are evaluated with Q_b, the between class fit statistic. Q_b is distributed as chi-square with $p - 1$ df, where p is the number of categories specified in the model. Q_w is the measure of within class heterogeneity, a chi-square with $K - p$ df. A model is correctly specified when Q_b is large and Q_w nonsignificant.

If there are no moderator variables, then one constructs a 95% confidence interval around the overall mean ES to determine if it includes zero. One can construct confidence intervals for the mean ESs for each level of a categorical variable as well.

The Durlak et al. (1991) study sample included treatments that sought to produce behavioral change by overtly and actively teaching children to change their thoughts. To be included, studies must have used a control group from the same population as the participants treated and employed social and/or behavioral measures. Participants must have met some criterion of maladjustment, been 13 years old or younger, and been the sole and direct recipient of treatment. There were 64 studies, including 15 unpublished dissertations.

Good methodological features were given 1 point each; those coded were sample size of 30 or larger, randomized assignment to groups, low and equal attrition rates, use of at least one normed or blinded behavioral outcome measure, use of attention placebo controls, and repeating the gathering of all pretest data at posttest. Interrater agreement on coding study variables was very good, and disagreements were resolved by discussion. Where effect sizes (ESs) were reported only as nonsignificant (17% of 312 ESs), the ES was set at zero, a very conservative procedure.

The average study had 41 children, most of whom were 9-year-old boys. Sixty-six percent of the studies treated externalizing problems, 17% treated internalizing problems, and the remainder mixed kinds of problems. Thirty-eight percent of the children had clinically significant presenting problems. Most treatment occurred in schools and averaged 10 hours of service. Eight techniques (e.g., social skills, self-instructions) were used in varying combinations. In terms of design rigor, the studies averaged 4.8 on a 6-point scale.

There were eight types of outcome measure (e.g., behavioral ratings, sociometric ratings, normed tests, cognitive–performance measures). Because ES was not significantly related to outcome measure type, effects were pooled within studies to obtain an average ES per study. The unit of analysis was the individual study.

Because Q_t indicated significant heterogeneity of ESs, the data were further examined by assessing age as a moderator variable. There were three levels: preoperational, ages 5 to 7; concrete operations, ages 7 to 11; and formal operations, ages 11 to 13. Heterogeneity of ESs was found across but not within age levels, indicating that age was a moderator of ES. The principal results are shown in the following table:

Level	K	Mean ES	95% Confidence
Preoperational	9	.57	0.27–0.86
Concrete operations	46	.55	0.44–0.66
Formal operations	9	.92	0.61–1.23

Data within 1 standard deviation (SD) of normative data were considered to be within normal limits. Considering only studies of children with clinically significant problems, most measures indicated that treated children but not controls were within the normal range following treatment. Although behavioral ratings, such as the Achenbach (1991) scale, showed that treated children's normative effect size (NES) was reduced 0.58 by treatment, their posttreatment scores were still outside the normal range (NES = 1.38). Although these outcome data were positive, particularly for older children, the expected significant positive correlation between cognitive and behavioral changes across studies was not found.

In summary, the effectiveness of CBT was moderated only by client age. Findings did not vary by methodological rigor, and no evidence of publication bias was found. CBT was as effective for clinical as for nonclinical samples. Effects of treatment were maintained an average of 4 months posttreatment. Durlak et al. (1991) concluded that future research should examine the effectiveness of varying combinations of CBT techniques and alternative techniques for younger children, and should attend to the integrity of interventions more explicitly.

Very similar conclusions were reached by Dush, Hirt, and Schroeder (1989) in a meta-analysis of self-statement modification in the treatment of children with behavioral disorders in the clinical range of severity. Forty-six controlled experimental studies were included. Participants averaged 10 years of age, and the majority were boys. Half of the studies focused on disruptive, aggressive, or delinquent children. The next most common problem was attention-deficit/hyperactivity disorder. The average ES was about 0.5 SD in comparison to data from placebo and untreated participants. Children under 11 were less improved than older children. Larger ESs were found for delinquency as the primary problem treated, female clients, behavioral as opposed to cognitive or self-report measures, recruited rather than referred clients, and doctoral-level service providers. Methodologically stronger studies found larger treatment effects. A nice example of a methodologically strong comparison of relationship therapy and problem-solving skills training is provided by Kazdin, Esveldt-Dawson, French, and Unis (1987).

Effectiveness of Treatment for Young Offenders

A number of reviews of experiments addressing the effectiveness of intervention for juvenile delinquency have been conducted (e.g., Garrett, 1985; Lipsey, 1992; Lipsey & Wilson, 1993; Whitehead & Lab, 1989). Garrett (1985) performed one of the first meta-analyses in this area. She examined studies appearing between 1960 and 1983 on the effect of institutional or community residential treatments for juvenile delinquents. Garrett identified 111 studies involving 13,056 delinquents, who averaged 15.6 years of age. Of these studies, 85 were of males, 16 were of females, and 12 involved both. In terms of methodology, 84 of the studies compared an additional treatment to regular treatment and 27 used a pre–post design. Fifty-two percent of the studies used random assignment, matched assignment, or a pretest group equation. Eighty-one percent of the programs were in institutional settings. In terms of treatment methods, 21% used contingency contracting,

16% group treatment, and 14% CBT. The outcome measures were psychological adjustment, 31%; institutional adjustment, 21%; and recidivism, 18%. An ES was calculated for each type of outcome measure.

The overall average ES was .37, indicating that, following treatment, treated participants performed at the 64th percentile of the control group. The 58 more rigorous designs yielded an average ES of .24, and the 53 less rigorous designs yielded an average ES of .65. The remaining discussion is limited to rigorous studies.

The average ES associated with different outcome measures among the more rigorous studies varied a great deal. Community adjustment was the most sensitive (ES = .72), followed by psychological adjustment (.45), academic improvement (.42), institutional adjustment (.27), recidivism (.10), and vocational adjustment (.06). In terms of broad treatment categories, the average ESs across outcome measures in the more rigorous studies were life skills (.32), behavioral (.30), other (.27), and psychodynamic (.17). The small number of studies per cell identified by using more specific treatment methods preclude meaningful discussion at a more detailed level.

Whitehead and Lab (1989) identified 50 studies involving the treatment of juvenile delinquents that collected recidivism data and used a control group. To be included, studies had to have a codeable description of the treatment used; studies involving only drug or alcohol treatments were excluded. Studies were categorized according to whether they were non-system-diversion programs (ending the youth's involvement with the justice system), system-diversion programs, community corrections (probation or parole), institutional or residential treatment programs, and novel/specialty interventions such as scared straight or Outward Bound programs. Most of the ESs (in this case Φ coefficients) for studies in these categories were small and some were negative. Studies were categorized according to whether they used behavioral or another type of intervention. Behavioral interventions had larger Φ coefficients but were more likely to be negative than other types of intervention. Whitehead and Lab concluded that system diversion was the most promising intervention. Half of the studies had Φ coefficients greater than .20 and all were in the positive direction. The investigators speculated that this finding might result from the right mix of deterrence and reduction of stigma (expected from labeling theory). In view of Schneider's (1990) work, summarized earlier in this section, this explanation is unlikely to be correct.

The meta-analytic techniques used by Garrett (1985) and Whitehead and Lab (1989) are considerably less statistically sophisticated than those employed by Durlak et al. (1991). The techniques used in the former two studies make quantitative conclusions difficult to reach. Izzo and Ross (1990) have briefly reported on a meta-analysis of 46 published studies that met the following criteria: They were published between 1970 and 1985, were experimental or quasi-experimental in design, contained measures of changes in recidivism, and evaluated an intervention for adjudicated delinquents.

Treatment programs formulated on some theoretical basis were not different from each other but were 5 times more effective than treatment programs with no theoretical rationale. A regression analysis indicated that two variables accounted for 19% of the variance. Cognitive programs (containing any of problem solving, negotiation skills training, interpersonal skills training, rational-emotive therapy, role playing and modeling, or cognitive behavior modification) accounted for 6% of the variance in recidivism outcome and were twice as effective as noncognitive programs. The second variable was setting, accounting for 13% of the variance; community programs were more effective than institutional programs.

Although this evaluation supports a cognitive approach to the treatment of delinquents, it is too briefly reported to be interpreted with confidence. A more substantive issue is conceptual; it is puzzling that any theoretical framework is as good as any other but better than none, that the type of theoretical framework was not a variable in the analysis, and that the cognitive label covers such a variety of interventions.

More complete meta-analyses have been reported by Gottshalk and his colleagues. The first of these analyzed data on community-based interventions for delinquents (Gottshalk, Davidson, Gensheimer, & Mayer, 1987). Ninety published and unpublished studies from 1967 to 1983 were included. Studies had to include outcome data from outside the treatment setting and focus on adjudicated delinquents. The meta-analysis used a treatment orientation in which, for example, if two treatments were compared to a control treatment in a given study, two ESs were calculated. Interrater agreement on study coding was good for all variables included.

The average sample was 76% male with an average age of 14.6 years. Fifty-two percent of the studies involved some form of diversion. The median intervention lasted 15 weeks and involved 15 hours of contact. The most common interventions were behavioral or nonspecific. Most of the studies suffered from multiple methodological problems.

The authors' ballot box review of these studies was considerably more positive than the meta-analytic results. Outcome variables in the analysis were recidivism; behavioral (in-program behavior, academic performance, and so on); and attitudinal (self-esteem, ratings of global adjustment, etc.). The 95% confidence interval for the mean ES of each outcome measure for pre–post and control group studies always included zero. Average ESs were always positive but were larger for pre–post than for control group designs.

Because sampling error did not account for a large percentage of variation in ES, moderator variables were searched for by correlating study variables with ES. Higher ESs were associated with older studies; nonadjudicated (i.e., diverted) versus adjudicated youths; being male; hours of intervention;

and use of behavioral, educational/vocational, or group psychotherapeutic interventions versus individual psychotherapeutic, probation/parole casework, or other.

Gottshalk, Davidson, Gensheimer, and Mayer (1987) concluded that the effects of community interventions for delinquents, although positive, were very small. They observed that the interventions that they evaluated were neither intense nor of long duration; more important, program implementation was seldom measured directly. A subset of 25 behavioral studies (involving 30 ESs) from the above sample were analyzed by Gottshalk, Davidson, Mayer, and Gensheimer (1987). Similar to the findings in the larger sample, zero was included in the 95% confidence interval of all average ESs, save experimental-control comparisons of in-program behaviors and experimental-control comparisons of postprogram social behaviors. As a consequence of these observations, Davidson et al. (1987) addressed many of these problems directly in an experimental comparison of a number of different treatments administered to juvenile offenders diverted from the criminal justice system. In brief, interventions that were specific and focused on positive (as opposed to pathological) processes by providing social support or activities and skills to serve social control functions successfully reduced officially recorded (but not self-reported) delinquency so long as the interventions were conducted outside the influence of the court.

Lipsey and Wilson (1993) conducted an analysis of treatment outcome in 156 meta-analyses on juvenile delinquency and other behavioral, psychological, and educational treatments. Of the 443 studies reviewed on treatments for juvenile delinquency, the average ES was .18. The average ES for patients hospitalized for mental problems and interventions for children at risk (i.e., failing, handicaps) was at least twice as large as that of juvenile delinquents. It appeared from this analysis that treatment for juvenile delinquency is much less effective than treatments designed to help other individuals with adjustment problems.

With the exception of Izzo and Ross's (1990) study, the meta-analyses of the effectiveness of treatment for juvenile delinquents indicate small, although positive effects. In all reviews, save Whitehead and Lab's (1989), treatment type moderator variables were found or suggested by the analyses. Garrett (1985) found that treatment type was related to outcome. Izzo and Ross found a theoretically interesting moderator variable, a cognitive component in the intervention, although it had a smaller effect than the setting in which treatment was delivered. Gottshalk, Davidson, Mayer, and Gensheimer (1987) found that hours of intervention and type of treatment were positively related to ES. The finding that treatment characteristics act as moderator variables suggests that average ES across all of these studies may obscure what may be effective interventions.

In order to increase the lawfulness of the treatment outcome data, Andrews and his colleagues (1990a) have taken G. Paul's famous message on psychotherapy outcome evaluation seriously (G. Paul, 1967) and conceptualized the treatment literature in terms of the principles of risk, need, and responsivity. *Risk* refers to the likelihood of recidivism, *need* refers to specific offender problem areas that require remediation because of their relationship with criminal behavior, and *responsivity* refers to the likelihood of particular offenders to improve with a specific type of intervention. Andrews and his colleagues (Andrews, Kiessling, Robinson, & Mickus, 1986) have provided evidence that the intensity of supervision is positively related to reductions in recidivism rates for high-risk offenders and negatively related to reduced recidivism for low-risk offenders.

Andrews and his colleagues (Andrews et al., 1990a, 1990b; J. K. Hill, Andrews, & Hoge, 1991) applied the principles of risk, need, and responsivity in a meta-analysis of 45 of the 50 studies in Whitehead and Lab's (1989) sample and an additional sample of 35 treatment studies that included a measure of recidivism. Coded variables were setting (system diversion, probation/parole/community corrections, etc.); year of publication; quality of research design; juvenile or adult correctional system; behavioral–nonbehavioral intervention; and type of treatment. Type of treatment was coded as (a) criminal sanction; (b) inappropriate service (service delivery to low-risk cases, nondirective, relationship-dependent or unstructured psychodynamic counseling, all milieu and group approaches emphasizing within-group communication and not controlling procriminal modeling and reinforcement, nondirective or poorly targeted academic and vocational approaches, and scared straight); (c) appropriate service (service to high-risk cases, all behavioral programs, not to low-risk cases, comparisons of specific responsivity-treatment comparisons, and nonbehavioral programs targeting criminogenic needs), and (d) unspecified.

It was predicted that type of treatment would have larger effects on recidivism than all of the other variables. In the Whitehead and Lab (1989) sample, the correlation between type of treatment and Φ coefficients was strong ($\eta = .69$). Controlling for the effects of the other variables in an analysis of covariance produced a stronger correlation (beta = .72). In sample 2, a stepwise regression yielded the largest effect for type of treatment (beta = .69). Scheffe tests indicated that appropriate treatment was significantly better than criminal sanctions, inappropriate treatment, and other treatment. Behavioral treatments were more effective than nonbehavioral treatments. Although behavioral treatment and type of treatment were highly correlated ($r = .62$), when controls were introduced for type of treatment, the effect of behavioral treatment was nonsignificant. As in Izzo and Ross (1990), treatment provided in residential settings was less effective than that provided in community settings.

Most recently, Lipsey and Wilson (1997) conducted a meta-analysis on interventions with serious offenders, namely programs for offenders in the community (K = 117) and programs for institutionalized offenders (K = 83). A regression analysis indicated that the strongest predictor of ES was the type of prior offenses. ESs were larger for juvenile offenders with mixed priors (mostly person offenses) compared to those with property offenses and those with many prior offenses. The ES also was larger for samples with larger concentration of offenses. With respect to amount of treatment, three variables were important and present a contrasting picture. First, duration of treatment was positively associated with ES. Second, the mean hours of treatment per week was negatively associated with ES, thus fewer contact hours were related to increased ES. Difficulties in treatment delivery such as following treatment protocol were associated with smaller ESs. Third, general program characteristics such as the researcher's role in treatment (i.e., delivered, planned, supervised, influential but did not design or supervise, and independent) were examined. The less involved the researcher was in the design, planning, and delivery, the smaller the ES. In addition, Lipsey and Wilson examined the mean ES and the consistency of the estimates within each treatment. Treatments with the largest ES were interpersonal skills, individual counseling, and behavioral programs. Some treatments such as deterrence and vocational programs had negative ESs (i.e., outcome was worse).

Similar analyses were conducted with programs for institutionalized offenders. In this model none of the characteristics of the juvenile delinquents contributed to the ES, suggesting that with incarcerated individuals treatments need not differentiate between age, sex, ethnicity, and prior offense history. With regard to the amount of treatment, treatment integrity and duration of treatment were positively associated with ES. Finally, in contrast to the noninstitutionalized model, administration and involvement of mental health workers was positively associated with ES. Treatments with the largest ES were interpersonal skills and programs that occurred in the home.

This research extends previous research in that it not only addresses the question of what works but also asks what type of programs work for whom. Given that the serious, chronic offenders represent the major costs to society, this distinction is important. The good news is that the majority of programs do have a positive effect on recidivism, although the mean ES is modest and there is considerable variance around it. Interestingly, the mean ESs for noninstitutionalized offenders (.14) and for institutionalized offenders (.10) were similar. The factors related to the ESs were different, with characteristics of the juvenile as the strongest predictors for the noninstitutionalized group. General program characteristics were the most important for the institutionalized offenders, probably reflecting their greater homogeneity. This review supported Andrews's (1980) risk principle: Treatment for delinquent behavior is most effective for offenders of higher risk.

The meta-analytic literature leads to some important conclusions. On the methodological side, statistical sophistication cannot substitute for an empirically based conceptualization of the important issues involved in treatment effectiveness. Data do not speak for themselves and cannot be coaxed to do so with statistical analysis. On the substantive side, there are interactions that affect treatment effectiveness involving setting, client characteristics, and program characteristics.

Cost–Benefit Analysis of Treatment for Juvenile Delinquency

While the primary goal of treatment programs for delinquency is the reduction of delinquent behavior, policymakers, taxpayers, and scientists are also interested in the cost of such programs. In a comprehensive report by the Washington State Institute for Public Policy, Aos, Phipps, Barnoski, and Lieb (2001) reviewed the economics of programs intended to reduce crime. They reviewed programs in four broad areas: early childhood programs, middle childhood and adolescent (nonjuvenile) programs, juvenile programs, and adult offender programs. The first three are relevant to this review. The inclusion criteria were limited to evaluations that measured criminality, although many of the programs reviewed had additional goals. Aos et al. reviewed more than 400 program evaluations conducted primarily in North America in the last 25 years. For each type of program, the average ES, the direct cost of the program per participant, and the cost of the program were calculated.

With respect to early childhood programs, nurse home visits had an average ES of .29, with a cost of approximately $7,733 per participant. However, taking into account the cost savings with respect to fewer victims, the payoff for this program is about $3.06 per dollar of cost. Early childhood programs, including the Perry Preschool Project, had an average ES of .12 and a cost of $8,939 per participant. The cost–benefit ratio of the program was $1.78 per dollar spent. It is important to note that the benefits of these programs are unlikely to be limited to crime reduction.

Five types of programs were reviewed for the middle childhood and adolescent programs. The Seattle Social Development Program involves teachers, parents, and students in grades one through six in high-crime urban areas. Training is provided for teachers to manage classrooms and promote students' bonding to the school, for parents to promote bonding to family and school, and for children to affect attitudes toward school, behavior in school, and academic achievement. The program had an ES of .13, a $4,355 cost per participant, and a cost–benefit ratio of $4.25 per dollar spent. The four other programs, Quantum Opportunities, Mentoring, National Job Corps, and Job Training Partnership Act, had ESs ranging from .04 to .31.

Two types of juvenile offender programs were evaluated, namely, off-the-shelf programs (multisystemic therapy, functional family therapy, aggression replacement therapy, multidimensional foster care, and adolescent diversion) and general types of programs (diversion with services, intensive probation, intensive parole supervision, coordinated services, scared straight, other family approaches, juvenile sex offender programs, and boot camps). The off-the-shelf programs have prescribed approaches described in manuals and training protocols and offer telephone support. The ESs for the off-the-shelf programs (ranging from .18 to .37) were larger than those for the general types of treatment programs (ranging from –.13 to .17). One general program, scared straight, had a negative ES. With respect to cost–benefit ratios, the off-the-shelf programs ranged from $24.91 (adolescent diversion project) to $45.91 (aggression replacement therapy) per dollar spent. Two general programs, scared straight and boot camps, actually cost the taxpayers $3,587 and $24,531, respectively, per year per dollar spent; there was no benefit either in treatment effect or cost to these types of programs. Diversion and coordinated youth services saved the taxpayers approximately $5,679 and $18,000, respectively, per dollar spent. The remaining programs have cost–benefit ratios ranging from $3.38 (sex offenders) to $25.59 (coordinated services) per dollar spent.

Aos et al. (2001) concluded that there are some good investments in treating delinquency. From a dollar perspective, the largest returns are for juvenile delinquency programs. Furthermore, there are some programs that cost the taxpayer but do not lower delinquency. These programs typically were not developed from a theoretical perspective and did not address known risk factors of crime. An important caveat in comparing these figures is that they measure crime costs only. For the infant and childhood programs, there are many other possible benefits. A third conclusion by these researchers was that even a relatively small ES or crime reduction can have important cost benefits.

SUMMARY

In 1990, Gottfredson and Hirschi derived eight principles of crime prevention from their general theory of crime: Do not attempt to control crime by incapacitating or rehabilitating adults or altering the severity of criminal penalties. Instead, supervise teenagers' activities, limit proactive policing, skeptically evaluate the criminal justice system's and media's characterization of crime, support early education and effective child care programs, and promote two-parent families and an increase in the number of caregivers relative to the number of children. Subsequent research has supported some of these principles, qualified some, and not supported others. We now know that rehabilitation and treatment programs vary according to the characteristics of the target population, particularly risk level, and according to the nature of the programs themselves. Multisystemic-behavior-oriented or cognitive–behavior-oriented programs focused on the criminogenic needs of relatively high-risk individuals perform best. These programs must be implemented precisely in order to be effective.

Accumulating evidence points to the importance of preventing delinquency by acting early through reducing risk factors and promoting protective factors. The most effective strategy for the future involves the evaluation of both the efficacy and the underlying etiological theories of prevention interventions (Coie & Jacobs, 1993; Tremblay & Craig, 1995). The success of interventions depends on the accuracy of the screening methods used to identify those most at risk for chronic antisocial conduct. If our proposed taxonomy is correct, prevention and intervention efforts will need to be adjusted to the characteristics and developmental course of the three main groups of juvenile offenders. Although we have made a great deal of progress in understanding individual differences in antisociality and linking these to interventions, there is much work that remains to be done.

EPILOGUE

We began this book by stating that a theoretical and analytical framework derived from evolutionary psychology, behavioral genetics, and developmental psychology could enhance our understanding of individual differences in antisocial behavior and the development of juvenile delinquency. Our book has summarized a substantial part of the very large literature that documents stable differences among individuals in antisociality, including variations in its development. Although the empirical literature on the correlates of juvenile delinquency is rich and progress has been made in understanding some of the proximal causes of antisocial behavior, theoretical insights from basic science have only recently been applied in aid of identifying possible ultimate causes of individual differences. Because Darwinian evolution provides the unifying theory of the life sciences, such application offers the promise of conceptual advances from fields of inquiry that may at first appear unrelated to delinquency.

It will be apparent to readers who have persevered to this point that the promise of these conceptual advances is only partially fulfilled. However, we believe that an important beginning has been made, in part by identifying the questions that are central to the development of a complete theory of juvenile delinquency and providing at least tentative answers to some of them.

Stable individual differences in antisociality are observable early in development. They are partly heritable, but there is evidence that particular environments make these heritable differences more likely to manifest themselves in behavior. The weight of the evidence to date suggests that most of the environmental influences that have a lasting influence on development are not shared by family members; for example, prenatal events, differential parental treatment, and peers account for much more variance than household socioeconomic status of origin, neigborhood conditions, or family adversity. If we are to fully understand the origins and maintenance of delinquent behavior, then we will need to consider individual, contextual, situational, and neighborhood factors.

The empirical evidence reviewed in this book is consistent with the existence of two subgroups of persistently antisocial males. Both subgroups begin their antisocial behavior early in life and persist in it through adolescence and into adulthood. However, the first comprises antisocial individuals who suffer from various neurodevelopmental difficulties. The second subgroup comprises individuals who appear neurodevelopmentally healthy but whose constellation of characteristic—including early reproduction, low parental investment, high risk acceptance, and aggressiveness—make them qualitatively different from other males. It is possible that these individuals are pursuing a qualitatively different life history, one molded by natural selection in ancestral environments.

To date, we have neither theoretical nor empirical reasons to support the notion that a similar taxon of persistent antisocial females exists. However, recent evidence does suggest that there is also a group, albeit much smaller, of persistently antisocial females who, like their male counterparts, are characterized by neurological difficulties and developmental contexts that support antisocial behavior.

Male adolescents who begin their antisocial behavior in adolescence and who later desist from delinquency as young adults show many of the characteristics of persistently antisocial males but in a temporally and situationally limited form. Although these individuals engage in significant antisocial behavior in adolescence, they desist by adulthood. Antisocial behaviors of male adolescents are likely part of intermale competition for status, resources, and mating opportunities and may be exacerbated by perceived competitive disadvantage.

The less violent antisocial behavior exhibited by adolescent females is in keeping with the aversion to risk associated with the demands of motherhood and females' lower fitness variance. The ultimate cause of their aggression is likely the differential reproductive success of ancestral females who adopted strategies that diminished the fitness of rival females and increased their own fitness through the acquisition of desirable mateships to men with social and material resources.

The frequency and type of antisocial behaviors involved in juvenile delinquency appear to be anything but random. These behaviors are often related directly (as in pursuing sexual opportunities) or indirectly (as in establishing a fearsome reputation) to fitness enhancing goals. For the majority of the population, antisocial behaviors vary in a sensible way with age, sex, and long-term prospects. Members of the taxon of persistently antisocial individuals, however, do not show the adolescent peak in antisociality followed by adult desistance, suggesting that they are on a different life history trajectory, albeit one similarly sculpted by selective forces.

Some intervention programs are effective in reducing delinquent acts. We now know that the programs that perform best are those behavioral- or cognitive-behavioral-oriented programs that target not only the youth but also systems that interact with the youth and that are focused on the criminogenic needs of relatively high-risk individuals. However, we also know that these programs must be implemented exactly as specified in order to be effective. There is still much room for improvement in our intervention efforts. An effective strategy for the future must involve evaluating not only the efficacy of interventions but also the etiological theories that provide their rationale. The success of interventions also depends on the accuracy of the screening methods used to identify those most at risk for chronic antisocial conduct. If our proposed taxonomy is correct, prevention and intervention efforts will need to focus on the characteristics and developmental course of the three main groups of juvenile offenders. Different approaches to adolescence-limited and the two groups of life-course-persistent delinquents seem warranted. In addition, we will also need to emphasize early identification and intervention, to focus on the possible functions of delinquent acts, and to recognize that much antisocial behavior is a manifestation of the self-interest that we all share.

REFERENCES

Achenbach, T. M. (1991). *Manual for the child behavior checklist and 1991 profile.* Burlington: University of Vermont, Department of Psychiatry.

Adler, F. (1975). *Sisters in crime.* New York: McGraw-Hill.

Aguilar, B., Sroufe, L. A., Egeland, B., & Carlson, E. (2000). Distinguishing the early-onset/persistent and adolescence-onset antisocial behavior types: From birth to 16 years. *Development & Psychopathology, 12,* 109–132.

Akman, D. D., & Normandeau, A. (1967). The measurement of crime and delinquency in Canada. *British Journal of Criminology, 7,* 129–149.

Alcock, J. (2001). *The triumph of sociobiology.* New York: Oxford University Press.

Alessi, G. (1992). Models of proximate and ultimate causation in psychology. *American Psychologist, 47,* 1359–1370.

Alexander, J. F., & Parsons, B. V. (1973). Short-term behavioral intervention with delinquent families: Impact on family process and recidivism. *Journal of Abnormal Psychology, 81,* 219–225.

Alexander, J. F., & Parsons, B. V. (1982). *Functional family therapy.* Monterey, CA: Brooks/Cole.

Alexander, R. D. (1979). *Darwinism and human affairs.* Seattle: University of Washington Press.

Alexander, R. M. (1995). *The "girl problem": Female sexual delinquency in New York, 1900–1930.* Ithaca, NY: Cornell University Press.

American Psychiatric Association. (1994). *Diagnostic and statistical manual of mental disorders* (4th ed.). Washington, DC: Author.

Anderson, L., & Snart, F. (1999). Sensory and perceptual difficulties, academic deficits, and delinquency: An overview. *Developmental Disabilities Bulletin, 27,* 56–74.

Andersson, M. B. (1982). Female choice selects for extreme tail length in a widow bird. *Nature, 99,* 818–820.

Andersson, M. B. (1994). *Sexual selection.* Princeton, NJ: Princeton University Press.

Andrews, D. A. (1980). Some experimental investigations of the principles of differential association through deliberate manipulations of the structure of service systems. *American Sociological Review, 45,* 448–462.

Andrews, D. A., & Bonta, J. (1994). *The psychology of criminal conduct.* Cincinnati: Anderson.

Andrews, D. A., Kiessling, J. J., Robinson, D., & Mickus, S. (1986). The risk principle of case classification: An outcome evaluation with young adult probationers. *Canadian Journal of Criminology, 28,* 377–384.

Andrews, D. A., & Wormith, J. S. (1989). Personality and crime: Knowledge destruction and construction in criminology. *Justice Quarterly, 6,* 289–309.

Andrews, D. A., Zinger, I., Hoge, R. D., Bonta, J., Gendreau, P., & Cullen, F. T. (1990a). Does correctional treatment work? A clinically relevant and psychologically informed meta-analysis. *Criminology, 28,* 369–404.

Andrews, D. A., Zinger, I., Hoge, R. D., Bonta, J., Gendreau, P., & Cullen, F. T. (1990b). A human science approach or more punishment and pessimism: A rejoinder to Lab and Whitehead. *Criminology, 28,* 419–429.

Anthony, E. J., & Cohler, B. J. (1987). *The invulnerable child.* New York: Guilford Press.

Aos, S., Phipps, P., Barnoski, R., & Lieb, R. (2001). *The comparative costs and benefits of programs to reduce crime: A review of national programs with implications for Washington State.* Olympia: Washington State Institute for Public Policy.

Archer, J. (1991). The influence of testosterone on human aggression. *British Journal of Psychology, 82,* 1–28.

August, G. J., Realmuto, G. M., Crosby, R. D., & MacDonald, A. W. (1995). Community-based multiple-gate screening of children at risk for conduct disorder. *Journal of Abnormal Child Psychology, 23,* 521–544.

Axelrod, R. (1984). *The evolution of cooperation.* New York: Basic Books.

Bailey, J. M., Kirk, K. M., Zhu, G., Dunne, M. P., & Martin, N. G. (2000). Do individual differences in sociosexuality represent genetic or environmentally contingent strategies? Evidence from the Australian twin registry. *Journal of Personality and Social Psychology, 78,* 537–545.

Bangert-Drowns, R. L., Wells-Parker, E., & Chevillard, I. (1997). Assessing the methodological quality of research in narrative reviews and meta-analyses. In K. J. Bryant, M. Windle, & S. G. West (Eds.), *The science of prevention: Methodological advances from alcohol and substance abuse research.* Washington, DC: American Psychological Association.

Barr, K. N., & Quinsey, V. L. (in press). Is psychopathy a pathology or a life strategy? Implications for social policy. In C. Crawford & C. Salmon (Eds.), *Evolutionary psychology, public policy, and private decisions.* Hillsdale, NJ: Erlbaum.

Barth, R. P. (1990). Theories guiding home-based intensive family preservation services. In J. K. Whittaker, J. Kinney, E. M. Tracy, & C. Brooth (Eds.), *Reaching high-risk families* (pp. 89–112). New York: Aldine de Gruyter.

Bartley, P. (2000). *Prostitution: Prevention and reform in England, 1860–1914.* NY: Routledge.

Basta, J. M., & Davidson, W. S. (1988). Treatment of juvenile offenders: Study outcomes since 1980. *Behavioral Sciences and the Law, 6,* 355–384.

Batten, M. (1992). *Sexual strategies: How females choose their mates.* New York: Putnam.

Beevor, A. (2002). *The fall of Berlin 1945.* New York: Viking.

Bell, G. (1997). *Selection: The mechanism of evolution.* New York: Chapman and Hall.

Belovsky, G. E., Slade, J. B., & Chase, J. M. (1996). Mating strategies based on foraging abilities: An experiment with grasshoppers. *Behavioral Ecology, 7,* 438–444.

Belsky, J., Steinberg, L., & Draper, P. (1991). Childhood experience, interpersonal development, and reproductive strategy: An evolutionary theory of socialization. *Child Development, 62,* 647–670.

Benjamin, J., Osher, Y., Belmaker, R. H., & Ebstein, R. (1998). No significant associations between two dopamine receptor polymorphisms and normal temperament. *Human Psychopharmacology, 13,* 11–15.

Benjamin, J., Li, L., Patterson, C., Greenberg, B. D., Murphy, D. L., & Hamer, D. H. (1996). Population and familial association between the D4 dopamine receptor gene and measures of novelty seeking. *Nature Genetics, 12,* 81–84.

Bereczkei, T. (2001). Maternal trade-off in treating high-risk children. *Evolution and Human Behavior, 22,* 197–212.

Berrueta-Clement, J. R., Schweinhart, L. J., Barnett, W. S., Epstein, E. S., & Weikart, D. P. (1984). *Changed lives: The effects of the Perry Preschool Program on youths through age 19.* Ypsilanti, MI: High School Press.

Berrueta-Clement, J. R., Schweinhart, L. J., Barnett, W. S., & Weikart, D. P. (1987). The effects of early educational intervention on crime and delinquency in adolescence and early adulthood. In J. D. Burchard & S. N. Burchard (Eds.), *Prevention of delinquent behavior* (pp. 220–240). Newbury Park, CA: Sage.

Bettencourt, B. A., & Miller, N. (1996). Gender differences in aggression as a function of provocation: A meta-analysis. *Psychological Bulletin, 119,* 422–447.

Bianchi, M., Sacerdote, P., & Panerai, A. E. (1996). Peripherally administered GM-CSF interferes with scopolamine-induced amnesia in mice: Involvement of interleukin-1. *Brain Research, 729,* 285–288.

Biederman, J., Mick, E., Faraone, S. V., & Burback, M. (2001). Patterns of remission and symptom decline in conduct disorder: A four-year prospective study of an ADHD sample. *Journal of the American Academy of Child and Adolescent Psychiatry, 40,* 290–298.

Bierman, K. L. (1990). Using the clinical interview to assess children's interpersonal reasoning and emotional understanding. In C. R. Reynolds & R. W. Kamphaus (Eds.), *Handbook of psychological and educational assessment of children* (Vol. 2, pp. 204–222). New York: Guilford Press.

Bierman, K. L., Greenberg, M. T., & Conduct Problems Prevention Research Group. (1996). Social skills training in the Fast Track Program. In R. DeV. Peters & R. J. McMahon (Eds.), *Preventing childhood disorders, substance abuse, and delinquency* (pp. 65–89). Thousand Oaks, CA: Sage.

Bingham, C. R., & Crockett, L. J. (1996). Longitudinal adjustment patterns of boys and girls experiencing early, middle, and late sexual intercourse. *Developmental Psychology, 32,* 647–658.

Bjerregaard, B., & Smith, C. (1993). Gender differences in gang participation, delinquency, and substance use. *Journal of Quantitative Criminology, 9*, 329–355.

Blanchard, J. J., Gangestad, S. W., Brown, S. A., & Horan, W. P. (2000). Hedonic capacity and schizotypy revisited: A taxometric analysis of social anhedonia. *Journal of Abnormal Psychology, 109*, 87–95.

Blum, K., Sheridan, P. J., Chen, T. H. J., Wood, R. C., Braverman, E. R., Cull, J. G., et al. (1997). The dopamine D2 receptor gene locus in reward deficiency syndrome: Meta-analyses. In K. Blum & E. P. Noble (Eds.), *Handbook of psychiatric genetics* (pp. 407–434). New York: CRC Press.

Blumstein, A., & Wallman, J. (Eds.). (2000). *The crime drop in America.* New York: Cambridge University Press.

Bock, G. R., & Cardew, G. (Eds.). (1997). *Characterizing human psychological adaptations.* Rexdale, Ontario: Wiley.

Bodmer, W., & McKie, R. (1994). *The book of man: The quest to discover our genetic heritage.* Toronto, Ontario, Canada: Penguin.

Bogaert, A. F. (1993). Personality, delinquency, and sexuality: Data from three Canadian samples. *Personality and Individual Differences, 15*, 353–356.

Bogaert, A. F., & Fisher, W. A. (1995). Predictors of university men's number of sexual partners. *Journal of Sex Research, 32*, 119–130.

Bogaert, A. F., & Rushton, J. P. (1989). Sexuality, delinquency and r/K reproductive strategies: Data from a Canadian university sample. *Personality and Individual Differences, 10*, 1071–1077.

Bohman, M. (1996). Predisposition to criminality: Swedish adoption studies in retrospect. In G. R. Bock & J. A. Goode (Eds.), *Genetics of criminal and antisocial behavior* (pp. 99–114). Chichester, England: Wiley.

Book, A. S., Starzyk, K. B., & Quinsey, V. L. (2001). The relationship between testosterone and aggression: A meta-analysis. *Aggression and Violent Behavior, 6*, 579–599.

Borduin, C. M., Mann, B. J., Cone, L. T., Henggeler, S. W., Fucci, B. R., Blaske, D. M., et al. (1995). Multisystemic treatment of serious juvenile offenders: Long-term prevention of criminality and violence. *Journal of Consulting and Clinical Psychology, 63*, 569–578.

Borduin, C. M., & Schaeffer, C. M. (1998). Violent offending in adolescence: Epidemiology, correlates, outcomes and treatment. In T. P. Gulotta, G. R. Adams, & R. Montemayor (Eds.), *Delinquent violent youth: Theory and interventions.* Thousand Oaks, CA: Sage.

Bouchard, T. J. (1983). Do environmental similarities explain the similarity in intelligence of identical twins reared apart? *Intelligence, 7*, 175–184.

Bouchard, T. J. (1997). The genetics of personality. In K. Blum & E. P. Noble (Eds.), *Handbook of psychiatric genetics* (pp. 273–296). New York: CRC Press.

Bouchard, T. J., Jr., Lykken, D. T., McGue, M., Segal, N. L., & Tellegen, A. (1990). Sources of human psychological differences: The Minnesota Study of twins reared apart. *Science, 250*, 223–228.

Bowker, L. H., & Klein, M. W. (1983). The etiology of female juvenile delinquency and gang membership: A test of psychological and social structural explanations. *Adolescence, 18,* 739–751.

Braungart–Rieker, J., Rende, R. D., Plomin, R., DeFries, J. C., & Fulker, D. W. (1995). Genetic mediation of longitudinal associations between family environment and childhood behavior problems. *Development and Psychopathology, 7,* 233–245.

Breland, K., & Breland, M. (1961). The misbehavior of organisms. *American Psychologist, 16,* 681–684.

Brendgen, M., Vitaro, F., & Bukowski, W. M. (2000). Deviant friends and early adolescents' emotional and behavioral adjustment. *Journal of Research on Adolescence, 10,* 173–189.

Brennan, P. A., Mednick, S. A., & Jacobsen, B. (1996). Assessing the role of genetics in crime using adoption cohorts. In G. R. Bock & J. A. Goode (Eds.), *Genetics of criminal and antisocial behavior* (pp. 115–128). Chichester, England: Wiley.

Brennan, P. A., Mednick, B. R., & Mednick, S. A. (1993). Parental psychopathology, congenital factors, and violence. In S. Hodgins (Ed.), *Mental disorder and crime* (pp. 244–261). Thousand Oaks, CA: Sage.

Breslau, N., Davis, G. C., Andreski, P., & Peterson, E. (1991). Traumatic events and posttraumatic stress disorder in an urban population of young adults. *Archives of General Psychiatry, 48,* 216–222.

Brickman, A. S., Mcmanus, M. M., Grapentine, W., & Alessi, N. (1984). Neurological assessment of seriously delinquent adolescents. *Journal of the Academy of Child Psychiatry, 23,* 453–457.

Brown, S. A., Tate, S. R., Vik, P. W., Haas, A. L., & Aarons, G. A. (1999). Modeling of alcohol use mediates the effect of family history of alcoholism on adolescent alcohol expectancies. *Experimental and Clinical Psychopharmacology, 7,* 20–27.

Bugental, D. B. (2000). Acquisition of the algorithms of social life: A domain-based approach. *Psychological Bulletin, 126,* 187–219.

Burbank, V. (1987). Female aggression in cross-cultural perspective. *Behavioral Science Research, 21,* 70–100.

Burr, C. (1996). *A separate creation: The search for the biological origins of sexual orientation.* New York: Hyperion.

Buss, A. H., & Plomin, R. (1975). *A temperament theory of personality development.* New York: Wiley.

Buss, D. M. (1987). Sex differences in human mate selection criteria: An evolutionary perspective. In C. Crawford, M. Smith, & D. Krebs (Eds.), *Sociobiology and psychology: Ideas, issues, and applications* (pp. 335–351). Hillsdale, NJ: Erlbaum.

Buss, D. M. (1989). Sex differences in human mate preferences: Evolutionary hypotheses tested in 37 cultures. *Behavioral and Brain Sciences, 12,* 1–49.

Buss, D. M. (1994). *The evolution of desire*. New York: Basic Books.

Buss, D. M. (1995). Psychological sex differences: Origins through sexual selection. *American Psychologist, 50*, 164–168.

Buss, D. M. (1999). *Evolutionary psychology: The new science of the mind*. Toronto, Ontario, Canada: Allyn & Bacon.

Buss, D. M., Larsen, Westen, D., & Semmelroth, J. (1992). Sex difference in jealousy: Evolution, physiology, and psychology. *Psychological Science, 3*, 251–255.

Buss, D. M., & Schmitt, D. P. (1993). Sexual strategies theory: An evolutionary perspective on human mating. *Psychological Review, 100*, 204–232.

Buunk, B. P., Angleitner, A., Oubaid, V., & Buss, D. M. (1996). Sex differences in jealousy in evolutionary and cultural perspective: Tests from the Netherlands, Germany, and the United States. *Psychological Science, 7*, 359–363.

Byock, J. L. (1995). Egil's bones. *Scientific American, 272*, 82–87.

Byrne, J. M., & Sampson, R. J. (Eds.). (1986). *The social ecology of crime*. New York: Springer-Verlag.

Cadoret, R. J., Yates, W. R., Troughton, E., Woodworth, G., & Stewart, M. A. (1995). Genetic-environmental interaction in the genesis of aggressivity and conduct disorders. *Archives of General Psychiatry, 52*, 916–924.

Cairns, R. B. (1996). Aggression from a developmental perspective: Genes, environments and interactions. In G. R. Bock & J. A. Goode (Eds.), *Genetics of criminal and antisocial behavior* (pp. 45–60). Chichester, England: Wiley.

Cairns, R. B., & Cairns, B. D. (1991). Social cognition and social networks: A developmental perspective. In D. J. Pepler & K. H. Rubin (Eds.), *The development and treatment of childhood aggression* (pp. 249–278). Hillsdale, NJ: Erlbaum.

Cairns, R. B., Cairns, B. D., Neckerman, H. J., Ferguson, L. L., & Gariepy, J. (1989). Growth and aggression: 1. Childhood to early adolescence. *Developmental Psychology, 25*, 320–330.

Cairns, R. B., & Gariepy, J. L. (1990). Dual genesis and the puzzle of aggressive mediation. In M. E. Hahn et al. (Eds.), *Developmental behavior genetics: Neural, biometrical, and evolutionary approaches* (pp. 40–59). New York: Oxford University Press.

Cairns, R. B., Gariepy, J. L., & Hood, K. E. (1990). Development, microevolution, and social behavior. *Psychological Review, 97*, 49–65.

Campbell, A. (1981). *Girl delinquents*. Oxford: Basil Blackwell.

Campbell, A. (1984). *The girls in the gang*. Oxford: Basil Blackwell.

Campbell, A. (1995). A few good men: Evolutionary psychology and female adolescent aggression. *Ethology and Sociobiology, 16*, 99–123.

Campbell, A. (1999). Staying alive: Evolution, culture, and women's intrasexual aggression. *Behavioral and Brain Sciences, 22*, 203–252.

Campbell, S. B., Pierce, E. W., March, C. L., Ewing, L. J., & Szumowski, E. K. (1994). Hard-to-manage preschool boys: Symptomatic behavior across contexts and time. *Child Development, 65*, 836–851.

Canadian Psychological Association (1988). *Canadian codes of ethics for psychologists*. Old Chelsea, Québec: Author.

Capaldi, D. M., & Patterson, G. R. (1994, March). *The violent adolescent male: Specialist or generalist?* Paper presented at the biennial meeting of the Society for Research in Child Development, New Orleans, LA.

Capaldi, D. M., & Patterson, G. R. (1996). Can violent offenders be distinguished from frequent offenders: Predictions from childhood to adolescence. *Journal of Research in Crime and Delinquency, 33,* 206–231.

Caplan, G. (1964). *Principles of preventive psychiatry*. New York: Basic Books.

Carey, G., & Goldman, D. (1997). The genetics of antisocial behavior. In D. M. Stoff, J. Breiling, & J. D. Maser (Eds.), *Handbook of antisocial behavior* (pp. 243–254). New York: Wiley.

Carlson, M., Earls, F., & Todd, R. D. (1988). The importance of regressive changes in the development of the nervous system: Towards a neurobiological theory of child development. *Psychiatric Development, 1,* 1–22.

Carter, C. S., Kirkpatrick, B., & Lederhendler, I. I. (Eds.). (1997). The Integrative Neurobiology of Affiliation. *Annals of the New York Academy of Sciences, 807,* 1–418.

Caspi, A., Lynam, D., Moffitt, T. E., & Silva, P. A. (1993). Unravelling girls' delinquency: Biological, dispositional, and contextual contributions to adolescent misbehavior. *Developmental Psychology, 29,* 19–30.

Caspi, A., McClay, J., Moffitt, T. E., Mill, J., Martin, J., Craig, I. W., et al. (2002). Role of genotype in the cycle of violence in maltreated children. *Science, 29,* 851–854.

Caspi, A., & Moffitt, T. E. (1995). The continuity of maladaptive behaviour: From description to explanation in the study of antisocial behaviour. In D. Cicchetti & D. Cohen (Eds.), *Developmental psychopathology* (Vol. 2, pp. 472–511). New York: Wiley.

Caspi, A., Moffitt, T. E., Newman, D. L., & Silva, P. A. (1996). Behavioral observations at age 3 predict adult psychiatric disorders: Longitudinal evidence from a birth cohort. *Archives of General Psychiatry, 53,* 1033–1039.

Caspi, A., Taylor, A., Moffitt, T. E., & Plomin, R. (2000). Neighbourhood deprivation affects children's mental health: Environmental risks identified in a genetic design. *Psychological Science, 11,* 338–342.

Castellanos, F. X., Lau, E., Tayebi, N., Lee, P., Long, R. E., Giedd, J. N., et al. (1998). Lack of an association between a dopamine 4 receptor polymorphism and attention deficit/hyperactivity disorder: genetic and brain morphometric analyses. *Molecular Psychiatry, 3,* 431–434.

Chang, I. (1997). *The rape of Nanking: The forgotten holocaust of World War II*. New York: Basic Books.

Chen, C., Burton, M., Greenberger, E., & Dmitrieva, J. (1999). Population migration and the variation of dopamine D4 receptor (DRD4) allele frequencies around the globe. *Evolution and Human Behavior, 20,* 309–324.

Cheney, D. L., & Seyfarth, R. M. (1990). *How monkeys see the world: Inside the mind of another species*. Chicago: University of Chicago Press.

Chesney-Lind, M., & Shelden, R. G. (1992). *Girls, delinquency, and juvenile justice*. Pacific Grove, CA: Brooks/Cole.

Clark, R. D. (1990). The impact of AIDS on gender differences in willingness to engage in casual sex. *Journal of Applied Social Psychology, 20,* 771–782.

Clark, R. D., & Hatfield, E. (1989). Gender differences in receptivity to sexual offers. *Journal of Psychology and Human Sexuality, 2,* 39–55.

Cloninger, C. R. (1995). The psychobiological regulation of social cooperation. *Nature Medicine, 1,* 623–625.

Cloninger, R. C., Bayon, C., & Przybeck, T. R. (1997). Epidemiology and axis I comborbidity of antisocial personality. In D. M. Stoff, J. Breiling, & J. D. Maser (Eds.), *Handbook of antisocial behavior* (pp. 12–21). New York: Wiley.

Cloninger, C. R., Christiansen, K. O., Reich, T., & Gottesman, I. I. (1978) Implications of sex differences in the prevalences of antisocial personality, alcoholism, and criminality for familial transmission. *Archives of General Psychiatry, 35,* 941–951.

Clutton-Brock, T. H., & Vincent, A. C. (1991). Sexual selection and the potential reproductive rates of males and females. *Nature, 351,* 58–60.

Coen, E. (1999). *The art of genes: How organisms make themselves*. Toronto, Ontario, Canada: Oxford University Press.

Cohen, D. (1998). Culture, social organization, and patterns of violence. *Journal of Personality and Social Psychology, 75,* 408–419.

Cohen, D. (2001). Cultural variation: Considerations and implications. *Psychological Bulletin, 127,* 451–472.

Coid, J. (1993). Current concepts and classifications of psychopathic disorder. In P. Tyrer & G. Stein (Eds.), *Personality disorder reviewed* (pp. 113–164). London: Gaskell.

Coie, J. D., & Jacobs, M. R. (1993). The role of social context in the prevention of conduct disorder. *Development and Psychopathology, 5,* 263–275.

Coie, J. D., & Kupersmidt, J. B. (1983). A behavioral analysis of emerging social status in boys' groups. *Child Development, 54,* 1400–1416.

Colman, A. M., & Wilson, J. C. (1997). Antisocial personality disorder: An evolutionary game theory analysis. *Legal and Criminological Psychology, 2,* 23–34.

Comings, D. E. (1997). Polygenic inheritance in psychiatric disorders. In K. Blum & E. P. Noble (Eds.), *Handbook of psychiatric genetics* (pp. 235–260). New York: CRC Press.

Conduct Problems Prevention Research Group. (1992). A developmental and clinical model for the prevention of conduct disorder: The FAST track program. *Development and Psychopathology, 4,* 509–527.

Conger, R. D., Lorenz, F. O., Elder, G. H., Melby, J. N., Simons, R. L., & Conger, K. J. (1991). A process model of family economic pressure and early adolescent alcohol use. *Journal of Early Adolescence, 11,* 430–449.

Cosmides, L., & Tooby, J. (1987). Evolutionary psychology and the generation of culture, Part II. *Ethology and Sociobiology, 10*, 51–97.

Cosmides, L., & Tooby, J. (1992). Cognitive adaptations for social exchange. In J. Barkow, L. Cosmides, & J. Tooby (Eds.), *The adapted mind* (pp. 163–228). New York: Oxford University Press.

Costa, P. T., & McCrae, R. R. (1985). *The NEO personality inventory manual.* Odessa, FL: Psychological Assessment Resources.

Cowan, B. R., & Underwood, M. K. (1995). *Sugar and spice and everything nice? A developmental investigation of social aggression among girls.* Unpublished manuscript, Reed College.

Cowie, J., Cowie, V., & Slater, E. (1968). *Delinquency in girls.* London: Heinemann.

Cox, C. R., & LeBoeuf, B. J. (1977). Female incitation of male competition: Mechanism in sexual selection. *American Naturalist, 111*, 317–335.

Crawford, C. B., & Anderson, J. L. (1989). Sociobiology: An environmentalist discipline? *American Psychologist, 44*, 1449–1459.

Crawford, C. B., & Krebs, D. L. (Eds.). (1998). *Handbook of evolutionary psychology: Ideas, issues, and applications.* Mahwah, NJ: Erlbaum.

Crockenberg, S., & Litman, C. (1990). Autonomy as competence in 2-year-olds: Maternal correlates of child defiance, compliance, and self-assertion. *Developmental Psychology, 26*, 961–971.

Dabbs, J. M. (1992). Testosterone measurements in social and clinical psychology. *Journal of Social & Clinical Psychology, 11*, 302–321.

Dabbs, J. M., Jurkovic, G. J., & Frady, R. L. (1991). Salivary testosterone and cortisol among late adolescent male offenders. *Journal of Abnormal Child Psychology, 19*, 469–478.

Dabbs, J. M., Jr., & Morris, R. (1990). Testosterone, social class, and antisocial behavior in a sample of 4,462 men. *Psychological Sciences, 1*, 209–211.

Daly, M. (1996). Evolutionary adaptationism: Another biological approach to criminal and antisocial behavior. In G. R. Bock & J. A. Goode (Eds.), *Genetics of criminal and antisocial behavior* (pp. 183–195). Chichester, England: Wiley.

Daly, M., & Wilson, M. (1980). Discriminative parental solicitude: A biological perspective. *Journal of Marriage and the Family, 42*, 277–288.

Daly, M., & Wilson, M. (1982). Homicide and kinship. *American Anthropologist, 84*, 372–378.

Daly, M. & Wilson, M. (1983). *Sex, evolution, and behavior.* Belmont, CA: Wadsworth.

Daly, M., & Wilson, M. (1988). *Homicide.* New York: Aldine.

Daly, M., Wilson, M., & Vasdev, S. (2001). Income inequality and homicide rates in Canada and the United States. *Canadian Journal of Criminology, 43*, 219–236.

Daly, M., Wilson, M., & Weghorst, S. J. (1982). Male sexual jealousy. *Ethology and Sociobiology, 3*, 11–27.

Daniels, D., Dunn, J., Furstenberg, F. F., & Plomin, R. (1985). Environmental differences within the family and adjustment differences within pairs of adolescent siblings. *Child Development, 56,* 764–774.

Daniels, D., & Plomin, R. (1985). Differential experience of siblings in the same family. *Developmental Psychology, 21,* 747–760.

Daugherty, T. K., & Quay, H. (1991). Response preservation and delayed responding in childhood behavior disorders. *Journal of Child Psychiatry and Psychology, 32,* 453–461.

David, H. P. (1994). Reproductive rights and reproductive behavior: Clash or convergence of private values and public policies? *American Psychologist, 49,* 343–349.

Davidson, W. S., Redner, R., Blakely, C. H., Mitchell, C. M., & Emshoff, J. G. (1987). Diversion of juvenile offenders: An experimental comparison. *Journal of Consulting and Clinical Psychology, 55,* 68–75.

Dawkins, R. (1978). *The selfish gene.* Oxford: Oxford University Press.

Dawkins, R. (1986). *The blind watchmaker.* New York: Norton.

Dawkins, R. (1995). *River out of Eden: A Darwinian view of life.* New York: Basic Books.

DeMaris, A. (1992). Male versus female initiation of aggression: The case of courtship violence. In E. Viano (Ed.), *Intimate violence: Interdisciplinary perspectives* (pp. 11–120). Washington, DC: Hemisphere.

DeMulder, E. K., & Radke-Yarrow, M. (1991). Attachment with affectively ill and well mothers: Concurrent behavioral correlates. *Development & Psychopathology, 3,* 227–242.

Dennett, D. C. (1995). *Darwin's dangerous idea: Evolution and the meanings of life.* New York: Simon and Schuster.

Denno, D. W. (1990). *Biology and violence: From birth to adulthood.* Cambridge, England: Cambridge University Press.

Denno, D. W., & Clelland, R. C. (1986). Longitudinal evaluation of a delinquency prevention program by self-report. *Journal of Offender Counselling, Services and Rehabilitation, 10,* 59–82.

Devlin, B., Daniels, M., & Roeder, K. (1997). The heritability of IQ. *Nature, 388,* 468–471.

deVries, M. W. (1984). Temperament and infant mortality among the Masai of East Africa. *American Journal of Psychiatry, 141,* 1189–1194.

Dishion, T. J. (1990). The family ecology of boys' peer relations in middle childhood. *Child Development, 61,* 874–892.

Dishion, T. J., Eddy, J. M., Haas, E., Li, F., & Spracklen, K. (1997). Friendships and violent behavior during adolescence. *Social Development, 6,* 207–223.

Dishion, T. J., French. D. C., & Patterson, G. R. (1995). The development and ecology of antisocial behavior. In D. Cicchetti and D. J. Cohen (Eds.), *Wiley series on personality processes: Developmental psychopathology, Vol. 2: Risk, disorder and adaptation* (pp. 421–471). New York: Wiley.

Dishion, T. J., McCord, J., & Poulin, F. (1999). When interventions harm: Peer groups and problem behavior. *American Psychologist, 54,* 755–764.

Dishion, T. J., & Patterson, G. R. (1997). The timing of severity on antisocial behaviour: Three hypotheses within an ecological framework. In D. M. Stoff & J. Breiling (Eds.), *Handbook of antisocial behavior* (pp. 205–217). New York: Wiley.

Dishion, T. J., Patterson, G. R., & Kavanagh, K. A. (1992). An experimental test of the coercion model: Linking theory, measurement, and intervention. (pp. 253–282) In J. McCord & R. Tremblay (Eds.), *Preventing antisocial behaviour.* New York: Guilford Press.

Dishion, T. J., Spracklen, K., Andrews, D. M., & Patterson, G. R. (1996). Deviancy training in adolescent male friendships. *Behavior Therapy, 27,* 373–390.

Dodge, K. A. (1983). Behavioral antecedents of peer social status. *Child Development, 54,* 1386–1399.

Dodge, K. A., Bates, J. E., & Pettit, G. S. (1990). Mechanisms in the cycle of violence. *Science, 250,* 1678–1683.

Donahue, J. J., & Levitt, S. D. (2001). The impact of legalized abortion on crime. *Quarterly Review of Economics, 116,* 379–420.

Donovan, J. E., Jessor, R., & Costa, F. M. (1988). Syndrome of problem behavior in adolescence: A replication. *Journal of Consulting and Clinical Psychology, 56,* 762–765.

Downey, G., & Coyne, J. C. (1990). Children of depressed parents: An integrative review. *Psychological Bulletin, 108,* 50–76.

Dumas, J. E., & Wahler, R. G. (1983). Predictors of treatment outcome in parent training: Mother insularity and socioeconomic disadvantage. *Behavioral Assessment, 5,* 301–313.

Dunbar, R. I. M., Clark, A., & Hurst, N. L. (1995). Conflict and cooperation among the Vikings: Contingent behavioral decisions. *Ethology and Sociobiology, 16,* 233–246.

Dunn, J., Stocker, C., & Plomin, R. (1990). Nonshared experiences within the family: Correlates of behavioral problems in middle childhood. *Development & Psychopathology, 2,* 113–126.

Dunne, M. P., Martin, N. G., Statham, D. J., Slutske, W. S., Dinwiddie, S. H., Bucholz, K. K., et al. (1997). Genetic and environmental contributions to variance in age at first sexual intercourse. *Psychological Science, 8,* 211–216.

Durdle, B. M. (1998). *Measuring the severity of inter-spousal physical aggression.* Unpublished doctoral dissertation, Queen's University, Kingston, Ontario.

Durlak, J. A., Fuhrman, T., & Lampman, C. (1991). Effectiveness of cognitive-behavior therapy for maladapting children: A meta-analysis. *Psychological Bulletin, 110,* 204–214.

Durlak, J. A., & Lipsey, M. W. (1991). A practitioner's guide to meta-analysis. *American Journal of Community Psychology, 19*, 291–332.

Dush, D. M., Hirt, M. L., & Schroeder, H. E. (1989). Self-statement modification in the treatment of child behavior disorders: A meta-analysis. *Psychological Bulletin, 106*, 97–106.

Dzik, D. (1975). Optometric intervention in the control of juvenile delinquents. *Journal of the American Optometric Association, 46*, 629–634.

Eagly, A. H., & Steffen, V. (1986). Gender and aggressive behavior: A meta-analytic review of the social psychological literature. *Psychological Bulletin, 100*, 309–330.

Earls, C. M., & Lalumière, M. L. (2002). A case study of preferential bestiality (zoophilia). *Sexual Abuse: A Journal of Research and Trauma, 14*, 83–88.

East, M. L., & Hofer, H. (1991). Loud calling in a female-domianted mammalian society: Behavioural contexts and functions of whooping of spotted hyaenas, *Crocuta crocuta. Animal Behaviour, 42*, 651–659.

East, M. L., & Hofer, H. (1997). The peniform clitoris of female spotted hyaenas. *Trends in Ecology and Evolution, 12*, 401–402.

Ebstein, R. P., Novick, O., Umansky, R., Priel, B., Osher, Y., Blaine, D., et al. (1996). Dopamine D4 receptor (D4DR) exon III polymorphism associated with the human personality trait of Novelty Seeking. *Nature Genetics, 12*, 78–80.

Ebstein, R. P., Levine, J., Geller, V., Auerbach, J., Gritsenko, I., & Belmaker, R. H. (1998). Dopamine D4 receptor and serotonin transporter promoter in the determination of neonatal temperament. *Molecular Psychiatry, 3*, 238–246.

Edelbrock, C., Rende, R., Plomin, R., & Thompson, L. A. (1995). A twin study of competence and problem behavior in childhood and early adolescence. *Journal of Child Psychology and Psychiatry, 36*, 775–785.

Ekman, P. (1992). Are there basic emotions? *Psychological Review, 99*, 550–553.

Ekman, P. (1993). Facial expression and emotion. *American Psychologist, 48*, 384–392.

Eley, T. C. (1998). General genes: A new theme in developmental psychopathology. *Current Directions in Psychological Science, 6*, 90–95.

Elliott, D. S. (1994). Serious violent offenders: Onset, developmental course, and termination. *Criminology, 32*, 1–21.

Elliott, D. S., Dunford, F. W., & Huizinga, D. (1987). The identification and prediction of career offenders utilizing self-reported and official data. In J. D. Burchard & S. N. Burchard (Eds.), *Prevention of delinquent behavior* (pp. 90–121). Newbury Park, CA: Sage.

Elliott, D. S., Huizinga, D., & Ageton, S. S. (1985). *Explaining delinquency and drug use*. Newbury Park, CA: Sage.

Elliott, D. S., Huizinga, D., & Menard, S. (1989). *Multiple-problem youth: Delinquency, substance use, and mental health problems*. New York: Springer-Verlag.

Elliott, D. S., Huizinga, D., & Morse, B. (1986). Self-reported violent offending: A descriptive analysis of juvenile violent offenders and their offending careers. *Journal of Interpersonal Violence, 1,* 472–514.

Ellis, B. J., & Symons, D. (1990). Sex differences in sexual fantasy: An evolutionary psychological approach. *Journal of Sex Research, 27,* 527–555.

Ellis, L. (1988). The victimful–victimless crime distinction, and seven universal demographic correlates of victimful criminal behavior. *Personality and Individual Differences, 9,* 525–548.

Ellis, L. (1991). Monoamine oxidase and criminality: Identifying an apparent biological marker for antisocial behavior. *Journal of Research in Crime and Delinquency, 28,* 227–251.

Ellis, L., & Walsh, A. (2000). *Criminology: A global perspective.* Needham Heights, MA: Allyn & Bacon.

Fagot, B. I., Pears, K. C., Capaldi, D. M., Crosby, L., & Leve, C. S. (1998). Becoming an adolescent father: Precursors and parenting. *Developmental Psychology, 34,* 1209–1219.

Faraone, S. V., Biederman, J., Weiffenbach, B., Keith, T., Chu, M. P., Weaver, A., et al. (1999). Dopamine D4 gene 7repeat allele and attention deficit hyperactivity disorder. *American Journal of Psychiatry, 156,* 768–770.

Farrington, D. P. (1986). Stepping stones to criminal adult criminal careers. In D. Olweus, J. Block, & M. R. Yarrow (Eds.), *From children to citizens: Families, schools, and delinquency prevention* (pp. 27–57). New York: Springer-Verlag.

Farrington, D. P. (1987). Early precursors of frequent offending. In J .Q. Wilson & G. C. Loury (Eds.), *Families, schools and delinquency prevention* (pp. 27–50). New York: Springer-Verlag.

Farrington, D. P. (1991). Childhood aggression and adult violence: Early precursors and later life outcomes. In D. J. Pepler & K. H. Rubin (Eds.) *The development and treatment of childhood aggression* (pp. 5–30). Hillsdale, NJ: Erlbaum.

Farrington, D. P. (1997). Early prediction of violent and nonviolent youthful offending. *European Journal on Criminal Policy and Research, 5,* 51–66.

Farrington, D. P., Gallagher, B., Morley, L., St. Ledger, R. J., & West, D. J. (1988). Are there any successful men from criminogenic backgrounds? *Psychiatry, 51,* 116–130.

Farrington, D. P., Loeber, R., & Van Kammen, W. B. (1990). Long-term criminal outcomes of hyperactivity-impulsivity-attention deficit and conduct problems in childhood. In L. N. Robins & M. Rutter (Eds.), *Straight and devious pathways to adulthood.* New York: Cambridge University Press.

Fergusson D. M., Lynskey M. T., & Horwood, L. J. (1996). Alcohol misuse and juvenile offending in adolescence. *Addiction, 91,* 483–494.

Fergusson, D. M. & Woodward, L. J. (2000). Educational, psychosocial, and sexual outcomes of girls with conduct problems in early adolescence. *Journal of Child Psychology and Psychiatry and Allied Disciplines, 41,* 779–792.

Firestone, P., Levy, F., & Douglas, V. I. (1976). Hyperactivity and physical anomalies. *Canadian Psychiatric Association Journal, 21*, 23–26.

Fisher, R. A. (1930). *The genetical theory of natural selection*. Oxford: Clarendon Press.

Forth, A. E., Hart, S. D., & Hare, R. D. (1990). Assessment of psychopathy in male young offenders. *Psychological Assessment: A Journal of Consulting and Clinical Psychology, 2*, 1–3.

Frank, L. G. (1986). Social organization of the spotted hyena *Crocuta crocuta*. II. Dominance and reproduction. *Animal Behavior, 34*, 1510–1527.

Frank, L. G. (1994). When hyenas kill their own. *New Scientist, 141*, 38–41.

Frank, L. G., Weldele, M. L. & Glickman, S. E. (1995). Masculinization costs in hyaenas. *Nature, 377*, 584–585.

Frank, R. H. (1988). *Passions within reason: The strategic role of the emotions*. New York: Norton.

Frick, P. J. (1995). Callous-unemotional traits and conduct problems: A two-factor model of psychopathy in children. *Issues in Criminological & Legal Psychology, 24*, 47–51.

Frick, P. J., Lahey, B. B., Loeber, R., Stouthamer-Loeber, M., Christ, M. A. G., & Hanson, K. (1992). Familial risk factors to oppositional defiant disorder and conduct disorder: Parental psychopathology and maternal parenting. *Journal of Consulting and Clinical Psychology, 60*, 49–55.

Frick, P. J., O'Brien, B. S., Wootton, J. M., & McBurnett, K. (1994). Psychopathy and conduct problems in children. *Journal of Abnormal Psychology, 103*, 700–707.

Furlow, B. F., Armijo-Prewitt, T., Gangestad, S. W., & Thornhill, R. (1997). Fluctuating asymmetry and psychometric intelligence. *Proceedings of the Royal Society of London B., 264*, 823–829.

Gabor, T. (1999). Trends in youth crime: Some evidence pointing to increases in the severity and volume of violence on the part of young people. *Canadian Journal of Criminology, 41*, 385–392.

Gangestad, S. W. (1997). Evolutionary psychology and genetic variation: Non-adaptive, fitness-related and adaptive. In G. R. Bock & G. Cardew (Eds.), *Characterizing human psychological adaptations*. New York: Wiley (Ciba Foundation).

Gangestad, S. W., Bailey, J. M., & Martin, N. G. (2000). Taxometric analyses of sexual orientation and gender identity. *Journal of Personality & Social Psychology, 78*, 1109–1121.

Gangestad, S. W., & Snyder, M. (1985). "To carve nature at its joints": On the existence of discrete classes in personality. *Psychological Review, 92*, 317–349.

Gangestad, S. W., & Thornhill, R. (1997). The evolutionary psychology of extra-pair sex: The role of fluctuating asymmetry. *Evolution & Human Behavior, 18*, 69–88.

Gardner, F. E. (1987). Positive interactions between mothers and conduct problem children: Is there harmony as well as fighting? *Journal of Abnormal Psychology, 21*, 245–270.

Garmezy, N. (1985). Stress resistant children: The search for protective factors. In J. E. Stevenson (Ed.), *Recent research in developmental psychopathology* (pp. 213–233). New York: Pergamon.

Garrett, C. J. (1985). Effects of residential treatment on adjudicated delinquents: A meta-analysis. *Journal of Research in Crime and Delinquency, 22,* 287–308.

Geary, D. C., Rumsey, M., Bow-Thomas, C. C., & Hoard, M. K. (1995). Sexual jealousy as a facultative trait: Evidence from the pattern of sex differences in adults from China and the United States. *Ethology and Sociobiology, 16,* 355–383.

Gerhart, J., & Kirschner, M. (1997). *Cells, embryos, and evolution.* Malden, MA: Blackwell Science.

Ghodsian-Carpey, J., & Baker, L. A. (1987). Genetic and environmental influences on aggression in 4- to 7-year-old twins. *Aggressive Behavior, 13,* 173–186.

Giancola, P. R., & Parker, A. M. (2001). A six-year prospective study of pathways toward drug use in adolescent boys with and without a family history of a substance use disorder. *Journal of Studies on Alcohol, 62,* 166–178.

Ginsburg, G. P. (1997). Faces: An epilogue and reconceptualization. In J. A. Russell & J. M. Fernández-Dols (Eds.), *The psychology of facial expression* (pp. 349–382). New York: Cambridge Univeristy Press.

Gleaves, D. H., Lowe, M. R., Snow, A. C., Green, B. A., & Murphy-Eberenz, K. P. (2000). Continuity and discontinuity models of bulimia nervosa: A taxometric investigation. *Journal of Abnormal Psychology, 109,* 56–68.

Glueck, S., & Glueck, E. (1934). *Five hundred delinquent girls.* New York: Knopf.

Glueck, S., & Glueck, E. (1950). *Unravelling juvenile delinquency.* Cambridge, MA: Harvard University Press.

Glueck, S., & Glueck, E. (1967). *Predicting delinquency and crime.* Cambridge, MA: Harvard University Press.

Gold, M. (1987). Social ecology. In H. C. Quay (Ed.), *Handbook of juvenile delinquency* (pp. 62–105). Toronto, Ontario, Canada: Wiley.

Golden, R. R. (1982). A taxometric model for the detection of a conjectured latent taxon. *Multivariate Behavioral Research, 17,* 389–416.

Golden, R. R., & Meehl, P. E. (1979). Detection of the schizoid taxon with MMPI indicators. *Journal of Abnormal Psychology, 88,* 217–233.

Goldhagen, D. J. (1997). *Hitler's willing executioners: Ordinary Germans and the Holocaust.* New York: Vintage.

Goos, L. M., & Silverman, I. (2001). The influence of genomic imprinting on brain development and behavior. *Evolution and Human Behavior, 22,* 385–407.

Gordon, D. A., & Arbuthnot, J. (1987). Individual, group, and family interventions. In H. C. Quay (Ed.), *Handbook of juvenile delinquency* (pp. 290–324). New York: Wiley.

Gordon, D. A., & Arbuthnot, J. (1988). The use of paraprofessionals to deliver home-based family therapy to juvenile delinquents. *Criminal Justice and Behavior, 15,* 364–378.

Gordon, D. A., Arbuthnot, J., Gustafson, K. E., & McGreen, P. (1988). Home-based behavioral-systems family therapy with disadvantaged juvenile delinquents. *The American Journal of Family Therapy, 16,* 243–255.

Gottfredson, D. (1984). A theory-ridden approach to program evaluation: A method for stimulating researcher-implementer collaboration. *American Psychologist, 39,* 1101–1112.

Gottfredson, M. R., & Hirschi, T. (1990). *A general theory of crime.* Stanford, CA: Stanford University Press.

Gottshalk, R., Davidson, W. S., Gensheimer, L. K., & Mayer, J. P. (1987). Community-based interventions. In H. C. Quay (Ed.), *Handbook of juvenile delinquency* (pp. 266–289). Toronto, Ontario, Canada: Wiley.

Gottshalk, R., Davidson, W. S., Mayer, J., & Gensheimer, L. K. (1987). Behavioral approaches with juvenile offenders: A meta-analysis of long-term treatment efficacy. In E. K. Morris & C. J. Braukmann (Eds.), *Behavioral approaches to crime and delinquency: A handbook of application, research, and concepts* (pp. 399–422). New York: Plenum.

Gough, H. G. (1969). *Manual for the California Psychological Inventory.* Palo Alto, CA: Consulting Psychologists Press.

Gray, P. (1991). *Psychology.* New York: Worth.

Gray, P. B., Kahlenberg, S. M., Barrett, E. S., Lipson, S. F., & Ellison, P. T. (2002). Marriage and fatherhood are associated with lower testosterone in males. *Evolution and Human Behavior, 23,* 193–201.

Greenberg, M., Speltz, M., & DeKlyen, M. (1993). The role of attachment in the early development of disruptive behavior problems. *Development and Psychopathology, 5,* 191–213.

Gretton, H. M., McBride, M., Hare, R. D., O'Shaughnessy, R., & Kumka, G. (2001). Psychopathy and recidivism in adolescent sex offenders. *Criminal Justice and Behavior, 28,* 427–449.

Gross, M. R. (1991). Evolution of alternative reproductive strategies: Frequency-dependent sexual selection in male bluegill sunfish. *Philosophical Transactions of the Royal Society of London B, 332,* 59–66.

Grove, W. M., Andreasen, N. C., Young, M., Endicott, J., Keller, M. B., Hirschfeld, R. M. A., et al. (1987). Isolation and characterization of a nuclear depressive syndrome. *Psychological Medicine, 17,* 471–484.

Gualtieri, T., & Hicks, R. E. (1985). An immunoreactive theory of selective male affliction. *The Behavioral and Brain Sciences, 8,* 427–441.

Gurr, T. R. (1989). Historical trends in violent crime: Europe and the United States. In T. R. Gurr (Ed.), *Violence in America: The history of crime* (pp. 11–21). Newbury Park, CA: Sage.

Guy, J. D., Majorski, L. V., Wallace, C. J., & Guy, M. P. (1983). The incidence of minor physical anomalies in adult male schizophrenic. *Schizophrenia Bulletin, 9,* 571–582.

Gwynne, D. T. (1991). Sexual competition among females: What causes courtship-role reversal? *Trends in Ecology and Evolution*, 6, 118–121.

Hahn, M. E., Hewitt, J. K., Henderson, N. D., & Benno, R. (1990). *Developmental behavior genetics: Neural, biometrical, and evolutionary approach*. Toronto, Ontario, Canada: Oxford Univeristy Press.

Haig, D. (1992). Genomic imprinting and the theory of parent-offspring conflict. *Developmental Biology*, 68, 153–160.

Haig, D. (1993). Genetic conflicts in human pregnancy. *Quarterly Review of Biology*, 68, 495–532.

Haig, D. (1995, June). *Genetic conflicts in human pregnancy*. Paper presented at the meeting of the Human Behavior and Evolution Society, Santa Barbara, CA.

Haig, D. (1997). Parental antagonism, relatedness asymmetries, and genomic imprinting. *Proceedings of the Royal Society of London B*, 264, 1657–1662.

Haig, D. (1999). Assymetric relations: Internal conflicts and the horror of incest. *Evolution and Human Behavour*, 20, 83–98.

Halverson, C. F., & Victor, J. B. (1976). Minor physical anomalies and problem behavior in elementary school children. *Child Development*, 47, 281–285.

Hamer, D. (1997). The search for personality genes: Adventures of a molecular biologist. *Current Directions in Psychological Science*, 6, 111–114.

Hamilton, W. D. (1964). The genetical theory of social behavior, I, II. *Journal of Theoretical Biology*, 12, 12–45.

Hare, R. D. (1984). Performance of psychopaths on cognitive tasks related to frontal lobe function. *Journal of Abnormal Psychology*, 93, 133–140.

Hare, R. D. (1991). *Manual for the Revised Psychopathy Checklist*. Toronto, Ontario, Canada: Multi-Health Systems.

Hare, R. D. (1993). *Without conscience: The disturbing world of the psychopaths among us*. New York: Pocket Books.

Hare, R. D. (1996). Psychopathy: A clinical construct whose time has come. *Criminal Justice & Behavior*, 23, 25–54.

Hare, R. D., Clark, D., Grann, M., & Thornton, D. (2000). Psychopathy and the predictive validity of the PCL-R. *Behavioral Sciences and the Law*, 18, 623–645.

Harpending, H. C., & Sobus, J. (1987). Sociopathy as an adaptation. *Ethology and Sociobiology*, 8, 63–72.

Harris, M. G. (1994). Cholas, Mexican-American girls, and gangs. *Sex Roles*, 30, 289–301.

Harris, G. T., Rice, M. E., & Lalumière, M. L. (2001). Criminal violence: The roles of psychopathy, neurodevelopmental insults, and antisocial parenting. *Criminal Justice and Behavior*, 28, 402–426.

Harris, G. T., Rice, M. E., & Quinsey, V. L. (1993). Violent recidivism of mentally disordered offenders: The development of a statistical prediction instrument. *Criminal Justice and Behavior*, 20, 315–335.

Harris, G. T., Rice, M. E., Quinsey, V. L., Lalumière, A., Boer, D., & Lang, C. (in press). Multi-site comparison of actuarial risk instruments for sex offenders. *Psychological Assessment*.

Harris, G. T., Rice, M. E., & Quinsey, V. L. (1994). Psychopathy as a taxon: Evidence that psychopaths are a discrete class. *Journal of Consulting and Clinical Psychology, 62*, 387–397.

Harris, G. T., Rice, M. E., Quinsey, V. L., & Chaplin, T. C. (1996). Viewing time as a measure of sexual interest among child molesters and normal heterosexual men. *Behaviour Research and Therapy, 34*, 389–394.

Haslam, N., & Beck, A. T. (1994). Subtyping major depression: A taxometric analysis. *Journal of Abnormal Psychology, 103*, 686–692.

Hawkins, J. D., & Catalano, R. F. (1990). Intensive family preservation services: Broadening the vision for prevention. In J. K. Whittaker, J. Kinney, E. M. Tracy, & C. Brooth (Eds.), *Reaching high-risk families* (pp. 179–192). New York: Aldine de Gruyter.

Hawkins, J. D., Catalano, R. F., & Miller, J. Y. (1992). Risk and protective factors for alcohol and other drug problems in adolescence and early adulthood: Implications for substance abuse prevention. *Psychological Bulletin, 112*, 64–105.

Hawkins, J. D., Farrington, D. P., & Catalano, R. F. (1991). Reducing violence through the schools. In D. S. Elliott, B. A. Hamburg, & K. R. Williams (Eds.), *Youth violence: New perspectives for schools and communities*. Cambridge, England: Cambridge University Press.

Hawkins, J. D., Herrenkohl, T., Farrington, D. P., Brewer, D., Catalano, R. F., & Harachi, T. (1998). A review of predictors of youth violence. In R. Loeber & D. P. Farrington (Eds.), *Serious and violent juvenile offenders: Risk factors and successful interventions*. Thousand Oaks, CA: Sage.

Hawkins, J. D., Von Cleve, E., & Catalano, R. F. (1991). Reducing early childhood aggression: Results of a primary prevention program. *Journal of the American Academy of Child and Adolescent Psychiatry, 30*, 208–217.

Hawkins, J. D., & Weiss, J. G. (1985). The social development model: An integrated approach to delinquency prevention. *Journal of Primary Prevention, 6*, 73–97.

Hazelrigg, M. D., Cooper, H. M., & Borduin, C. M. (1987). Evaluating the effectiveness of family therapies: An integrative review and analysis. *Psychological Bulletin, 101*, 428–442.

Heino, M., Metz, J. A., & Kaitala, V. (1998). The enigma of frequency-dependent selection. *TREE, 13*, 367–370.

Hejmadi, A., Davidson, R. J., & Rozin, P. (2000). Exploring Hindu Indian emotion expressions: Evidence for accurate recognition by Americans and Indians. *Psychological Science, 11*, 183–187.

Helzer, J. E., Robins, L. N., & McEvoy, L. (1987). Post-traumatic stress disorder in the general population: Findings of the Epidemiologic Catchment Area Survey. *The New England Journal of Medicine, 317*, 1630–1634.

Henggeler, S. W. (1989). *Delinquency in adolescence*. Newbury Park, CA: Sage.

Henggeler, S. W. (1999). Multisystemic therapy: An overview of clinical procedures, outcomes, and policy implications. *Child Psychology & Psychiatry Review, 4*, 2–10.

Henggeler, S. W., Melton, G. B., Brondino, M. J., Scherer, D. G., & Hanley, J. H. (1997). Multisystemic therapy with violent and chronic juvenile offenders and their families: The role of treatment fidelity in successful dissemination. *Journal of Consulting and Clinical Psychology, 65*, 821–833.

Henggeler, S. W., Melton, G. B., & Smith, L. A. (1992). Family preservation using multisystemic therapy: An effective alternative to incarcerating serious juvenile offenders. *Journal of Consulting and Clinical Psychology, 60*, 953–961.

Henggeler, S. W., Melton, G. B., Smith, L. A., Schoenwald, S. K., & Hanley, J. H. (1993). Family preservation using multisystemic treatment: Long-term follow-up to a clinical trial with serious juvenile offenders. *Journal of Child and Family Studies, 2*, 283–293.

Henggeler, S. W., Schoenwald, S. K., Borduin, C. M., Rowland, M. D., & Cunningham, P. B. (1998). *Multisystemic treatment of antisocial behavior in children and adolescents*. New York: Guilford Press.

Henington, C., Hughes, J. N., Cavell, T. A., & Thompson, B. (1998). The role of relational aggression in identifying aggressive boys and girls. *Journal of School Psychology, 36*, 457–477.

Herpertz, S. C., Werth, U., Lukas, G., Qunaibi, M., Schuerkens, A., Kunert, H. J., et al. (2001). Emotion in criminal offenders with psychopathy and borderline personality disorder. *Archives of General Psychiatry, 58*, 737–745.

Hertwig, R., Davis, J. N., & Sulloway, F. J. (2002). Parental investment: How an equity motive can produce inequality. *Psychological Bulletin, 128*, 728–745.

Hetherington, E. M., & Clingempeel, W. G. (1992). Coping with marital transitions: A family systems perspective. *Monographs of the Society for Research in Child Development, 57*(2–3, Serial No. 227).

Hill, J. K., Andrews, D. A., & Hoge, R. D. (1991). Meta-analysis of treatment programs for young offenders: The effect of clinically relevant treatment on recidivism, with controls for various methodological variables. *Canadian Journal of Program Evaluation, 6*, 97–109.

Hill, K., & Hurtado, A. M. (1996). *Ache life history: The ecology and demography of a foraging people*. Hawthorne, NY: Aldine de Gruyter.

Hindelang, M. J., Hirschi, T., & Weis, J. (1981). *Measuring Delinquency*. Beverly Hills, CA: Sage Publications.

Hinshaw, S. P. (1992). Externalizing behavior problems and academic underachievement in childhood and adolescence: Causal relationships and underlying mechanisms. *Psychological Bulletin, 111*, 127–155.

Hirschi, T. (1969). *Causes of delinquency*. University of California Press, Berkeley.

Hirschi, T., & Gottfredson, M. (1983). Age and the explanation of crime. *American Journal of Sociology, 89*, 552–584.

Hirschi, T., & Hindelang, M. J. (1977). Intelligence and delinquency: A revisionist review. *American Sociological Review, 42*, 571–587.

Hoffman-Bustamente, D. (1973). The nature of female criminology. *Issues in Criminology, 8*, 1117–1136.

Hoge, R. D. (1999). An expanded role for psychological assessments in juvenile justice systems. *Criminal Justice and Behavior, 26*, 251–266.

Hoge, R. D. (2002). Standardized instruments for assessing risk and need in youthful offenders. *Criminal Justice and Behavior, 29*, 380–396.

Hoge, R. D., & Andrews, D. A. (2001). *The Youth Level of Service/Case Management Inventory manual—revised*. Ottawa, Ontario, Canada: Department of Psychology, Carleton University.

Holekamp, K. E., & Smale, L. (1995). On hyenas. *The American Naturalist, 145*, 261–278.

Holekamp, K. E., Cooper, S. M., Katona, C. I., Berry, N. A., Frank, L. G., & Smale, L. (1997). Patterns of association among female spotted hyenas (*Crocuta crocuta*). *Journal of Mammology, 78*, 55–64.

Horowitz, R., & Pottieger, A. E. (1991). Gender bias in juvenile justice handling of seriously crime-involved youths. *Journal of Research in Crime and Delinquency, 28*, 75–100.

Hrdy, S.B. (1981). *The Woman that Never Evolved*. Cambridge, Massachusetts: Harvard University Press.

Huesmann, L. R., & Eron, L. D. (1984). Cognitive processes and the persistence of aggressive behavior. *Aggressive Behavior, 10*, 243–251.

Huesmann, L. R., Eron, L. D., Lefkowitz, M. M., & Walder, L. O. (1984). Stability of aggression over time and generations. *Developmental Psychology, 20*, 1120–1134.

Huesmann, L. R., Eron, L. D., & Yarmel, P. W. (1987). Intellectual functioning and aggression. *Journal of Personality and Social Psychology, 52*, 232–240.

Hughes, K. A., & Burleson, M. H. (2000). Evolutionary causes of genetic variation in fertility and other fitness components. In J. L. Rodgers, D. C. Rowe, & W. B. Miller (Eds.), *Genetic influences on human fertility and sexuality: Theoretical and empirical contributions from the biological and behavioral sciences* (pp. 7–33). Boston: Kluwer.

Hunter, J. E., & Schmidt, F. L. (1990). *Methods of meta-analysis*. Newbury Park, CA: Sage.

Hyde, J. S. (1984). How large are gender differences in aggression? A developmental meta-analysis. *Developmental Psychology, 20*, 722–736.

Iacono, W. G., Carlson, S. R., Taylor, J., Elkins, I. R., & McGue, M. (1999). Behavioral disinhibition and the development of substance-use disorder: Findings from the Minnesota twin family study. *Development and Psychopathology, 11*, 869–900.

Infant Health and Development Program. (1990). Enhancing the outcomes of low-birth-weight, premature infants: A multisite, randomized trial. *Journal of the American Medical Association, 263*, 3035–3042.

Izzo, R. L., & Ross, R. R. (1990). Meta-analysis of rehabilitation programs for juvenile delinquents: A brief report. *Criminal Justice and Behavior, 17,* 134–142.

Jaffe, P. G., Suderman, M., Reitzel, D., & Killip, S. M. (1992). An evaluation of a secondary school primary prevention program on violence in intimate relationships. *Violence and Victims, 7,* 129–146.

Jensen, A. R. (1997). The puzzle of nongenetic variance. In R. J. Sternberg & E. Grigorenko (Eds.), *Intelligence, heredity, and environment* (pp. 42–88). Cambridge, England: Cambridge University Press.

Jensen, A. R. (1998). *The g factor: The science of mental ability.* London: Praeger.

Jessor, R., Costa, F., Jessor, L., & Donovan, J. E. (1983). Time of first intercourse: A prospective study. *Journal of Personality and Social Psychology, 44,* 618–626.

Joel, S. (1985). The female offender. In M. H. Ben-Aron, S. J. Hucker, & C. D. Webster (Eds.), *Clinical criminology: The assessment and treatment of criminal behavior* (pp. 239–254). Toronto, Ontario, Canada: M & M Graphics.

John, O. P. (1990). The "Big Five" factor taxonomy: Dimensions of personalty in the natural language and in questionnaires. In L. A. Pervin (Ed.), *Handbook of personality: Theory and research* (pp. 66–100). New York: Guilford Press.

Johnson, R. C. (1963). Similarity in IQ of separated identical twins as related to length of time spent in same environment. *Child Development, 34,* 745–749.

Johnson, V. S. (1999). *Why we feel: The science of human emotions.* Reading, MA: Perseus.

Johnson, D. J., & Walker, T. (1987). Primary prevention of behavior problems in Mexican-American children. *American Journal of Community Psychology, 15,* 375–385.

Jones, M. B., & Offord, D. R. (1998). Reduction of antisocial behavior in poor children by nonschool skill development. *Journal of Child Psychology and Psychiatry, 30,* 737–750.

Jonsson, E. G., Nothen, M. M., Gustavsson, J. P., Neidt, H., Brene, S., Tylec, A., Propping, P., & Sedvall, G. C. (1997). Lack of evidence for allelic association between personality traits and the dopamine D-4 receptor gene polymorphisms. *American Journal of Psychiatry, 154,* 697–699.

Kanazawa, S., & Still, M. C. (2000). Why men commit crimes and why they desist. *Sociological Theory, 18,* 434–447.

Kandel, E., Brennan, P. A., Mednick, S. A., & Michelson, N. M. (1989). Minor physical abnormalities and recidivistic adult violent criminal behavior. *Acta Psychiatricia Scandinavia, 79,* 103–109.

Kandel, E., & Mednick, S. A. (1991). Perinatal complications predict violent offending. *Criminology, 29,* 519–529.

Kandel, E., Mednick, S. A., Kirkegaard-Sorensen, L., Hutchings, B., Knop, J., Rosenberg, R., et al. (1988). IQ as a protective factor for subjects at high risk for antisocial behavior. *Journal of Consulting and Clinical Psychology, 56,* 224–226.

Karniski, W. M., Levine, M. D., Clarke, S., Palfrey, J. S., & Meltzer, L. J. (1982). A study of neurodevelopmental findings in early adolescent delinquents. *Journal of Adolescent Health Care, 3*, 151–159.

Kasen, S., Cohen, P., Skodol, A. E., Johnson, J. G., Smailes, E., & Brook, J. S. (2001). Childhood depression and adult personality disorder: Alternative pathways of continuity. *Archives of General Psychiatry, 58*, 231–236.

Kaseno, S. L. (1985). The visual anatomy of the juvenile delinquent. *Academic Therapy, 21*, 99–105.

Kazdin, A. E. (1985). *Treatment of antisocial behavior in children and adolescents*. Homewood, IL: Dorsey Press.

Kazdin, A. E. (1987). Treatment of antisocial behavior in children: Current status and future directions. *Psychological Bulletin, 102*, 187–203.

Kazdin, A. E. (1993a). Adolescent mental health: Prevention and treatment programs. *American Psychologist, 48*, 127–141.

Kazdin, A. E. (1993b). Treatment of conduct disorder: Progress and directions in psychotherapy research. *Development and Psychopathology, 5*, 277–310.

Kazdin, A. E., Esveldt-Dawson, K., French, N. H., & Unis, A. S. (1987). Problem-solving skills training and relationship therapy in the treatment of antisocial child behavior. *Journal of Consulting and Clinical Psychology, 55*, 76–85.

Keenan, K., & Shaw, D. S. (1994). The development of aggression in toddlers: A study of low-income families. *Journal of Abnormal Child Psychology, 22*, 53–77.

Kellam, S. G., & Van Horn, Y. V. (1997). Life course development, community epidemiology, and preventive trials: A scientific structure for prevention research. *American Journal of Community Psychology, 25*, 177–188.

Kelly, M. L., Embry, L. H., & Baer, D. M. (1979). Skills for child management and family support: Training parents for maintenance. *Behavior Modification, 3*, 373–396.

Kenrick, D. T., & Keefe, R. C. (1992). Age preferences in mates reflect sex differences in human reproductive strategies. *Behavioral and Brain Sciences, 15*, 75–133.

Kety, S. S. (1988). Schizophrenic illness in the families of schizophrenic adoptees: Findings from the Danish national sample. *Schizophrenia Bulletin, 14*, 217–222.

Kety, S. S., Rosenthal, D., Wender, P. H., Schulsinger, F., & Jacobsen, B. (1978). The biological and adoptive families of adopted individuals who become schizophrenic. In L. C. Wynne, R. L. Cromwell, & S. Matthysse (Eds.), *The nature of schizophrenia* (pp. 25–37). New York: Wiley.

King, D. W., King, L. A., Foy, D. W., & Gudanowski, D. M. (1996). Prewar factors in combat-related Posttraumatic Stress Disorder: Structural equation modeling with a national sample of female and male Vietnam veterans. *Journal of Consulting and Clinical Psychology, 64*, 520–531.

Klein, N. C., Alexander, J. F., & Parsons, B. V. (1977). Impact of family systems intervention on recidivism and sibling delinquency: A model of primary prevention and program evaluation. *Journal of Consulting and Clinical Psychology, 45*, 469–474.

Kolvin, I. (1981). *Help starts here: The maladjusted child in the ordinary school.* London: Tavistock.

Kolvin, I., Miller, F., Fleeting, M., & Kolvin, P. (1988). Social and parenting factors affecting criminal offending rates. *British Journal of Psychiatry, 152*, 80–90.

Konopka, G. (1966). *The adolescent girl in conflict.* Upper Saddle River, NJ: Prentice-Hall.

Korfine, L., & Lenzenweger, M. F. (1995). The taxonicity of schizotypy: A replication. *Journal of Abnormal Psychology, 104*, 26–31.

Krueger, R. F., Hicks, B. M., & McGue, M. (2001). Altruism and antisocial behavior: Independent tendencies, unique personality correlates, distinct etiologies. *Psychological Science, 12*, 397–402.

Kruesi, M. J., Rapoport, J. L., Hamburger, S., Hibbs, E. D., Potter, W. Z., Lenane, M., et al. (1990). Cerebrospinal fluid monoamine metabolites, aggression, and impulsivity in disruptive behavior of children and adolescents. *Archives of General Psychiatry, 47*, 419–426.

Krynicki, V. E. (1978). Cerebral dysfunction in repetitively assaultive adolescents. *Journal of Nervous & Mental Disease, 166*, 59–67.

Kuhn, K. U., Meyer, K., Noethen, M. M., Gaensicke, M., Papassotiropoulos, A., & Maier, W. (1999). Allelic variants of dopamine receptor D4 (DRD4) and serotonin receptor 5HT2c (HTR2c) and temperament factors: Replication tests. *American Journal of Medical Genetics, 88*, 168–172.

Lagerspetz, K. M. J., Bjorkqvist, K., & Peltonen, T. (1988). Is indirect aggression typical in females? Gender differences in aggressiveness in 11- to 12-year-old children. *Aggressive Behavior, 14*, 403–414.

Lalumière, M. L., Chalmers, L. J., Quinsey, V. L., & Seto, M. C. (1996). A test of the mate deprivation hypothesis of sexual coercion. *Ethology and Sociobiology, 17*, 299–318.

Lalumière, M. L., Harris, G. T., & Rice, M. E. (2001). Psychopathy and developmental instability. *Evolution & Human Behavior, 22*, 75–92.

Lalumière, M. L., & Quinsey, V. L. (1996). Sexual deviance, antisociality, mating effort, and the use of sexually coercive behaviors. *Personality and Individual Differences, 21*, 33–48.

Lalumière, M. L., & Quinsey, V. L. (2000). Good genes, mating effort, and delinquency. *Behavioral and Brain Sciences, 23*, 608–609.

Lalumière, M. L., Quinsey, V. L., & Craig, W. M. (1996). Why children from the same family are so different from one another: A Darwinian note. *Human Nature, 7*, 281–290.

Lalumière, M. L., Quinsey, V. L., Harris, G. T., & Rice, M. E. (In preparation). Sexual coercion: Understanding individual differences.

Landolt, M. A., Lalumière, M. L., & Quinsey, V. L. (1995). Sex differences and intra-sex variations in human mating tactics: An evolutionary approach. *Ethology and Sociobiology, 16*, 3–23.

Lane, R. (1989). On the social meaning of homicide trends in America. In T. R. Gurr (Ed.), *Violence in America: The history of crime* (pp. 21–54). Newbury Park, CA: Sage.

Langbehn, D. R., & Cadoret, R. J. (2001). The adult antisocial syndrome with and without antecedent conduct disorder: Comparisons from an adoption study. *Comprehensive Psychiatry, 42,* 272–282.

Langlois, J. H., & Roggman, L. A. (1990). Attractive faces are only average. *Psychological Science, 1,* 115–121.

Laub, J. H., Nagin, D. S., & Sampson, R. J. (1998). Trajectories of change in criminal offending: Good marriages and the desistance process. *American Sociological Review, 63,* 225–238.

Laub, J. H., & Sampson, R. J. (1988). Unraveling families and delinquency: A reanalysis of the Gluecks' data. *Criminology, 26,* 355–380.

Lawson, A. W., & Sanet, R. (1992). Vision problems, juvenile delinquency, and drug abuse. In G. W. Lawson & A. W. Lawson (Eds.), *Adolescent substance abuse: Etiology, treatment, and prevention* (pp. 337–350). Gaithersburg, MD: Aspen.

LeBlanc, M. (1998). Screening of serious and violent offenders: Identification, classification, and prediction. In R. Loeber & D. P. Farrington (Eds.), *Serious and violent juvenile offenders: Risk factors and successful interventions*. London: Sage.

Leitenberg, H. (1987). Primary prevention of delinquency. In J. D. Burchard & S. N. Burchard (Eds.), *Prevention of delinquent behavior* (pp. 312–330). Newbury Park, CA: Sage.

Lenzenweger, M. F., & Korfine, L. (1992). Confirming the latent structure and base rate of schizotypy: A taxometric analysis. *Journal of Abnormal Psychology, 101,* 567–571.

Lesch, K. P., Bengel, D., Heils, A., Sabol, S. Z., Greenberg, B. D., Petri, S., et al. (1996). Association of anxiety-related traits with a polymorphism in the serotonin transporter gene regulatory region. *Science, 274,* 1527–1531.

Leschied, A. W., Cummings, A. L., Van Brunschot, M., Cunningham, A., & Saunders, A. (2000). *Female adolescent aggression: A review of the literature and correlates of aggression*. Ottawa, Ontario, Canada: Solicitor General of Canada.

Lewis, C., Battistich, V., & Schaps, E. (1990). School-based primary prevention: What is an effective program? *New Directions for Child Development, 50,* 35–59.

Lewis, C. E. (1991). Neurochemical mechanisms of chronic antisocial behavior (psychopathy): A literature review. *Journal of Nervous and Mental Disease, 179,* 720–727.

Lewis, D. O., Yeager, C. A., Cobham-Portorreal, C. S., Klein, N., Showalter, C., & Anthony, A. (1991). A follow-up of female delinquents: Maternal contributions to the perpetuation of deviance. *Journal of the American Academy of Child and Adolescent Psychiatry, 30,* 197–201.

Lieberman, P. (1984). *The biology and evolution of language*. Cambridge, MA: Harvard University Press.

Lipsey, M. W. (1992). Juvenile delinquency treatment: A meta-analytic inquiry into the variability of effects. In T. D. Cook, H. Cooper, D. S. Cordray, H. Hartmann, L. V. Hedges, R. J. Light, et al. (Eds.), *Meta-analysis for explanation: A casebook* (pp. 83–127). New York: Russell Sage.

Lipsey, M. W., & Derzon, J. H. (1998). Predictors of violent or serious delinquency in adolescence and early adulthood: A synthesis of longitudinal research. In R. Loeber & D. P. Farrington (Eds.), *Serious & violent juvenile offenders: Risk factors and successful interventions* (pp. 86–105). Thousand Oaks, CA: Sage.

Lipsey, M. W., & Wilson, D. (1993). The efficacy of psychological, educational, and behavioral treatment: Confirmation from meta-analysis. *American Psychologist, 48,* 1181–1209.

Lipsey, M. W., & Wilson, D. B. (1997). *Effective intervention for serious juvenile offenders: A synthesis of research.* Paper prepared for the OJJDP study group on serious and violent juvenile offenders.

Livshits G., & Kobyliansky E. (1987). Dermatoglyphic traits as possible markers of developmental processes in humans. *American Journal of Medical Genetics, 26,* 111–122.

Livshits G., & Kobyliansky E. (1991). Fluctuating asymmetry as a possible measure of developmental homeostasis in humans: A review. *Human Biology, 63,* 441–466.

Loeber, R. (1982). The stability of antisocial and delinquent child behavior: A review. *Child Development, 53,* 1431–1446.

Loeber, R. (1990). Development and risk factors of juvenile antisocial behavior and delinquency. *Clinical Psychology Review, 10,* 1–41.

Loeber, R. (1999, May). *Youth violence: An overview of research.* Presentation to the Department of Child Psychiatry and the Institute for Anti-Social and Violent Youth, Toronto, Ontario, Canada.

Loeber, R., & Dishion, T. J. (1983). Early predictors of male delinquency: A review. *Psychological Bulletin, 94,* 68–99.

Loeber, R., & Dishion, T. J. (1987). Antisocial and delinquent youths: Methods for their early identification. In J. D. Burchard & S. N. Burchard (Eds.), *Prevention of delinquent behavior* (pp. 75–89). Newbury Park, CA: Sage.

Loeber, R., Dishion, T. J., & Patterson, G. R. (1984). Multiple gating: A multistage assessment procedure for identifying youths at risk for delinquency. *Journal of Research on Crime and Delinquency, 21,* 7–32.

Loeber, R., & Farrington, D. P. (1998). *Serious and violent juvenile offenders: Risk factors and successful interventions.* Thousand Oaks, CA: Sage.

Loeber, R., & Stouthamer-Loeber, M. (1986). Family factors as correlates and predictors of juvenile conduct problems and delinquency. In N. Morris & M. Tonry (Eds.), *Crime and justice: An annual review of research* (Vol. 7, pp. 29–149). Chicago: University of Chicago Press.

Loeber, R., & Stouthamer-Loeber, M. (1987). Prediction. In H. C. Quay (Ed.), *Handbook of juvenile delinquency* (pp. 325–382). New York: Wiley.

Loeber, R., Weissman, W., & Reid, J. B. (1983). Family interactions of assaultive adolescents, stealers, and nondelinquents. *Journal of Abnormal Child Psychology, 11*, 1–14.

Loeber, R., Wung, P., Keenan, K., Giroux, B., Stouthamer-Loeber, M., Van Kammen, W. B., et al. (1993). Developmental pathways in disruptive child behavior. *Development and Psychopathology, 5*, 103–133.

Loehlin, J. C. (1989). Partitioning environmental and genetic contributions to behavioral development. *American Psychologist, 44*, 1285–1292.

Lombroso, C., & Ferrero, G. (1895). *The female offender*. New York: Appleton.

Lorion, R. P., Tolan, P. H., & Whaler, R. G. (1987). Prevention. In H. C. Quay (Ed.), *Handbook of juvenile delinquency* (pp. 383–416). New York: Wiley.

Loucks, A. D. (1995). *Criminal behaviour, violent behaviour, and prison maladjustment in federal female offenders*. Unpublished doctoral dissertation, Queen's University, Kingston, Ontario, Canada.

Loy, J. D., & Peters, C. B. (Eds.). (1991). *Understanding behavior: What primate studies tell us about human behavior*. New York: Oxford University Press.

Lykken, D. T. (1995). *The antisocial personalities*. Hillsdale, NJ: Erlbaum.

Lynam, D. R. (1996). Early identification of chronic offenders: Who is the fledgling psychopath? *Psychological Bulletin, 120*, 209–234.

Lynam, D., Moffitt, T., & Stouthamer-Loeber, M. (1993). Explaining the relation between IQ and delinquency: Class, race, test motivation, school failure, or self-control? *Journal of Abnormal Psychology, 102*, 187–196.

Lynn, R., Hampson, S., & Agahi, E. (1989). Genetic and environmental mechanisms determining intelligence, neuroticism, extraversion and psychoticism: An analysis of Irish siblings. *British Journal of Psychology 80*, 499–507.

Lyons, M. J. (1996). A twin study of self-reported criminal behavior. In G. R. Bock & J. A. Goode (Eds.), *Genetics of criminal and antisocial behavior* (pp. 61–75). Chichester, England: Wiley.

Lyons, M. J., Goldberg, J., Eisen, S. A., True, W., Tsuang, M. T., Meyer, J. M., et al. (1993). Do genes influence exposure to trauma? A twin study of combat. *American Journal of Medical Genetics, 48*, 22–27.

Lyons-Ruth, K., Easterbrooks, M. A., & Cibelli, C. E. (1997). Infant attachment strategies, infant mental lag, and maternal depressive symptoms: Predictors of internalizing and externalizing problems at age 7. *Developmental Psychology, 33*, 681–692.

Lytton, H. (1990). Child and parent effects in boys' conduct disorder: A reinterpretation. *Developmental Psychology, 26*, 683–697.

Maccoby, E. E., & Martin, J. A. (1983). Socialization in the context of the family: Parent–child interaction. In E. M. Hetherington (Ed.), *Handbook of child psychology* (Vol. 4, pp. 1–101). New York: Wiley.

Magnusson, D. (1988). *Individual development from an interactional perspective*. Hillsdale, NJ: Erlbaum.

Mak, A. S. (1990). Testing a psychosocial control theory of delinquency. *Criminal Justice and Behavior, 17*, 215–230.

Malamuth, N. M., Heavy, C. L., & Linz, D. (1993). Predicting men's antisocial behavior against women: The interaction model of sexual aggression. In G. C. N. Hall, R. Hirschman, J. R. Graham, & M. S. Zaragoza (Eds.), *Sexual aggression: Issues in etiology, assessment, and treatment* (pp. 63–97). Bristol, PA: Taylor & Francis.

Manning, J. T., Koukourakis, K., & Brodie, D. A. (1998). Fluctuating asymmetry, metabolic rate and sexual selection in human males. *Evolution and Human Behavior, 18*, 15–21.

Martinson, R. (1974). What works? Questions and answers about prison reform. *The Public Interest, 36*, 22–54.

Mayr, E. (1983). How to carry out the adaptationist program. *American Naturalist, 121*, 324–334.

Mayr, E. (1988). *Toward a new philosophy of biology: Observations of an evolutionist.* Cambridge, MA: Belknap Press of Harvard University.

Mayr, E. (1991). *One long argument: Charles Darwin and the genesis of modern evolutionary thought.* Cambridge, MA: Harvard University Press.

Mazerolle, P., Brame, R., & Paternoster, R. (2000). Onset age, persistence, and offending versatility: Comparisons across gender. *Criminology, 38*, 1143–1172.

Mazur, A., & Booth, A. (1998). Testosterone and dominance in men. *Behavioral and Brain Sciences, 21*, 353–397.

Mazur, A., Halpern, C., Udry, J. R. (1994). Dominant-looking male teenagers copulate earlier. *Ethology and Sociobiology, 15*, 87–94.

McCartney, K., Harris, M. J., & Bernieri, F. (1990). Growing up and growing apart: A developmental meta-analysis of twin studies. *Psychological Bulletin, 107*, 226–237.

McCarton, C., Bennett, F., Donithan, M., Belt, P., Brooks-Gunn, J., Bauer, C., et al. (1997). Neurologic status at 36 months of age. In R. T. Gross, D. Spiker, & C. W. Haynes (Eds.), *Helping low birth weight, premature babies: The Infant Health and Development Program* (pp. 324–334). Stanford, CA: Stanford University Press.

McClintock, F. H. (1963). *Crimes of Violence.* London: MacMillan and Co.

McCord, J. (1978). A thirty-year follow-up of treatment effects. *American Psychologist, 33*, 284–289.

McCord, J., & McCord, W. (1959a). A follow-up on the Cambridge-Somerville youth study. *Annals of the American Academy of Political and Social Science, 322*, 89–96.

McCord, W., & McCord, J. (1959b). *Origins of crime.* New York: Columbia University Press.

McGlashan, T. H., Grilo, C. M., Skodol, A. E., Gunderson, J. G., Shea, M. T., Morey, L. C., et al. (2000). The Collaborative Longitudinal Personality Disorders Study: Baseline axis I/II and II/II diagnostic co-occurrence. *Acta Psychiatrica Scandinavica, 102*, 256–264.

McGue, M., Iacono, W. G., Legrand, L. N., Malone, S., & Elkins, I. R. (2001). Origins and consequences of age at first drink: I. Associations with substance use disorders, disinhibitory behavior and psychopathology, and P3 amplitude. *Alcoholism: Clinical Research and Experimental Research, 25,* 1156–1165.

McMahon, R. J., Slough, N., & Conduct Problems Prevention Research Group. (1996). Family-based intervention in the Fast Track Program. In R. DeV. Peters & R. J. McMahon (Eds.), *Preventing childhood disorders, substance abuse, and delinquency* (pp. 90–110). Thousand Oaks, CA: Sage.

Mealey, L. (1995). The sociobiology of sociopathy: An integrated evolutionary model. *Behavioral & Brain Sciences, 18,* 523–599.

Mealey, L. (2000). *Sex differences: Developmental and evolutionary strategies.* New York: Academic.

Mednick, S. A., Gabrielli, W. F., & Hutchings, B. (1983). Genetic influences in criminal behavior: Evidence from an adoption cohort. In K. T. Van Dusen & S. A. Mednick (Eds.), *Prospective studies of crime and delinquency* (pp. 39–71). Boston: Kluwer-Nijhoff.

Meehl, P. E. (1990a). Appraising and amending theories: The strategy of Lakatosian defense and two principles that warrant using it. *Psychological Inquiry, 1,* 108–141, 173–180.

Meehl, P. E. (1990b). Corroboration and verisimilitude: Against Lakatos' "sheer leap of faith" (Working Paper, MCPS–90–01). Minneapolis: University of Minnesota, Center for Philosophy of Science, (pp. 39–42).

Meehl, P. E. (1992). Factors and taxa, traits and types, differences in degree and differences in kind. *Journal of Personality, 60,* 117–173.

Meehl, P. E. (1995). Bootstraps taxometrics: Solving the classification problem in psychopathology. *American Psychologist, 50,* 266–275.

Meehl, P. E., & Golden, R. R. (1982). Taxometric methods. In J. N. Butcher & P. C. Kendall (Eds.), *The handbook of research methods in clinical psychology* (pp. 127–181). New York: Wiley.

Meehl, P. E., & Yonce, L. J. (1994). Taxometric analysis: I. Detecting taxonicity with two quantitative indicators using means above and below a sliding cut (MAMBAC procedure). *Psychological Reports, 74,* 1059–1274.

Meehl, P. E., & Yonce, L. J. (1996). Taxometric analysis: II. Detecting taxonicity using covariance of two quantitative indicators in successive intervals of a third indicator (Maxcov procedure). *Psychological Reports, 78,* 1091–1227.

Mel, H. & Horowitz, R. (1998). Additional evidence for an association between the dopamine D4 receptor (D4DR) exon III seven repeat allele and substance abuse in opioid dependent subjects: Relationship of treatment retention to genotype and personality. *Addiction Biology, 3,* 473–481.

Mellor, C. S. (1992). Dermatoglyphic evidence of fluctuating asymmetry in schizophrenia. *British Journal of Psychiatry, 160,* 467–472.

Merton, R. K. (1938). Social structure and anomie. *American Sociological Review, 3,* 672–682.

Metropolitan Area Child Study Research Group (2002). A cognitive-ecological approach to preventing aggression in urban settings: Initial outcomes for high-risk children. *Journal of Consulting and Clinical Psychology, 70,* 179–194.

Michelson, L. (1987). Cognitive-behavioral strategies in the prevention and treatment of antisocial disorders in children and adolescents. In J. D. Burchard & S. N. Burchard (Eds.), *Prevention of delinquent behavior* (pp. 275–310). Newbury Park, CA: Sage.

Miller, G. E., & Prinz, R. J. (1990). Enhancement of social learning family interventions for childhood conduct disorder. *Psychological Bulletin, 108,* 291–307.

Moffitt, T. E. (1987). Parental mental disorder and offspring criminal behavior: An adoption study. *Psychiatry, 50,* 346–360.

Moffitt, T. E. (1990). Juvenile delinquency and attention-deficit disorder: Developmental trajectories from age 3 to 15. *Child Development, 61,* 893–910.

Moffitt, T. E. (1993a). The neuropsychology of conduct disorder. *Development and Psychopathology, 5,* 135–151.

Moffitt, T. E. (1993b). Adolescence-limited and life-course-persistent antisocial behavior: A developmental taxonomy. *Psychological Bulletin, 100,* 674–701.

Moffitt, T. E., & Caspi, A. (2001). Childhood predictors differentiate life-course persistent and adolescence-limited antisocial pathways among males and females. *Development and Psychopathology, 13,* 355–375.

Moffitt, T. E., Caspi, A., Rutter, M., & Silva, P. A. (2001). *Sex Differences in Antisocial Behavior: Conduct Disorder, Delinquency, and Violence in the Dunedin Longitudinal Study.* Cambridge, UK: Cambridge University Press.

Moffitt, T. E., & Henry, B. (1989). Neuropsychological assessment of executive functions in self-reported delinquents. *Development & Psychopathology, 1,* 105–118.

Moffitt, T. E., & Silva, P. A. (1988). IQ and delinquency: A direct test of the differential detection hypothesis. *Journal of Abnormal Psychology, 97,* 330–333.

Moore, C., & Rose, M. R. (1995). Adaptive and nonadaptive explanations of sociopathy. *Behavioral and Brain Sciences, 18,* 566–567.

Morris, A. (1987). *Women, crime and criminal justice.* New York: Basil Blackwell.

Morrison, D., & Gilbert, P. (2001). Social rank, shame and anger in primary and secondary psychopaths. *The Journal of Forensic Psychiatry, 12,* 330–356.

Mrazek, P. J., & Haggerty, R. J. (Eds.). (1994). *Reducing the risks for mental disorders: Frontiers for preventive intervention research.* Washington, DC: National Academy Press.

Munn, D. H., Zhou, M., Attwood, J. T., Bondarev, I., Conway, S. J., Marshall, B., et al. (1998). Prevention of allogeneic fetal rejection by tryptophan catabolism. *Science, 281,* 1191–1193.

Naugler, C. T., & Ludman, M. D. (1996). Fluctuating asymmetry and disorders of developmental origins. *American Journal of Medical Genetics, 66,* 15–20.

Neiderhiser, J. M., Reiss, D., Hetherington, E. M., & Plomin, R. (1999). Relationships between parenting and adolescent adjustment over time: Genetic and environmental contributions. *Developmental Psychology, 35*, 680–692.

Nesse, R. M. (1990). Evolutionary explanations of emotions. *Human Nature, 1*, 261–289.

Nesse, R. M., & Williams, G. C. (1994). *Why we get sick*. New York: Times Books.

Noble, E. P., Ozkaragoz, T. Z., Ritchie, T. L., Zhang, X., Belin, T. R., & Sparkes, R. S. (1998). D2 and D4 dopamine receptor polymorphisms and personality. *American Journal of Medical Genetics, 81*, 257–267.

Nuffield, J. (1982). *Parole-decision making in Canada: Research towards decision guidelines*. Ottawa, Ontario, Canada: Supply and Services Canada.

O'Connor, T. G., Deater-Deckard, K., Fulker, D., Rutter, M., & Plomin, R. (1998). Genotype-environment correlations in late childhood and early adolescence: Antisocial behavioral problems and coercive parenting. *Developmental Psychology, 34*, 970–981.

Offord, D. R., Boyle, M. C., & Racine, Y. A. (1991). The epidemiology of antisocial behavior in childhood and adolescence. In D. J. Pepler & K. H. Rubin (Eds.), *The development and treatment of childhood aggression* (pp. 31–54). Hillsdale, NJ: Erlbaum.

Offord, D. R., Chimura-Kraemer, H., Kazdin, A. E., Jensen, P., & Harrington, R. (1998). Lowering the burden of suffering from child psychiatric disorder: Trade-offs among clinical, targeted, and universal interventions. *Journal of the American Academy of Child Adolescent Psychiatry, 37*, 686–694.

Ogloff, J. R., Wong, S., & Greenwood, A. (1990). Treating criminal psychopaths in a therapeutic community program. *Behavioral Sciences and the Law, 8*, 81–90.

Olds, D. L., Eckenrode, J., Henderson, C. R., Jr., Kitzman, H., Powers, J., Cole, R., et al. (1997). Long-term effects of home visitation on maternal life course, and child abuse and neglect. *Journal of American Medical Association, 278*, 637–643.

Olsen, S. L. (1992). Development of conduct problems and peer rejection in preschool children: A social systems analysis. *Journal of Abnormal Child Psychology, 20*, 327–350.

Olweus, D. (1992). Bullying among schoolchildren: Prevention and intervention. In R. DeV. Peters, R. J. McMahon, & V. L. Quinsey (Eds.), *Aggression and violence throughout the life span* (pp. 100–125). Newbury Park, CA: Sage.

Ono, Y., Manki, H., Yoshimura, K., Muramatsu, T., Mizushima, H., Higuchi, S., et al. (1997). Association between dopamine D4 receptor (D4DR) exon III polymorphism and novelty seeking in Japanese subjects. *American Journal of Medical Genetics, 74*, 501–503.

Osgood, D. W., Wilson, J. K., Bachman, J. G., O'Malley, P. M., & Johnston, L. D. (1996). Routine activities and deviant behavior. *American Sociological Review, 100*, 674–701.

O'Shea, S. (2000). *The perfect heresy: The revolutionary life and death of the medieval Cathars*. Toronto, Ontario, Canada: Douglas & McIntyre.

Pagani, L., Boulerice, B., Vitaro, F., & Tremblay, R. E. (1999). Effects of poverty on academic failure and delinquency in boys: A change and process model approach. *Journal of Child Psychology and Psychiatry, 40,* 1209–1219.

Pagani, L., Tremblay, R. E., & Vitaro, F. (1998). The impact of family transition on the development of delinquency in adolescent boys: A 9-year longitudinal study. *The Journal of Child Psychology and Psychiatry and Allied Disciplines, 39,* 489–499.

Palmer, C. T., & Tilley, C. F. (1995). Sexual access to females as a motivation for joining gangs: An evolutionary approach. *Journal of Sex Research, 32,* 213–217.

Palsson, H., & Edwards, P. (Trans.). (1976). *Egil's saga.* London: Penguin Classics.

Parke, R. D., & Tinsley, B. R. (1983). Fatherhood: Historical and contemporary perspectives. In K. A. McCluskey & H. W. Reese (Eds.), *Lifespan developmental psychology: Historical and generational effects* (pp. 203–248). New York: Academic Press.

Parish, A. R. (1994). Sex and food control in the "uncommon chimpanzee": How bonobo females overcome a phylogenetic legacy of male dominance. *Ethology and Sociobiology, 15,* 159–179.

Parish, A. R. (1996). Female relationships in bonobos (Pan paniscus). *Human Nature, 7,* 61–96.

Patterson, G. R. (1974). Interventions for boys with conduct problems: Multiple settings, treatments, and criteria. *Journal of Consulting and Clinical Psychology, 42,* 471–481.

Patterson, G. R. (1976). The aggressive child: Victim and architect of a coercive process. In E. J. Mash, L. A. Hamerlynck, & L. C. Handy (Eds.), *Behavior modification in families* (pp. 267–316). New York: Brunner/Mazel.

Patterson, G. R. (1982). *Coercive family process.* Eugene, OR: Castalia.

Patterson, G. R. (1986). Performance models for antisocial boys. *American Psychologist, 41,* 432–444.

Patterson, G. R. (1992). Developmental changes in antisocial behavior. In R. DeV. Peters, R. J. McMahon, & V. L. Quinsey (Eds.), *Aggression and violence throughout the life span* (pp. 52–82). Newbury Park, CA: Sage.

Patterson, G. R. (1997). Performance models for parenting: A social interactional perspective. In J. E. Grusec & L. Kuczynski (Eds.), *Parenting and children's internalization of values: A handbook of contemporary theory* (pp. 193–226). New York: Wiley.

Patterson, G. R., & Bank, L. I. (1989). Some amplifying mechanisms for pathologic processes in families. In M. Gunnar & E. Thelan (Eds.), *Systems and development: The Minnesota symposia on child psychology* (pp. 167–209). Hillsdale, NJ: Erlbaum.

Patterson, G. R., Capaldi, D., & Bank, L. (1991). An early starter model for predicting delinquency. In D. J. Pepler & K. H. Rubin (Eds.), *The development and treatment of childhood aggression* (pp. 139–168). Hillsdale, NJ: Erlbaum.

Patterson, G. R., DeBaryshe, B. D., & Ramsey, E. (1989). A developmental perspective on antisocial behavior. *American Psychologist, 44,* 329–335.

Patterson, G. R., & Dishion, T. J. (1985). Contributions of families and peers to delinquency. *Criminology, 23,* 63–79.

Patterson, G. R., Dishion, T. J., & Bank, L. (1984). Family interaction: A process model of deviance training. *Aggressive Behavior, 10,* 253–367.

Patterson, G. R., Dishion, T. J., & Yoerger, K. (2000). Adolescent growth in new forms of problem behavior: Macro and micro peer dynamics. *Prevention Science, 1,* 3–13.

Patterson, G. R., & Yoerger, K. (1997). A developmental model for late onset delinquency. In D. W. Osgood (Ed.), *Motivation and delinquency: Nebraska Symposium on Motivation* (Vol. 44, pp. 119–177). Lincoln: University of Nebraska Press.

Paul, G. (1967). Strategy of outcome research in psychotherapy. *Journal of Consulting and Clinical Psychology, 31,* 109–118.

Paul, L., Foss, M. A., & Baenninger, M. A. (1996). Double standards for sexual jealousy: Manipulative morality or a reflection of evolved sex differences. *Human Nature, 7,* 291–321.

Pedersen, N. L., Friberg, L., Floderus-Myrhed, B., McClearn, G. E., & Plomin, R. (1984). Swedish early separated twins: Identification and characterization. *Acta Geneticae Medicae et Gemellologiae: Twin Research, 33,* 243–250.

Pedersen, N. L., McClearn, G. E., Plomin, R., & Friberg, L. (1985). Separated fraternal twins: Resemblance for cognitive abilities. *Behavior Genetics, 15,* 407–419.

Pedersen, N. L., McClearn, G. E., Plomin, R., & Nesselroade, J. R. (1992). Effects of early rearing environment on twin similarity in the last half of the life span. *British Journal of Developmental Psychology, 10,* 255–267.

Penner, M. J. (1982). The role of selected health problems in the causation of juvenile delinquency. *Adolescence, 17,* 347–368.

Pepler, D. J., Craig, W. M., & Roberts, W. (1994). Social skills training and aggression in the peer group. In J. McCord (Ed.), *Coercion and punishment in long-term perspectives.* New York: Cambridge University Press.

Peters, R. D., & Russell, C. C. (1996). Promoting development and preventing disorder: The Better Beginnings, Better Futures Project. In R. D. Peters & R. J. McMahon (Eds.), *Preventing childhood disorders, substance abuse, and delinquency* (pp. 19–47). Thousand Oaks, CA: Sage.

Pettit, G., & Bates, J. (1989). Family interaction patterns and children's behavior problems from infancy to four years. *Developmental Psychology, 255,* 413–420.

Phelps, J. A., Davis, J. O., & Shartz, K. M. (1998). Nature, nurture, and twin research strategies. *Current Directions in Psychological Science, 6,* 117–121.

Pine, D. S., Cohen, E., Cohen, P., & Brook, J. S. (2000). Social phobia and the persistence of conduct problems. *Journal of Child Psychology and Psychiatry and Allied Disciplines, 41,* 657–665.

Plomin, R. (1989). Environment and genes. *American Psychologist, 44,* 105–111.

Plomin, R., & Daniels, D. (1987). Why are children in the same family so different from one another? *Behavioral and Brain Sciences, 10,* 1–60.

Plomin, R., DeFries, J. C., & McClearn, G. E. (1990). *Behavioral genetics* (2nd ed.). New York: W. H. Freeman.

Plomin, R., DeFries, J. C., McClearn, G. E., & McGuffin, P. (2000). *Behavioral genetics* (4th ed.). New York: W. H. Freeman.

Plomin, R., & Nesselroade, J. R. (1990). Behavioral genetics and personality change. *Journal of Personality, 58,* 191–220.

Plomin, R., Pedersen, N. L., McClearn, G. E., Nesselroade, J. R., & Bergeman, C. S. (1988). EAS temperaments during the last half of the life span: Twins reared apart and twins reared together. *Psychology & Aging, 3,* 43–50.

Pogue, G. M., Ferrell, R., Deka, R., Debski, T., & Manuck, S. (1998). Human novelty-seeking personality traits and dopamine D4 receptor polymorphisms: A twin and genetic association study. *American Journal of Medical Genetics, 81,* 44–48.

Pollack, O. (1950). *The criminality of women.* Philadelphia: University of Philadelphia Press.

Post, W. (1992). Dominance and mating success in male boat-tailed grackles. *Animal Behaviour, 44,* 917–929.

Prior, M., Smart, D., Sanson, A., & Oberklaid, F. (1993). Sex differences in psychological adjustment from infancy to 8 years. *Journal of the American Academy of Child and Adolescent Psychiatry, 32,* 291–304.

Pulkkinen, L. (1987). Offensive and defensive aggression in humans. *Aggressive Behavior, 13,* 197–212.

Pulkkinen, L. (1992). The path to adulthood for aggressively inclined girls. In K. Bjorkqvist & P. Niemela (Eds.), *Of mice and women: Aspects of female aggression* (pp. 113–121). San Diego, CA: Academic Press.

Quay, H .C. (1987). Intelligence. In H. C. Quay (Ed.), *Handbook of juvenile delinquency* (pp. 106–117). Toronto, Ontario, Canada: Wiley.

Quinsey, V. L. (1995). The prediction and explanation of criminal violence. *International Journal of Law & Psychiatry, 18,* 117–127.

Quinsey, V. L. (in press). Etiology of anomalous sexual preferences in men. In R. A. Prentky, M. Seto, & A. Burgess (Eds.), *Understanding and Managing Sexually Coercive Behavior.* Annals of the New York Academy of Sciences. New York: The New York Academy of Sciences.

Quinsey, V. L., Book, A. S., & Lalumière, M. L. (2001). A factor analysis of traits related to individual differences in antisocial behavior. *Criminal Justice and Behavior, 28,* 522–536.

Quinsey, V. L., & Chaplin, T. C. (1988). Preventing faking in phallometric assessments of sexual preference. In R. A. Prentky & V. L. Quinsey (Eds.), *Human sexual aggression: Current perspectives.* Annals of the New York Academy of Sciences, *528,* 49–58. New York: The New York Academy of Sciences.

Quinsey, V. L., Harris, G. T., Rice, M. E., & Cormier, C. (1998). *Violent offenders: Appraising and managing risk*. Washington, DC: American Psychological Association.

Quinsey, V. L., & Lalumière, M. L. (1995). Evolutionary perspectives on sexual offending. *Sexual Abuse, 7,* 301–315.

Quinsey, V. L., Lalumière, M. L., Querée, M., & McNaughton, J. K. (1999). Perceived crime severity and biological kinship. *Human Nature, 10,* 399–414.

Quinsey, V. L., Rice, M. E., Harris, G. T., & Reid, K. S. (1993). Conceptual and measurement issues in the phylogenetic and ontogenetic development of sexual age preferences in males. In H. E. Barbaree, W. L. Marshall, & S. M. Hudson (Eds.), *The juvenile sex offender* (pp. 143–163). New York: Guilford Press.

Quinsey, V. L., Steinman, C. M., Bergersen, S. G., & Holmes, T. F. (1975). Penile circumference, skin conductance, and ranking responses of child molesters and "normals" to sexual and nonsexual visual stimuli. *Behavior Therapy, 6,* 213–219.

Raine, A. (1993). *Psychopathology of crime: Criminal behavior as a clinical disorder*. San Diego, CA: Academic Press.

Raine, A., Brennan, P., & Mednick, S. A. (1994). Birth complications combined with early maternal rejection at age 1 predispose to violent crime at age 18 years. *Archives of General Psychiatry, 51,* 984–988.

Raine, A., Brennan, P., & Mednick, S. A. (1997). Interaction between birth complications and early maternal rejection in predisposing individuals to adult violence: Specificity to serious, early-onset violence. *American Journal of Psychiatry, 154,* 1265–1271.

Raine, A., & Dunkin, J. J. (1990). The genetic and psychophysiological basis of antisocial behavior: Implications for counseling and therapy. *Journal of Counseling and Development, 68,* 637–644.

Raine, A., & Venables, P. H. (1987). Contingent negative variation, P3 evoked potentials and antisocial behavior. *Psychophysiology, 24,* 191–199.

Raine, A., & Venables, P. H. (1988). Enhanced P3 evoked potentials and longer P3 recovery time in psychopaths. *Psychophysiology, 25,* 30–38.

Raine, A., Venables, P. H., & Mednick, S. A. (1997). Low resting heart rate at age 3 years predisposes to aggression at age 11 years: Evidence from the Mauritius Child Health Project. *Journal of the American Academy of Child & Adolescent Psychiatry, 36,* 1457–1464.

Raine, A., Venables, P., Williams, M. (1990a). Autonomic orienting responses in 15-year-old male subjects and criminal behavior at age 24. *American Journal of Psychiatry, 147,* 933–937.

Raine, A., Venables, P. H., & Williams, M. (1990b). Relationships between central and autonomic measures of arousal at age 15 and criminality at age 24. *Archives of General Psychiatry, 47,* 1003–1007.

Raine, A., Venables, P. H., & Williams, M. (1990c). Relationships between N1, P300 and contingent negative variation recorded at age 15 and criminal behavior at age 24. *Psychophysiology, 27,* 567–574.

Raine, A., Venables, P. H., & Williams, M. (1995). High autonomic arousal and electrodermal orienting at age 15 years as protective factors against criminal behavior at age 29 years. *American Journal of Psychiatry, 152*, 1595–1600.

Raine, A, Venables, P. H., & Williams, M. (1996). Better autonomic conditioning and faster electrodermal half-recovery time at age 15 years as possible protective factors against crime at age 29 years. *Developmental Psychology, 32*, 624–630.

Raine, A., Yaralian, P. S., Reynolds, C., Venables, P. H., & Mednick, S. A. (2002). Spatial but not verbal cognitive deficits at age 3 years in persistently antisocial individuals. *Development and Psychopathology, 14*, 25–44.

Rantakallio, P., Myhrman, A., & Koiranen, M. (1995). Juvenile offenders, with special reference to sex differences. *Social Psychiatry and Psychiatric Epidemiology, 30*, 113–120.

Reitsma-Street, M. (1999). Justice for Canadian girls: A 1990s update. *Canadian Journal of Criminology, 41*, 335–363.

Rice, M. E. (1997). Violent offender research and implications for the criminal justice system. *American Psychologist, 52*, 414–423.

Rice, M. E., & Harris, G. T. (1997). Cross-validation and extension of the Violence Risk Appraisal Guide for child molesters and rapists. *Law and Human Behavior, 21*, 231–241.

Rice, M. E., Harris, G. T., & Cormier, C. (1992). Evaluation of a maximum security therapeutic community for psychopaths and other mentally disordered offenders. *Law and Human Behavior, 16*, 399–412.

Rice, W. R. (1992). Sexually antagonistic genes: Experimental evidence. *Science, 256*, 1436–1439.

Rice, W. R. (1996a). Evolution of the Y sex chromosome in animals. *Bioscience, 46*, 331–343.

Rice, W. R. (1996b). Sexually antagonistic male adaptation triggered by experimental arrest of female evolution. *Nature, 381*, 232–234.

Richards, R. J. (1987). *Darwin and the emergence of evolutionary theories of mind and behavior*. Chicago: University of Chicago Press.

Ridley, M. (1993). *The red queen: Sex and the evolution of human nature*. New York: MacMillan.

Robins, L. N. (1966). *Deviant children grown up*. Baltimore: Williams & Wilkins.

Robins, L. N. (1978). Sturdy childhood predictors of adult antisocial behaviour: Replications from longitudinal studies. *Psychological Medicine, 8*, 611–622.

Robins, L. N. (1986). The consequences of conduct disorder in girls. In D. Olweus, J. Block, & M. Radke-Yarrow (Eds.), *Development of antisocial and prosocial behavior: Research, theories and issues*. San Diego, CA: Academic Press.

Robins, L. N. (1991). Conduct disorder. *Journal of Child Psychology and Psychiatry, 32*, 193–212.

Rodgers, J. L., Hughes, K., Kohler, H. P., Christensen, K., Doughty, D., Rowe, D. C., et al. (2001). Generic influence helps explain variation in human fertility:

Evidence from recent behavioral and molecular genetic studies. *Current Directions in Psychological Science, 10*, 184–188.

Rose, S. L., Rose, S. A., & Feldman, J. F. (1989). Stability of behavior problems in very young children. *Development and Psychopathology, 1*, 5–19.

Rosenfeld, R. (1986). Urban crime rates: Effects of inequality, welfare dependency, region, and race. In J. M. Byrne & R. J. Sampson (Eds.), *The social ecology of crime* (pp. 116–130). New York: Springer-Verlag.

Rowe, D. C. (1986). Genetic and environmental components of antisocial behavior: A study of 265 twin pairs. *Criminology, 24*, 513–532.

Rowe, D. C. (1994). *The limits of family influence: Genes, experience, and behavior.* New York: Guilford Press.

Rowe, D. C. (2002). *Biology and crime.* Los Angeles, CA: Roxbury.

Rowe, D. C., Stever, C., Giedinghagen, L. N., Gard, J. M., Cleveland, H. H., Terris, S. T., et al. (1998). Dopamine DRD4 receptor polymorphism and attention deficit hyperactivity disorder. *Molecular Psychiatry, 3*, 419–426.

Rowe, D. C., & Farrington, D. P. (1997). The familial transmission of criminal convictions. *Criminology, 35*, 177–201.

Rowe, D. C., & Rodgers, J. L. (1989). Behavioral genetics, adolescent deviance, and "d": Contributions and issues. In G. R. Adams, R. Montemayor, & T. P. Gullotta (Eds.), *Biology of adolescent behavior and development.* Newbury Park, CA: Sage.

Rowe, D. C., Rodgers, J. L., & Meseck-Bushey, S. (1992). Sibling delinquency and the family environment: Shared and unshared influences. *Child Development, 63*, 59–67.

Rowe, D. C., Rodgers, J. L., Meseck-Bushey, S., & St-John, C. (1989). Sexual behavior and nonsexual deviance: A sibling study of their relationship. *Developmental Psychology, 25*, 61–69.

Rowe, D. C., Vazsonyi, A. T., & Figueredo, A. J. (1997). Mating-effort in adolescence: A conditional or alternative strategy. *Personality and Individual Differences, 23*, 105–115.

Rowe, D. C., Vazsonyi, A. T., & Flannery, D. J. (1995). Sex differences in crime: Do means and within sex variation have similar causes? *Journal of Research in Crime and Delinquency, 32*, 84–100.

Russell, J. A., & Fernández-Dols, J. M. (Eds.). (1997). *The psychology of facial expression.* New York: Cambridge University Press.

Rutter, M. (1983). School effects on pupil progress: Research findings and policy implications. *Child Development, 54*, 1–29.

Rutter, M. (1985). Resilience in the face of adversity: Protective factors and resistance to psychiatric disorder. *British Journal of Psychiatry, 147*, 598–611.

Rutter, M. (1996). Introduction: concepts of antisocial behavior, of cause and of genetic influences. In G. R. Bock & J. A. Goode (Eds.), *Genetics of criminal and antisocial behavior* (pp. 1–15). Toronto, Ontario, Canada: Wiley.

Rutter, M. (1997). Antisocial behavior: Developmental psychopathology perspectives. In D. Stoff, J. Breiling, & J. Maser (Eds.), *Handbook of antisocial behavior*. New York: Wiley.

Rutter, M., & Giller, H. (1984). *Juvenile delinquency: Trends and perspectives*. New York: Guilford Press.

Rutter, M., Tizard, B., & Whitemore, K. (1970). *Education, health, and behavior*. London: Longmore.

Sacco, V. E., & Kennedy, L. W. (1998). *The criminal event* (2nd ed.). Toronto, Ontario, Canada: ITP Nelson.

Salmon, W. C. (1984). *Scientific explanation and the causal structure of the world* (pp. 213–227). Princeton: Princeton University Press.

Sampson, R. J., & Laub, J. H. (1993). *Crime in the making: Pathways and turning points through life*. Cambridge, MA: Harvard University Press.

Sander, T., Harms, H., Dufeu, P., Kuhn, S., Rommelspacher, H., & Schmidt, L. G. (1997). Dopamine D4 receptor exon III alleles and variation of novelty seeking in alcoholics. *American Journal of Medical Genetics, 74*, 483–487.

Saner, H., & Ellickson, P. (1996). Concurrent risk factors for adolescent violence. *Journal of Adolescent Health, 19*, 94–103.

Saudino, K. J. (1997). Moving beyond the heritability question: New directions in behavioral genetic studies of personality. *Current Directions in Psychological Science, 6*, 86–90.

Scalzitti, J. M., & Hensler, J. G. (1997). Serotonin receptors: Role in psychiatry. In K. Blum & E. P. Noble (Eds.), *Handbook of psychiatric genetics* (pp. 113–145). New York: CRC Press.

Scaramella, L. V., Conger, R. D., Simons, R. L., & Whitbeck, L. B. (1998). Predicting risk for pregnancy by late adolescence: A social contextual perspective. *Developmental Psychology, 34*, 1233–1245.

Scarr, S., & McCartney, K. (1983). How people make their own environments: A theory of genotype-environment effects. *Child Development, 54*, 424–435.

Schaal, B., Tremblay, R. E., Soussignan, R., & Susman, E. J. (1996). Male testosterone linked to high social dominance but low physical aggression in early adolescence. *Journal of the American Academy of Child & Adolescent Psychiatry, 35*, 1322–1330.

Schachter, F. F. (1982). Sibling deidentification and split-parent identification: A family tetrad. In M. D. Lamb & B. Sutton-Smith (Eds.), *Sibling relationships: Their nature and significance across the lifespan* (pp. 123–151). Hillsdale, NJ: Erlbaum.

Schneider, A. L. (1990). *Deterrence and juvenile crime: Results of a national policy experiment*. New York: Springer-Verlag.

Schoenwald, S. K., Henggeler, S. W., Brondino, M. J., & Rowland, M. D. (2000). Multisystemic therapy: Monitoring treatment fidelity. *Family Process, 39*, 83–103.

Schulsinger, F. (1972). Psychopathy: Heredity and environment. *International Journal of Mental Health, 1*, 190–206.

Schulsinger, F. (1977). Psychopathy: Heredity and environment. In S. Mednick & K. O. Christiansen (Eds.), *Biosocial bases of criminal behavior* (pp. 109–126). New York: Gardner Press.

Schweinhart, L. L., Barnes, H. V., & Weikart, D. P. (1993). *Significant benefits. The High/Scope Perry School Study through age 27.* Ypsilanti, MI: High/Scope.

Schweinhart, L. J., & Weikart, D. P. (1983). The effects of the Perry Preschool Program on youths through age 15: A summary. In Consortium for Longitudinal Studies, *As the twig is bent: Lasting effects of preschool programs* (pp. 1–31). Hillsdale, NJ: Erlbaum.

Segerstråle, U. (2000). *Defenders of the truth: The battle for science in the sociobiology debate and beyond.* New York: Oxford University Press.

Serbin, L. A., Cooperman, J. M., Peters, P. L., Lehoux, P. M., Stack, D. M., & Schwartzman, A. E. (1998). Intergenerational transfer of psychosocial risk in women with childhood histories of aggression, withdrawal, or aggression and withdrawal. *Developmental Psychology, 34,* 1246–1262.

Serbin, L. A., Moskowitz, D. S., Schwartzman, A. E., Ledingham, J. E. (1991). Aggressive, withdrawn, and aggressive/withdrawn children in adolescence: Into the next generation. D. Pepler & K. Rubin (Eds.) *The Development and Treatment of Childhood Aggression.* Hillsdale, NJ: Erlbaum.

Serbin, L. A., Peters, P. L., McAffer, V. J., & Schwartzman, A. E. (1991). Childhood aggression and withdrawal as predictors of adolescent pregnancy, early parenthood, and environmental risk for the next generation. *Canadian Journal of Behavioural Science, 23,* 318–331.

Serbin, L. A., Peters, P. L., & Schwartzman, A. E. (1996). Longitudinal study of early childhood injuries and acute illnesses in the offspring of adolescent mothers who were aggressive, withdrawn, or aggressive-withdrawn in childhood. *Journal of Abnormal Psychology, 105,* 500–507.

Serbin, L. A., Schwartzman, A. E., Moskowitz, D. S., & Ledingham, J. F. (1991). Aggressive, withdrawn and aggressive-withdrawn children in adolescence: Into the next generation. In D. Pepler & K. Rubin (Eds.), *The development and treatment of childhood aggression.* Hillsdale, NJ: Erlbaum.

Seto, M. C., & Barbaree, H. (1999). Psychopathy, treatment behavior and sex offender recidivism. *Journal of Interpersonal Violence, 14,* 1235–1248.

Shaw, C. R., & McKay, H. D. (1969). *Juvenille delinquency and urban areas* (Rev. ed.) Chicago, IL: University of Chicago Press.

Shaw, D. S., Keenan, K., & Vondra, J. I. (1994). Developmental precursors of externalizing behavior: Ages 1 to 3. *Developmental Psychology, 30,* 355–364.

Shaw, D. S., Owens, E. B., Vondra, J. I., Keenan, K., & Winslow, E. (1996). Early risk factors and pathways in the development of disruptive behaviors problems. *Development and Psychopathology, 8,* 679–699.

Shore, M. F., & Massimo, J. L. (1979). Fifteen years after treatment: A follow-up study of comprehensive vocationally-oriented psychotherapy. *American Journal of Orthopsychiatry, 49,* 240–245.

Siegel, L. J., & Senna, J. J. (1981). *Juvenile delinquency: Theory, practice, and law.* St. Paul: West.

Sigvardsson, S., Bohman, M., & Cloninger, C. R. (1987). Structure and stability of childhood personality: Prediction of later social adjustment. *Journal of Child Psychology and Psychiatry and Allied Disciplines, 28,* 929–946.

Silberg, J., Meyer, J., Pickles, A., Simonoff, E., Eaves, L., Hewitt, J., et al. (1996). Heterogeneity among juvenile antisocial behaviors: Findings from the Virginia twin study of adolescent behavioral development. In G. R. Bock & J. A. Goode (Eds.), *Genetics of criminal and antisocial behavior* (pp. 76–92). Chichester, England: Wiley.

Silverthorne, Z. A., & Quinsey, V. L. (2000). Sexual partner age preferences of homosexual and heterosexual men and women. *Archives of Sexual Behavior, 29,* 67–76.

Simourd, L., & Andrews, D. A. (1994). Correlates of delinquency: A look at gender differences. *Forum on Corrections Research, 6,* 26–31.

Singh, D. (1993). Adaptive significance of female physical attractiveness: Role of waist-to-hip ratio. *Journal of Personality and Social Psychology, 65,* 293–307.

Singh, D., & Luis, S. (1995). Ethnic and gender consensus for the effect of waist-to-hip ratio on judgment of women's attractiveness. *Human Nature, 6,* 51–65.

Skilling, T. A., Harris, G. T., Rice, M. E., & Quinsey, V. L. (2002). Identifying persistently antisocial offenders using the Hare Psychopathy Checklist and the DSM Antisocial personality disorder criteria. *Psychological Assessment, 14,* 27–38.

Skilling, T. A., Quinsey, V. L., & Craig, W. M. (2001). Evidence of a taxon underlying serious antisocial behavior in boys. *Criminal Justice & Behavior, 28,* 450–470.

Skinner, B. F. (1966). The phylogeny and ontogeny of behavior. *Science, 153,* 1205–1213.

Skoff, B., & Libon, J. (1987). Impaired executive functions in a sample of male juvenile delinquents. *Journal of Clinical and Experimental Neuropsychology, 9,* 60–64.

Skuse, D. H. (1999). Genomic imprinting of the X chromosome: A novel mechanism for the evolution of sexual dimorphism. *Journal of Laboratory and Clinical Medicine, 133,* 23–32.

Skuse, D. H., James, R. S., Bishop, D. V. M., Coppin, B., Dalton, P., Aamodt-Leeper, G., et al. (1997). Evidence from Turner's syndrome of an imprinted x-linked locus effecting cognitive function. *Nature, 387,* 705–707.

Slutske, W. S., Heath, A. C., Dinwiddie, S. H., Madden, P. A. F., Bucholz, K. K., Dunne, M. P., et al. (1997). Modeling genetic and environmental influences in the etiology of conduct disorder: A study of 2,682 adult twin pairs. *Journal of Abnormal Psychology, 106,* 266–279.

Smale, L., Frank, L. G., & Holekamp, K. E. (1993). Ontogeny of dominance in free-living spotted hyaenas: Juvenile rank relations with adult females and immigrant males. *Animal Behaviour, 46*, 467–477.

Smith, E. A., & Bliege Bird, R. L. (2000). Turtle hunting and tombstone opening: Public generosity as costly signalling. *Evolution and Human Behavior, 21*, 245–262.

Smuts, B. B., Cheney, D. L., Seyfarth, R. M., & Struhsaker, T. T. (Eds.). (1987). *Primate Societies*. Chicago: University of Chicago Press.

Snieder, H., MacGregor, A. J., & Spector, T. D. (1998). Genes control the cessation of a woman's reproductive life: A twin study of hysterectomy and age at menopause. *Journal of Clinical Endocrinology and Metabolism, 83*, 1875–1880.

Snyder, J., & Patterson, G. (1987). Family interaction and delinquent behavior. In H. C. Quay (Ed.), *Handbook of juvenile delinquency* (pp. 216–243). New York: Wiley.

Sobotowicz, W., Evans, J. R., & Laughlin, J. (1987). Neuropsychological function and social support in delinquency and learning disability. *International Journal of Clinical Neuropsychology, 9*, 178–186.

Spitzer, R. L., Gibbon, M., Skodol, A. E., Williams, J. B. W., & First, M. B. (Eds.). (1994). *DSM-IV casebook: A learning companion to the Diagnostic and Statistical Manual of Mental Disorders, 4th ed*. Washington, DC: American Psychiatric Press.

Sprecher, S., Sullivan, Q., & Hatfield, E. (1994). Mate selection preferences: Gender differences examined in a national sample. *Journal of Personality and Social Psychology, 66*, 1074–1080.

Stattin, H., & Magnusson, D. (1989). The role of early aggressive behavior in the frequency, seriousness, and types of later crime. *Journal of Consulting and Clinical Psychology, 57*, 710–718.

Sternberg, J., & Grigorenko, E. (Eds.). (1997). *Intelligence, heredity, and environment*. New York: Cambridge University Press.

Stoff, D. M., & Vitiello, B. (1996). Role of serotonin in the aggression of children and adolescents: Biochemical and pharmacological studies. In D. M. Stoff & R. B. Cairns (Eds.), *Aggression and violence: Genetic, neurobiological, and biosocial perspectives* (pp. 101–124). Mahwah, NJ: Erlbaum.

Storey, A. E., Walsh, C. J., Quinton, R. L., & Wynne-Edwards, K. E. (2000). Hormonal correlates of paternal responsiveness in new and expectant fathers. *Evolution and Human Behavior, 21*, 79–85.

Stouthamer-Loeber, M., & Wei, E. H. (1998). The precursors of young fatherhood and its effect on delinquency of teenage males. *Journal of Adolescent Health, 22*, 56–65.

Sullivan, P. F., Fifield, W. J., Kennedy, M. A., Mulder, R. T., Sellman, J. D., & Joyce, P. R. (1998). No association between novelty seeking and the type 4 dopamine receptor gene (DRD4) in two New Zealand samples. *American Journal of Psychiatry, 155*, 98–101.

Sulloway, F. J. (1996). *Born to rebel: Birth, order, family dynamics, and creative lives.* N.Y.: Random House.

Sutherland, E. H., & Cressey, D. (1974). *Principles of criminology* (8th ed.). Philadelphia: Lippincott.

Swanson, J. M., Sunohara, G. A., Kennedy, J. L., Regino, R., Fineberg, E., Wigal, T., et al. (1998). Association of the dopamine receptor D4 (DRD4) gene with a refined phenotype of attention deficit hyperactivity disorder (ADHD): A family based approach. *Molecular Psychiatry, 3,* 384.

Symons, D. (1979). *The evolution of human sexuality.* New York: Oxford University Press.

Tarter, R., Vanyukov, M., Giancola, P., Dawes, M., Blackson, T., Mezzich, A., et al. (1999). Etiology of early age of onset substance use disorder: A maturational perspective. *Development and Psychopathology, 11,* 657–683.

Taylor, C. S. (1993). *Girls, gangs, women and drugs.* East Lansing: Michigan State University Press.

Teicher, M. H. (2002). Scars that won't heal: The neurobiology of child abuse. *Scientific American, 287,* 68–75.

Thornberry, T., Huizinga, D., & Loeber, R. (1995). The prevention of serious delinquency and violence. In J. Howell, B. Krisberg, & D. J. Hawkins (Eds.), *Source book on serious, chronic, and violent offenders.* Thousand Oaks, CA: Sage.

Thornberry, T. P., & Krohn, M. D. (1997). Peers, drug use, and delinquency. In D. M. Skoff, J. Breiling & J. D. Maser (Eds.), *Handbook of antisocial behavior* (pp. 218–233). New York: Wiley.

Thornhill, R., Gangestad, S., & Comer, R. (1995). Human female orgasm and mate fluctuating asymmetry. *Animal Behaviour, 50,* 1601–1615.

Thornhill, R., & Moller, A. P. (1997). Developmental stability, disease and medicine. *Biological Review, 72,* 497–548.

Thornhill, R., & Palmer, C. T. (2000). *A natural history of rape: Biological bases of sexual coercion.* Cambridge, MA: MIT Press.

Thornhill, R., & Thornhill, N. W. (1992). Evolutionary psychology of men's coercive sexuality. *Behavioral and Brain Sciences, 15,* 363–421.

Tolan, P. H. (1987). Implications of age onset for delinquency risk. *Journal of Abnormal Child Psychology, 15,* 47–65.

Tolan, P. H. (1988). Socioeconomic, family, and social stress correlates of adolescent antisocial and delinquent behavior. *Journal of Abnormal Child Psychology, 16,* 317–331.

Tolan, P. H., & Gorman-Smith, D. (1998). Development of serious and violent offending careers. In R. Loeber, & D. P. Farrington (Eds.), *Serious and violent juvenile offenders: Risk factors and successful interventions* (pp. 68–85). Thousand Oaks, CA: Sage.

Tolan, P. H., & Lorion, R. P. (1988). Multivariate approaches to the identification of delinquency proneness in adolescent males. *American Journal of Community Psychology, 16,* 547–561.

Tolan, P. H., Perry, M. S., & Jones, T. (1987). Delinquency prevention: An example of consultation in rural community mental health. *Journal of Community Psychology, 15,* 43–50.

Tooby, J., & Cosmides, L. (1990). The past explain the present: Emotional adaptations and the structure of ancestral environments. *Ethology and Sociobiology, 11,* 375–424.

Tremblay, R. E. (2000). The development of aggressive behaviour during childhood: What have we learned in the past century? *International Journal of Behavioral Development, 24,* 129–141.

Tremblay, R. E., & Craig, W. (1995). Developmental crime prevention. In M. Tonry & D. P. Farrington (Eds.), *Building a safer society: Strategic approaches to crime prevention* (pp. 151–236). Chicago: University of Chicago Press.

Tremblay, R. E., LeMarquand, D., & Vitaro, F. (1999). The prevention of oppositional defiant disorder and conduct disorder. In H. C. Quay & A. E. Hogan (Eds.), *Handbook of disruptive behavior disorders* (pp. 525–555). New York: Plenum.

Tremblay, R. E., Masse, B., Perron, D., Leblanc, M., Schwartzman, A. E., & Ledingham, J. E. (1992). Early disruptive behavior, poor school achievement, delinquent behavior, and delinquent personality: Longitudinal analyses. *Journal of Consulting and Clinical Psychology, 60,* 64–72.

Tremblay, R. E., Masse, L. C., Vitaro, F., & Dobkin, P. L. (1995). The impact of friends' deviant behavior on early onset of delinquency: Longitudinal data from 6 to 13 years of age. *Development and Psychopathology, 7,* 649–668.

Tremblay, R. E., Pagani-Kurtz, L., Vitaro, F. Masse, L. C., & Pihl, R. O. (1995). A bimodal prevention intervention for disruptive kindergarten boys: Its impact through mid-adolescence. *Journal of Consulting and Clinical Psychology, 63,* 560–568.

Trivers, R. L. (1971). The evolution of reciprocal altruism. *The Quarterly Review of Biology, 46,* 35–57.

Trivers, R. L. (1972). Parental investment and sexual selection. In B. Campbell (Ed.), *Sexual selection and the descent of man* (pp. 136–179). Chicago: Aldine.

Trivers, R. L. (1974). Parent–offspring conflict. *American Zoologist, 14,* 249–264.

Trivers, R. L. (1985). *Social evolution.* Menlo Park, CA: Benjamin/Cummings.

Tyrka, A. R., Cannon, T. D., Haslam, N., Mednik, S. A., Schulsinger, F., Schulsinger, H., et al. (1995). The latent structure of schizotypy: I. Premorbid indicators of a taxon of individuals at risk for schizophrenia-spectrum disorders. *Journal of Abnormal Psychology, 104,* 173–183.

Underwood, M. K., Kupersmidt, J. B., & Coie, J. D. (1996). Childhood peer sociometric status and aggression as predictors of adolescent childbearing. *Journal of Research on Adolescence, 6,* 201–223.

Vandenberg, S. G., & Johnson, R. C. (1968). Further evidence on the relation between age of separation and similarity in IQ among pairs of separated identical twins. In S. G. Vandenberg (Ed.), *Progress in human behavior genetics* (pp. 215–219). Baltimore: John Hopkins University Press.

Van Dusen, K. T., & Mednick, S. A. (Eds.). (1983). *Prospective studies of crime and delinquency*. Boston: Kluwer-Nijhoff.

Vanyukov, M. M., Moss, H. B., Plail, J. A., Blackson, T., Mezzick, A. C., & Turter, R. E. (1993). Antisocial symptoms in preadolescent boys and in their parents: Associations with cortisol. *Psychiatry Research, 46*, 9–17.

Vedder, C. B., & Somerville, D. B. (1973). *The delinquent girl* (2nd ed.). Springfield, IL: Charles C. Thomas.

Venables, P. H. (1981). Studies of children at high risk for schizophrenia: Some methodological considerations. In M. J. Christie & P. Mellett (Eds.), *Foundations of psychosomatics* (pp. 111–127). London: Wiley.

Virkkunen, M. (1985). Urinary free cortisol secretion in habitually violent offenders. *Acta Psychiatrica Scandinavica, 72* (1), 40–44.

Virkkunen, M., de Jong, J., Bartko, J. J., Goodwin, F. K., & Linnoila, M. (1989). Relationship of psychobiological variables to recidivism in violent offenders and impulsive fire setters: A follow-up study. *Archives of General Psychiatry, 46*, 600–603.

Wakefield, J. C. (1992a). The concept of mental disorder: On the boundary between biological facts and social values. *American Psychologist, 47*, 373–388.

Wakefield, J. C. (1992b). Disorder as harmful dysfunction: A conceptual critique of *DSM-III-R*'s definition of mental disorder. *Psychological Review, 99*, 232–247.

Waldman, I. D., Rowe, D. C., Abramowitz, A., Kozel, S. T., Mohr, J. H., Sherman, S. L., et al. (1998). Association and linkage of the dopamine transporter gene and attention deficit hyperactivity disorder in children: Heterogeneity owing to diagnostic subtype and severity. *American Journal of Human Genetics, 63*, 1767–1776.

Waldrop, M. F., Bell, R. Q., McLaughlin, B., & Halverson, C. F. (1978). Newborn minor physical anomalies predict short attention span, peer aggression, and impulsivity at age 3. *Science, 199*, 563–564.

Waller, N. G., Kojetin, B. A., Bouchard, T. J., Jr., Lykken, D. T., & Tellegen, A. (1990). Genetic and environmental influences on religious interests, attitudes, and values: A study of twins reared apart and together. *Psychological Science, 1*, 138–142.

Waller, N. G., & Meehl, P. E. (1998). *Multivariate taxometric procedures: Distinguishing types from continua*. Thousand Oaks, CA: Sage.

Waller, N. G., Putnam, F. W., & Carlson, E. B. (1996). Types of dissociation and dissociative types: A taxometric analysis of dissociative experiences. *Psychological Methods, 1*, 300–321.

Waller, N. G., & Ross, C. A. (1997). The prevalence and biometric structure of pathological dissociation in the general population: Taxometric and behavior genetic findings. *Journal of Abnormal Psychology, 106* (4), 499–510.

Walters, G. D., & White, T. W. (1989). Heredity and crime: Bad genes or bad research. *Criminology, 27*, 455–485.

Warr, M. (1998). Life-course transitions and desistance from crime. *Criminology, 36*, 183–216.

Webster-Stratton, C. (1985). Predictors of treatment outcome in parent training for conduct disordered children. *Behavior Therapy, 16*, 223–243.

Webster-Stratton, C. (1990). Stress: A potential disrupter of parent perceptions and family interactions. *Journal of Child Clinical Psychology, 19*, 302–319.

Webster-Stratton, C. (1997). Preventing conduct problems in Head Start children: Strengthening parenting competencies. Manuscript submitted for publication.

Weiner, J. (1994). *The beak of the finch: A story of evolution in our time.* New York: Alfred A. Knopf.

Weitekamp, E. G. M., Kerner, H. J., Schindler, V., & Schubert, A. (1995). On the "dangerousness" of chronic/habitual offenders: A re-analysis of the 1945 Philadelphia birth cohort data. *Journal of the Study of Crime and Crime Prevention, 4*, 159–175.

Werner, E. E. (1987). Vulnerability and resiliency in children at risk for delinquency: A longitudinal study from birth to young adulthood. In J. D. Burchard & S. N. Burchard (Eds.), *Prevention of delinquent behavior* (pp. 16–43). Newbury Park, CA: Sage.

Werner, E. E. (1989a). High-risk children in young adulthood: A longitudinal study from birth to 32 years. *American Journal of Orthopsychiatry, 59*, 72–81.

Werner, E. E. (1989b). Children of the Garden Island. *Scientific American, 260*, 106–111.

Werner, E. E., & Smith, R. S. (1982). *Vulnerable but invincible: A longitudinal study of resilient children and youth.* New York: McGraw-Hill.

White, J. L., Moffitt, T. E., Earls, F., Robins, L. N., & Silva, P. A. (1990). How early can we tell? Preschool predictors of boys' conduct disorder and delinquency. *Criminology, 28*, 507–533.

White, J. L., Moffitt, T. E., & Silva, P. A. (1989). A prospective replication of the protective effects of IQ in subjects at high risk for juvenile delinquency. *Journal of Consulting and Clinical Psychology, 57*, 719–724.

Whitehead, J. T., & Lab, S. P. (1989). A meta-analysis of juvenile correctional treatment. *Journal of Research in Crime and Delinquency, 26*, 276–295.

Whitney, G. (1990). A contextual history of behavior genetics. In M. E. Hahn, J. K. Hewitt, N. D. Henderson, & R. Benno (Eds.), *Developmental behavior genetics: Neural, biometrical, and evolutionary approaches* (pp. 7–24). New York: Oxford University Press.

Whittaker, J. K., Kinney, J., Tracy, E. M., & Brooth, C. (1990). *Reaching high-risk families.* New York: Aldine de Gruyter.

Widom, C. S. (1989a). Does violence beget violence? A critical examination of the literature. *Psychological Bulletin, 106*, 3–28.

Widom, C. S. (1989b). Child abuse, neglect, and violent criminal behavior. *Criminology, 27,* 251–272.

Widom, C. S. (1991, February). *Long-term consequences of early childhood victimization.* Presented to the American Association for the Advancement of Science, Washington, DC.

Williams, G. C. (1966). *Adaptation and natural selection.* Princeton, NJ: Princeton University Press.

Williams, G. C. (1992). *Natural selection.* Oxford: Oxford University Press.

Williams, S., Anderson, J., McGee, R., & Silva, P. (1990). Risk factors for behavioral and emotional disorders in preadolescent children. *Journal of the American Academy of Child and Adolescent Psychiatry, 29,* 413–419.

Wilson, E. O. (1975). *Sociobiology: The new synthesis.* Cambridge: Harvard University Press.

Wilson, J. Q. (1983). *Thinking about crime* (Rev. ed.). New York: Basic Books.

Wilson, J. Q., & Herrnstein, R. J. (1985). *Crime and human nature.* New York: Simon & Schuster.

Wilson, M., & Daly, M. (1985). Competitiveness, risk taking, and violence: The young male syndrome. *Ethology and Sociobiology, 6,* 59–73.

Wilson, M., & Daly, M. (1993). Lethal confrontational violence among young men. In N. J. Bell (Ed.), *Adolescent risk taking* (pp. 84–106). Thousand Oaks, CA: Sage.

Wilson, M., & Daly, M. (1997). Life expectancy, economic inequality, homicide, and reproductive timing in Chicago neighborhoods. *British Medical Journal, 314,* 1271–1274.

Windle, M. (1994). Temperamental inhibition and activation: Hormonal and psychosocial correlates and associated psychiatric disorder. *Personality and Individual Differences, 17,* 61–70.

Wolff, P. H., Waber, D., Bauermeister, M., Cohen, C., & Ferber, R. (1982). The neuropsychological status of adolescent delinquent boys. *Journal of Child Psychology and Psychiatry, 23,* 267–279.

Wolfgang, M. E., & Ferracuti, F. (1967/82). *The subculture of violence: Towards an integrated theory in criminology.* Newbury Park, CA: Sage.

Wolfgang, M. E., Figlio, R. M., & Sellin, T. (1972). *Delinquency in a birth cohort.* Chicago: University of Chicago Press.

Wolfgang, M. E., Figlio, R. M., Tracy, P. E., & Singer, S. I. (1985). *The national survey of crime severity.* Washington, DC: U.S. Department of Justice, Bureau of Justice Statistics.

Wootton, J. M., Frick, P. J., Shelton, K. K., & Silverthorn, P. (1997). Ineffective parenting and childhood conduct problems: The moderating role of callous-unemotional traits. *Journal of Consulting and Clinical Psychology, 65,* 301–308.

Wright, R. (1994). *The moral animal.* New York: Pantheon Books.

Wright, J. D. (1995). Ten essential observations on guns in America. *Society, 32,* 63–68.

Yalcinkaya, T. M., Siiteri, P. K., Vigne, J. L., Licht, P., Pavgi, S., Frank, L. G., et al. (1993). A mechanism for virilization of female spotted hyenas in utero. *Science, 260,* 1929–1931.

Yeo, R. A., Gangestad, S. W., & Daniel, W. F. (1993). Hand preference and developmental instability. *Psychobiology, 21,* 161–168.

Yoshikawa, H. (1994). Preventions as cumulative protection: Effects of early family support and education on chronic delinquency and its risks. *Psychological Bulletin, 115,* 28–54.

Young, L. J., Nilsen, R., Waymire, K. G., MacGregor, G. R., & Insel, T. R. (1999). Increased affiliative response to vasopressin in mice expressing the V-1a receptor from a monogamous vole. *Nature, 400,* 766–768.

Young, L. J., Wang, Z., & Insel, T. R. (1998). Neuroendocrine bases of monogamy. *Trends in Neurosciences, 21,* 71–75.

Young, S. E., Smolen, A., Corley, R. P., Krauter, K. S., DeFries, J. C., Crowley, T. J, et al. (2002). Dopamine transporter polymorphism associated with externalizing behavior problems in children. *American Journal of Medical Genetics, 114,* 44–149.

Zahavi, A., & Zahavi, A. (1997). *The handicap principle: A missing piece of Darwin's puzzle.* New York: Oxford University Press.

Zahn-Waxler, C., Iannotti, R. J., Cummings, E. M., & Denham, S. (1990). Antecedents of problem behaviors in children of depressed mothers. *Development and Psychopathology, 2,* 271–291.

Zahn-Waxler, C., Mayfield, A., Radke-Yarrow, M., McKnew, D., Cytryn, L., & Davenport, Y. (1988). A follow-up investigation of offspring of parents with bipolar disorder. *American Journal of Psychiatry, 145,* 506–509.

Zajonc, R. B., & Mullally, P. R. (1997). Birth order: Reconciling conflicting effects. *American Psychologist, 52,* 685–699.

Zigler, E., Taussig, C., & Black, K. (1992). Early childhood intervention: A promising preventative for juvenile delinquency. *American Psychologist, 47,* 997–1006.

Zimring, F. M. (1984). The effect of attending to feeling on memory for internally generated stimuli. *Journal of Research in Personality, 19,* 170–184.

Zinger, I., & Forth, A. E. (1998). Psychopathy and Canadian criminal proceedings: The potential for human rights abuses. *Canadian Journal of Criminology, 40,* 237–276.

Zingraff, M. T., Leiter, J., Johnsen, M. C., & Myers, K. A. (1994). The mediating effect of good school performance on the maltreatment-delinquency relationship. *Journal of Research in Crime and Delinquency, 31,* 62–91.

Zoccolillo, M. (1993). Gender and the development of conduct disorder. *Development and Psychopathology, 5,* 65–78.

Zuckerman, M. (1989). Personality in the third dimension: A psychobiological approach. *Personality and Individual Differences*, *10*, 391–418.

Zuckerman, M. (1995). Good and bad humors: Biochemical bases of personality and its disorders. *Psychological Science*, *6*, 325–332.

Zuckerman, M., Kuhlman, D. M., Joireman, J., Teta, P., & Kraft, M. (1993). A comparison of three structural models for personality: The Big Three, the Big Five, and the Alternative Five. *Journal of Personality and Social Psychology*, *65*, 757–768.

AUTHOR INDEX

Bock, G. R., 3, 178
Bodmer, W., 24
Bogaert, A. F., 30, 71
Bohman, M., 40, 51
Book, A. S., 71, 111
Booth, 99
Borduin, C. M., 122, 149–150
Bouchard, T. J., 42–43
Boulerice, B., 81
Bow-Thomas, C. C., 29
Bowker, L. H., 125
Boyle, M. C., 81
Brame, R., 136
Braungart-Rieker, J., 47
Breland, K., 34
Brendgen, M., 90
Brennan, P. A., 67–68, 100
Breslau, N., 50
Brickman, A. S., 69
Brodie, D. A., 109
Brondino, M. J., 150
Brook, J. S., 100
Brooth, C., 149
Brown, S. A., 87, 104, 122
Bugental, D. B., 106–107
Bukowski, W. M., 90
Burback, M., 74
Burbank, V., 132
Burleson, M. H., 36
Burman, 122
Burr, C., 72
Buss, A. H., 42–43, 47
Buss, D. M., 9, 11–12, 15, 28–30
Buunk, B. P., 29
Byock, J. L., 106
Byrne, J. M., 59

Cadoret, R. J., 55
Cairns, B. D., 34–35, 89, 118–119
Campbell, A., 115, 118, 125, 132–134
Capaldi, D. M., 31, 81–83
Caplan, G., 139
Cardew, G., 9
Carey, G., 47, 49
Carlson, E., 67, 74–75, 102
Carter, C. S., 153
Caspi, A., 65, 74, 77–78, 128, 130, 136
Castellanos, F. X., 53
Catalano, R. F., 74, 142, 150–151
Cavell, T. A., 122
Chalmers, L. J., 12
Chance, 81

Chaplin, T. C., 13
Chase, J. M., 17
Cheney, D. L., 19, 135
Chesney-Lind, M., 117, 122–123, 125, 127, 134
Chevillard, I., 158
Chimura-Kraemer, H., 139
Christiansen, K., 120
Cibelli, C. D., 85
Clark, A., 30, 106
Clarke, S., 70
Clelland, R. C., 152
Clingempeel, W. G., 83
Cloninger, C. R., 40, 52, 100, 120
Clutton-Brock, T. H., 14, 46
Coen, E., 44
Cohen, C., 69
Cohen, D., 63
Cohen, E., 100
Cohen, P., 100
Cohler, B. J., 145
Coie, J. D., 89, 120, 169
Colman, A. M., 108
Comer, R., 17
Comings, D. E., 53
Conger, K. J., 31
Cooper, H. M., 149
Cormier, C., 79, 105, 114
Cosmides, L., 11–12, 19
Costa, F. M., 31, 42
Cowie, J., 124
Cox, C. R., 14
Coyne, J. C., 82
Craig, I. W., 150
Craig, W. M., 44, 89, 104, 150, 152, 169
Crawford, C. B., 9, 11, 36
Cressey, D., 59
Crockenberg, S., 84
Crockett, L. J., 31
Crosby, L., 31, 148
Cummings, A. L., 86, 118
Cunningham, A., 118, 150

Dabbs, J. M, 71
Daly, M., 12, 14–15, 19, 28–29, 36, 45, 97–98, 131
Daniel, W. F., 109
Daniels, D., 37, 39, 44–45
Daugherty, T. K., 70
David, H. P., 84
Davidson, R. J., 27
Davidson, W. S., 157, 163–164

SUBJECT INDEX

ABOUT THE AUTHORS

Vernon L. Quinsey received his PhD in biopsychology from the University of Massachusetts at Amherst in 1970. He was director of research of the Mental Health Centre in Penetanguishene, Ontario, Canada. In 1988, he moved to Queen's University in Kingston, where he is professor of psychology and psychiatry. He is a fellow of the Canadian Psychological Association and has been on the editorial boards of numerous journals. He has chaired research review panels of the National Institute of Mental Health and the Ontario Mental Health Foundation. He received the Significant Achievement Award from the Association for the Treatment of Sexual Abusers in 1994. In 1997, he received a senior research fellowship from the Ontario Mental Health Foundation.

Tracey A. Skilling received her PhD in forensic psychology from Queen's University in Kingston in 2000. She was a research fellow at the Mental Health Centre in Penetanguishene, Ontario, Canada, for two years where she was the first nonmedical fellow to receive the Clinical Investigators Training Program Award from McMaster University at Hamilton. In 2001, she became a psychologist in the Child Psychiatry Program at the Centre for Addiction and Mental Health in Toronto, Ontario, Canada. She is also an assistant professor of psychiatry at the University of Toronto.

Martin L. Lalumière received his PhD from Queen's University in Kingston, where he was awarded the Governor General's Academic Gold Medal. He is a research psychologist at the Centre for Addiction and Mental Health in Toronto, Ontario, Canada, and an assistant professor of psychiatry and criminology at the University of Toronto. His research examines the causes of sexual aggression, the development of sexual preferences, and the link between developmental instability and violence. He is on the editorial boards of *Archives of Sexual Behavior* and *Sexual Abuse*. Some of his recent work appears in *Evolution and Human Behavior*, the *Journal of Abnormal Psychology*, *Psychological Assessment*, and *Psychological Bulletin*.

Wendy M. Craig received her PhD in clinical developmental psychology from York University in Toronto in 1993. After completing a postdoctoral fellowship at the University of Montreal, she moved to Queen's University in Kingston, where she currently is an associate professor of psychology. She is chair of the research review panel for the Ontario Mental Health Foundation. In 2001, she received a Research Investigator Award from the Canadian Institute of Health Research. Currently, she is conducting a longitudinal study of bullying and victimization.